Collins

Year 9, Pupil Book 2

NEW MATHS FRAMEWORKING

Matches the revised KS3 Framework

Kevin Evans, Keith Gordon, Trevor Senior, Brian Speed

Contents

Introduction   vi

CHAPTER 1 Algebra 1 & 2

Sequences   1
Quadratic sequences   4
Functions   6
Graphs   8
Limits of sequences   11
National Test questions   12
Functional Maths – Mobile phone tariffs   14

CHAPTER 2 Number 1

Adding and subtracting fractions   16
Multiplying and dividing fractions   18
Percentages and compound interest   21
Reverse percentages   24
Ratio   26
Numbers between 0 and 1   29
Order of operations   31
Rounding and estimation   33
National Test questions   35
Functional Maths – The London Olympics 2012   38

CHAPTER 3 Algebra 3

Equations, formulae and identities   40
Solving problems using equations   43
Equations involving fractions   44
Equations involving x^2 46
Trial and improvement   48
Graphs showing direct proportion   50
National Test questions   54

CHAPTER 4 Geometry and Measures 1

Angles of polygons	55
Angles of regular polygons	59
The circle and its parts	61
Tessellations and regular polygons	63
Constructing right-angled triangles	64
Loci	66
Geometrical reasoning	69
National Test questions	71
Functional Maths – Garden design	74

CHAPTER 5 Statistics 1

Scatter graphs and correlation	76
Time series graphs	79
Two-way tables	83
Comparing two or more sets of data	85
Statistical investigations	88
National Test questions	90
Functional Maths – Rainforest deforestation	94

CHAPTER 6 Geometry and Measures 2

Circumference of a circle	96
Formula for the circumference of a circle	97
Formula for the area of a circle	99
Metric units for area and volume	101
Volume and surface area of prisms	103
National Test questions	106
Functional Maths – Athletics stadium	108

CHAPTER 7 Number 2

Powers of 10	110
Rounding	112
Multiplying decimals	114
Dividing decimals	115
Efficient use of calculators	117
Solving problems	118
National Test questions	121
Functional Maths – Paper	124

CHAPTER 8 Algebra 4

Factorisation	126
Index notation with algebra	128
Square roots and cube roots	130
Constructing graphs involving time	132
National Test questions	134
Functional Maths – Packages	136

CHAPTER 9 Statistics 2

Probability statements	138
Mutually exclusive events and exhaustive events	140
Estimates of probability	143
National Test questions	145
Functional Maths – Class test	148

CHAPTER 10 Geometry and Measures 3

Enlargements	150
Planes of symmetry	155
Map scales	157
Congruent triangles	160
National Test questions	162
Functional Maths – Map reading	166

CHAPTER 11 Algebra 5

Expansion	168
Factorisation	171
Quadratic expansion	173
Change of subject	175
Graphs from equations in the form $Ay \pm Bx = C$	177
National Test questions	179
Functional Maths – Trip to Rome	180

CHAPTER 12 Solving Problems and Revision

Number 1 – Fractions, percentages and decimals	182
Number 2 – Four rules, ratios and directed numbers	184
Algebra 1 – Rules of algebra and solving equations	186
Algebra 2 – Graphs	188
Geometry and measures	190
Statistics	193

CHAPTER 13 Statistics 3 and Revision

Statistical techniques	**186**
A handling data project	**201**

CHAPTER 14 Geometry and Measures 4 and Revision

Geometry and measures revision	**203**
Geometry and measures investigations	**205**
Symmetry revision	**206**
Symmetry investigations	**209**

CHAPTER 15 Statistics 4 and Revision

Revision of probability	**211**
A probability investigation	**214**

CHAPTER 16 GCSE Preparation

Long multiplication	**217**
Long division	**218**
Long multiplication and long division in real-life problems	**219**
Equivalent fractions	**221**
Adding and subtracting fractions	**223**
Multiplying and dividing fractions	**225**
Directed numbers	**227**
Basic percentages	**229**
Basic algebra	**230**
GCSE past-paper questions	**232**

CHAPTER 17 Functional Maths Practice

The Eden Project	**236**
Road safety	**238**
Squirrels	**240**
Mobile shop	**242**
Index	**244**
Garden design activity worksheet	**247**

Introduction

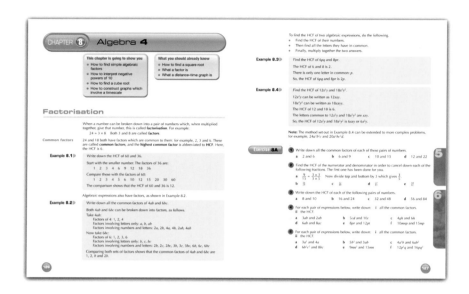

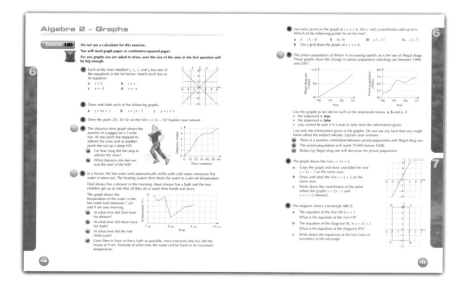

Learning objectives

See what you are going to cover and what you should already know at the start of each chapter. The purple and blue boxes set the topic in context and provide a handy checklist.

National Curriculum levels

Know what level you are working at so you can easily track your progress with the colour-coded levels at the side of the page.

Worked examples

Understand the topic before you start the exercises by reading the examples in blue boxes. These take you through how to answer a question step-by-step.

Functional Maths

Practise your Functional Maths skills to see how people use Maths in everyday life.

 Look out for the Functional Maths icon on the page.

Extension activities

Stretch your thinking and investigative skills by working through the extension activities. By tackling these you are working at a higher level.

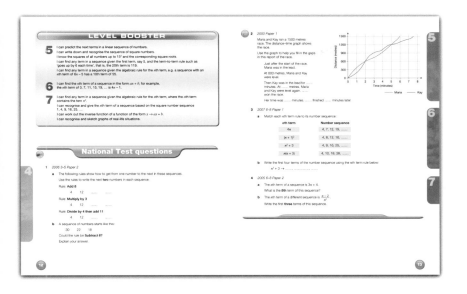

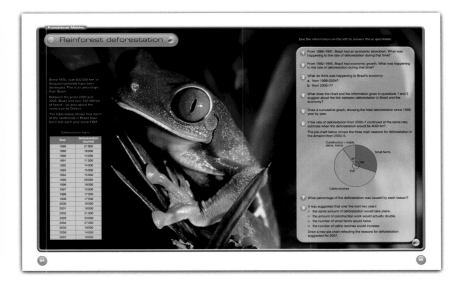

Level booster

Progress to the next level by checking the Level boosters at the end of each chapter. These clearly show you what you need to know at each level and how to improve.

National Test questions

Practise the past paper Test questions to feel confident and prepared for your KS3 National Curriculum Tests. The questions are levelled so you can check what level you are working at.

Extra interactive National Test practice

Watch and listen to the audio/visual National Test questions on the separate Interactive Book CD-ROM to help you revise as a class on a whiteboard.

 Look out for the computer mouse icon on the page and on the screen.

Functional Maths activities

Put Maths into context with these colourful pages showing real-world situations involving Maths. You are practising your Functional Maths skills by analysing data to solve problems.

Extra interactive Functional Maths questions and video clips

Extend your Functional Maths skills by taking part in the interactive questions on the separate Interactive Book CD-ROM. Your teacher can put these on the whiteboard so the class can answer the questions on the board.

See Maths in action by watching the video clips and doing the related Worksheets on the Interactive Book CD-ROM. The videos bring the Functional Maths activities to life and help you see how Maths is used in the real world.

 Look out for the computer mouse icon on the page and on the screen.

NEW

Hone your Functional Maths skills further by doing the four exciting tasks given in the new chapter – Functional Maths Practice.

CHAPTER 1 Algebra 1 & 2

This chapter is going to show you	What you should already know
● How to find the nth term of a linear sequence ● How to describe a sequence derived from a geometrical pattern ● How to find inverse functions ● The limits of some series	● How to continue a given pattern ● How to graph a simple relationship

Sequences

Arsenal had a sequence of 43 games in which they scored in every game. Is it possible to predict how many goals they would score in their next game?

A **sequence** is an ordered set of numbers or terms, such as the positive integers, 1, 2, 3…. Every number or term in a sequence is given by applying the same rule throughout the sequence. Look at Examples 1.1 and 1.2.

Example **1.1** ▷ What is the next number in the following sequence?

10, 100, 1000, 10 000, …   It is 100 000.

What is the term-to-term rule for the sequence?   Multiply by 10.

Example **1.2** ▷ What is the next number in this sequence?

1, 2, 4, 7, 11, 16, …   It is 22.

Show the differences between consecutive terms.   They are: 1, 2, 3, 4, 5,… .

The position of a term in a sequence can sometimes be used to find its value. The idea is to try to find a general term which represents the pattern, which is usually written as the **nth term**.

nth term of a sequence

A sequence is usually defined by its nth term. Look at Examples 1.3 to 1.5 to see how this works.

Example 1.3 ▷ Write down the first four terms of the sequence whose nth term is $4n + 2$.

The first term is given by $n = 1$. Hence, $4 \times 1 + 2 = 6$
The second term is given by $n = 2$. Hence, $4 \times 2 + 2 = 10$
The third term is given by $n = 3$. Hence, $4 \times 3 + 2 = 14$
The fourth term is given by $n = 4$. Hence, $4 \times 4 + 2 = 18$

So, the first four terms are 6, 10, 14, 18.

Example 1.4 ▷ Write down the nth term of the sequence 2, 5, 8, 11, ...

First, find the differences between consecutive terms. The sequence has the same difference, 3, between consecutive terms. This shows that the sequence is in the form $An + B$.

Since the common difference is 3, then $A = 3$.

So, in order to get the first term of 2, –1 must be added to 3. Hence $B = -1$.

That is, the nth term is given by $3n - 1$.

When a sequence has the same difference between consecutive terms, it can be defined by a general term that will be in the following form:

$An + B$

where A is the common difference between consecutive terms, B is the value which is added to A to give the first term, and n is the number of the term (that is, first, second, …).

Example 1.5 ▷ Write down the nth term of the sequence 5, 9, 13, 17, 21, … .

The difference between consecutive terms is 4.

To get the first term of 5, 1 must be added to 4.

Hence, the nth term is $4n + 1$.

Check this as follows: First term = $1 \times 4 + 1 = 5$
Second term = $2 \times 4 + 1 = 9$
Third term = $3 \times 4 + 1 = 13$

So, $4n + 1$ is correct.

Exercise 1A

1 Find the next three terms in each of the following sequences.

   a   1, 5, 9, 13, …   **b**   3, 8, 13, 18, …   **c**   2, 9, 16, 23, …
   d   4, 10, 16, 22, …   **e**   6, 14, 22, 30, …   **f**   5, 8, 11, 14, …

2 Write down the first four terms of each of the following sequences whose nth term is given below.

   a $2n + 3$ **b** $3n + 2$ **c** $4n + 5$ **d** $5n + 9$
   e $3n - 1$ **f** $5n - 3$ **g** $4n - 5$ **h** $2n - 4$

3 Find the *n*th term of each of the following sequences.

    a   6, 10, 14, 18, 22, …   **b**   8, 15, 22, 29, 36, …

    c   21, 19, 17, 15, 13, …   **d**   32, 28, 24, 20, 16, …

4 Find the *n*th term of each of the following sequences.

    a   43, 51, 59, 67, 75, …   **b**   57, 50, 43, 36, 29, …

    c   35, 48, 61, 74, 87, …   **d**   67, 76, 85, 94, 103, …

5 Find the *n*th term of each of the following sequences.

    a   9, 4, –1, –6, –11, …   **b**   –11, –9, –7, –5, –3, …

    c   –1, –5, –9, –13, –17, …   **d**   –15, –12, –9, –6, –3, …

6 Find the *n*th term of each of the following sequences.

    a   2.4, 2.6, 2.8, 3.0, 3.2, …   **b**   1.7, 2.0, 2.3, 2.6, 2.9, …

    c   6.8, 6.3, 5.8, 5.3, 4.8, …   **d**   5.3, 4.9, 4.5, 4.1, 3.7, …

7 Find the *n*th term of each of the following sequences of fractions.

    a $\frac{1}{2}, \frac{2}{5}, \frac{3}{8}, \frac{4}{11}, \frac{5}{14}$, …   **b** $\frac{3}{4}, \frac{5}{9}, \frac{7}{14}, \frac{9}{19}, \frac{11}{24}$, …

8 Look at each of the following sequences of squares.

 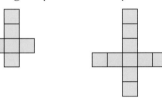 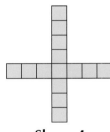

    Shape 1   **Shape 2**   **Shape 3**   **Shape 4**

    a   Find the number of squares in the *n*th shape.

    b   Find the number of squares in the 50th shape in the pattern.

9 Look at each of the following sequences of lines (blue) and crosses (green):

    Diagram 1   **Diagram 2**   **Diagram 3**   **Diagram 4**

    a   Find the number of lines in the *n*th shape.

    b   Find the number of crosses in the 50th shape in the pattern.

    c   Find the number of crosses in the *n*th shape in the pattern.

Extension Work

The *n*th term of a sequence is given by $\frac{1}{2}n(n + 1)$.

1 Work out the first 5 terms of the sequence.

2 Write down the term-to-term rule for the sequence.

3 Continue the sequence for 10 terms.

4 What special name is given to this sequence of numbers?

Quadratic sequences

You have already met the sequence of square numbers:

    1, 4, 9, 16, 25, 36, …

The nth term of this sequence is n^2.

Many sequences have nth terms that include n^2.

These are called quadratic sequences.

Example 1.6 ▷

The nth term of a quadratic sequence is given by $n^2 + 3n + 2$.

a Work out the first 5 terms of the sequence.

b Write down the term-to-term rule for this sequence.

c Continue the sequence for 10 terms.

d What is the 99th term in the sequence?

a By substituting $n = 1, 2, 3, 4$ and 5 into the expression for the nth term, we get the first 5 terms of the sequence to be 6, 12, 20, 30, 42.

b The sequence increases by 6, 8, 10 and 12, so the term-to-term rule is 'goes up in even numbers, starting with 6'.

c Carry on adding 14, 16, etc, to give:
    6, 12, 20, 30, 42, 56, 72, 90, 110, 132, …

d The 99th term is $(99 + 1)(99 + 2) = 100 \times 101 = 10\,100$.

Example 1.7 ▷

Write down the nth term of the following sequences.

a 1, 4, 9, 16, 25, …   **b** 3, 6, 11, 18, 27, …

c 2, 8, 18, 32, 50, …   **d** $\frac{1}{2}$, 2, $4\frac{1}{2}$, 8, $12\frac{1}{2}$, …

a This is the square number sequence, nth term $= n^2$

b This is 2 more than the square number sequence, nth term $= n^2 + 2$

c This is twice the square number sequence, nth term $= 2n^2$

d This is half the square number sequence, nth term $= \frac{1}{2}n^2$

Exercise 1B

1 For each of the following nth terms:

i   work out the first 5 terms of the sequence.

ii   write down the term-to-term rule for this sequence.

iii continue the sequence for 10 terms.

a $n(n + 3)$ **b** $3n^2$ **c** $n^2 + 5$

d $(n + 1)^2$ **e** $(n + 3)(n - 2)$ **f** $2n^2 + n + 1$

2 Write down the nth term of the following sequences.

a 1, 4, 9, 16, 25, …   **b** 2, 5, 10, 17, 26, …

c 5, 20, 45, 80, 125, …   **d** $\frac{1}{4}$, 1, $2\frac{1}{4}$, 4, $6\frac{1}{4}$ …

3 Look at the way straight lines can intersect one another.

| 1 line | 2 lines | 3 lines | 4 lines |
| 0 intersections | 1 intersection | 3 intersections | 6 intersections |

The maximum number of intersections for each set of lines is shown in the table below.

Number of lines	1	2	3	4
Maximum number of intersections	0	1	3	6

a Before drawing a diagram, can you predict, from the table, the maximum number of intersections you will have for five lines?

b Draw the five lines so that they all intersect one another. Count the number of intersections. Were you right?

c Now predict the maximum number of intersections for six and seven lines.

d Draw the diagram for 6 lines to confirm your result.

e Which of the following is the nth term of the sequence?

$$\tfrac{1}{2}n(n + 1) \qquad (n - 1)(n + 1) \qquad \tfrac{1}{2}n(n - 1)$$

Extension | **Work**

Look at the following polygons. Each vertex is joined to every other vertex with a straight line, called a diagonal.

| 3 sides | 4 sides | 5 sides | 6 sides | 7 sides |
| 0 diagonals | 2 diagonals | 5 diagonals | 9 diagonals | 14 diagonals |

The table below shows the number of diagonals drawn inside each polygon.

Number of sides	3	4	5	6	7
Number of diagonals	0	2	5	9	14

1 Before drawing a diagram, can you predict, from the table, the number of diagonals you will have for a polygon with eight sides?

2 Draw an eight-sided polygon and put in all the diagonals. Count the number of diagonals. Were you right?

3 Now predict the number of diagonals for polygons with nine and ten sides.

4 Check your results for part **3** by drawing the polygons with their diagonals and seeing how many diagonals there are in each case.

5 Which of the following is the nth term of the sequence?

$$\tfrac{1}{2}(n + 2)(n - 1) \qquad \tfrac{1}{2}n^2 + \tfrac{1}{2}n - 1 \qquad \tfrac{1}{2}(n^2 + n - 2)$$

Functions

A **function** is a rule which changes one number, called the **input**, to another number, called the **output**. For example, $y = 2x + 1$ is a function. So, when $x = 2$, a new number $y = 5$ is produced. Another way of writing this function is:

$$x \rightarrow 2x + 1$$

Identity function

$x \rightarrow x$ is called the **identity function** because it maps any number onto itself. In other words, it leaves the inputs unaltered.

$$0 \rightarrow 0$$
$$1 \rightarrow 1$$
$$2 \rightarrow 2$$
$$3 \rightarrow 3$$
$$4 \rightarrow 4$$

Inverse function

Every linear function has an **inverse function** which reverses the direction of the operation. In other words, the output is brought back to the input.

Example 1.8 ▷

The inverse of $x \rightarrow 4x$ is seen to be $y \rightarrow \frac{y}{4}$.

x	$\rightarrow$	$4x$		
0	$\rightarrow$	0	$\rightarrow$	0
1	$\rightarrow$	4	$\rightarrow$	1
2	$\rightarrow$	8	$\rightarrow$	2
3	$\rightarrow$	12	$\rightarrow$	3
	y	$\rightarrow$	$\frac{y}{4}$	

Note: The inverse function is sometimes written as $x \rightarrow \frac{x}{4}$, but we will use the letter y for inverse functions to avoid confusion.

Example 1.9 ▷

The inverse of $x \rightarrow x + 3$ is seen to be $y \rightarrow y - 3$.

x	$\rightarrow$	$x + 3$		
0	$\rightarrow$	3	$\rightarrow$	0
1	$\rightarrow$	4	$\rightarrow$	1
2	$\rightarrow$	5	$\rightarrow$	2
3	$\rightarrow$	6	$\rightarrow$	3
	y	$\rightarrow$	$y - 3$	

When a function is built up from two or more operations, you will need to consider the original operations and work backwards through these to find the inverse.

Example 1.10 ▶ Find the inverse of $x \rightarrow 4x + 3$.

The sequence of operations for this function is:

Input ⟶ ×4 ⟶ +3 ⟶ Output

Reversing this sequence gives:

Input ⟵ ÷4 ⟵ −3 ⟵ Output

Then give the output the value y:

$$\frac{y-3}{4} \longleftarrow y - 3 \longleftarrow y$$

So, the inverse function is:

$$y \longrightarrow \frac{y-3}{4}$$

Self-inverse

The inverses of some functions are the functions themselves. These are called **self-inverse** functions.

Example 1.11 ▶ The inverse of $x \rightarrow 8 - x$ can be seen to be itself, as $y \rightarrow 8 - y$.

x		$8 - x$		
0	→	8	→	0
1	→	7	→	1
2	→	6	→	2
3	→	5	→	3
4	→	4	→	4
5	→	3	→	5
		y	→	$8 - y$

Exercise 1C

① Write down the inverse of each of the following functions.

   a $\quad x \rightarrow 2x$ **b** $\quad x \rightarrow 5x$ **c** $\quad x \rightarrow x + 6$

   d $\quad x \rightarrow x + 1$ **e** $\quad x \rightarrow x - 3$ **f** $\quad x \rightarrow \frac{x}{5}$

② For each of the following functions:

   i   draw the flow diagram for the function.

   ii draw the flow diagram for the inverse function.

   iii write down the inverse function in the form $y \rightarrow$.

   a $\quad x \rightarrow 2x + 3$ **b** $\quad x \rightarrow 3x + 1$ **c** $\quad x \rightarrow 4x - 3$

   d $\quad x \rightarrow 5x - 2$ **e** $\quad x \rightarrow 4x + 7$ **f** $\quad x \rightarrow 6x - 5$

③ Show that the following are self inverse functions.

   a $\quad x \rightarrow 6 - x$ **b** $\quad x \rightarrow \frac{2}{x}$

④ Write down the inverse of each of the following functions.

   a $\quad x \rightarrow 2(x + 3)$ **b** $\quad x \rightarrow 3(x - 4)$ **c** $\quad x \rightarrow \frac{(x + 3)}{4}$

   d $\quad x \rightarrow \frac{(x - 2)}{5}$ **e** $\quad x \rightarrow \frac{1}{2}x + 3$ **f** $\quad x \rightarrow \frac{1}{2}x - 7$

7

1   The function $x \rightarrow 2x$ can also be expressed as $y = 2x$. Show this to be true by considering the input set {1, 2, 3, 4, 5}.

   a   What is the output set from {1, 2, 3, 4, 5} with the function $x \rightarrow 2x$?

   b   Find the value of y when x has values {1, 2, 3, 4, 5}, where $y = 2x$.

   c   Are the two sets of values found in parts **a** and **b** the same? If so, then you have shown that $y = 2x$ is just another way of showing the function $x \rightarrow 2x$.

2   Draw a graph of the function $x \rightarrow 2x$ by using $y = 2x$. On the same pair of axes, draw the graph of the inverse of $x \rightarrow 2x$.

3   On the same pair of axes, draw the graphs representing the function $x \rightarrow 4x$ and its inverse.

4   On the same pair of axes, draw the graphs representing the function $x \rightarrow 5x$ and its inverse.

5   Look at the two lines on each graph you have drawn for Questions **2**, **3** and **4**. Do you notice anything special about each pair of lines?

Graphs

The distance–time graph below illustrates three people in a race.

The graph shows how quickly each person ran, who was ahead at various times, who won and by how many seconds.

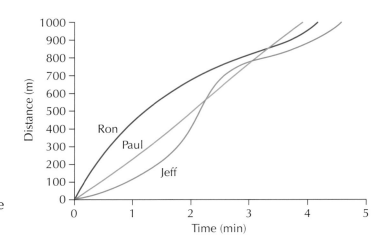

Paul

Notice that Paul's graph is a straight line. This means that he ran at the same speed throughout the race. Paul won the race, finishing about 20 seconds in front of Ron.

Ron

The shape of Ron's graph indicates that he started quickly and then slowed down. He was in the lead for the first 850 metres, before Paul overtook him.

Jeff

Jeff started slowly, but then picked up speed to overtake Paul for a minute before running out of steam and slowing down to come in last, about 30 seconds behind Ron.

Note: The steeper the graph, the faster the person is running.

Exercise 1D

 1 Look at the distance–time graph, which illustrates how two rockets flew during a test flight. Rocket D flew higher than Rocket E.

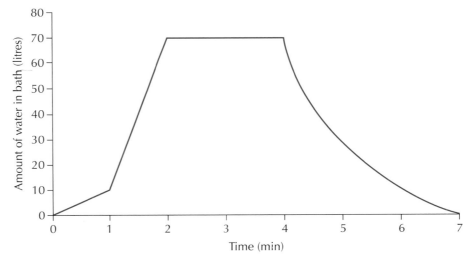

- **a** Estimate the height reached by Rocket D.
- **b** Estimate how much higher than Rocket E Rocket D went.
- **c** How long after the launch were both rockets at the same height?
- **d** For how long was each rocket higher than 150 m?
- **e** Can you tell which rocket travelled further? Explain your answer.

 2 Look at the graph below, which illustrates the amount of water in a bath after it has started to be filled.

- **a** Explain what might have happened 1 minute after the start.
- **b** When was the plug pulled out for the bath to start emptying?
- **c** Why do you think the graph shows a curved line while the bath was emptying?
- **d** How long did the bath take to empty?

3 Water drips steadily into the container shown. The graph shows how the depth of water varies with time.

 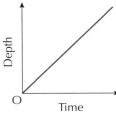

Sketch similar graphs for bottles with the following shapes.

a   **b**   **c**   **d**

FM **4** Suggest which graph below best fits each situation given.

a 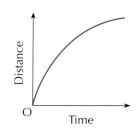   b 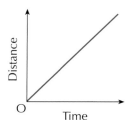   c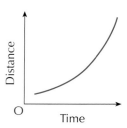

    A   The distance travelled by a train moving at a constant speed

    B   The distance travelled by a motorbike accelerating to overtake

    C   The distance travelled by an old car, which starts well, but gradually slows down

FM **5** Suggest which graph below best fits each situation given.

a 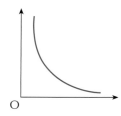   b 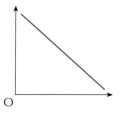   c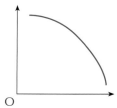

    A   The amount of fuel left in the tank of my car as I travel from Sheffield to Cornwall.

    B   The amount of infection in a body as it responds to medicine will first reduce gradually and then more quickly until it has all gone.

    C   The rate of cooling of a hot drink starts quickly and then slows down.

FM **6** Sketch graphs to illustrate the following situations.

    a   The number of euros that can be purchased with £x

    b   The temperature during the 24 hours of 21st July

    c   The temperature during the 24 hours of 12th February

    d   The number of empty car-park spaces in a supermarket on a Saturday between 8 am and 8 pm

    e   The amount of daylight each day of the year from 21st June to next 20th June

Extension Work

FM The UK population has been increasing over the last 200 years. The following table shows the population every 20 years.

Year	Population (millions)	Year	Population (millions)
1801	12	1901	38
1821	15.5	1921	44
1841	20	1941	47
1861	24.5	1961	53
1881	31	1981	56

    1   Draw a graph to show how the population has increased since 1801.

    2   From the graph, estimate what the population was in 2001.

    3   Try to find out what the actual population was in 2001.

Limits of sequences

Some sequences go on forever, as you have seen. These are called **infinite sequences**. Other sequences finish after so many numbers or terms. These are called **finite sequences**. Follow through Example 1.12, which shows an infinite sequence.

Example 1.12 ▷

> Using the term-to-term rule 'Divide by 5 and add 4', find the first 10 terms of this sequence, which starts at 1.
>
> This rule generates the following sequence:
>
> 1, 4.2, 4.84, 4.968, 4.9936, 4.998 72, 4.999 744, 4.999 948 8, 4.999 989 76, 4.999 997 952

Notice that the sequence gets closer and closer to 5, which is called the **limit** of the sequence.

1. Using the term-to-term rule 'Divide by 2 and add 3' to build a sequence and starting at 1.

   a   Find the first 12 terms generated by this sequence. Use a calculator or a spreadsheet.

   b   To what value does this sequence get closer and closer?

   c   Use the same term-to-term rule with different starting numbers. What do you notice?

2. Repeat Question **1**, but change the 'add 3' in the term-to-term rule to 'add 4'.

3. Repeat Question **1**, but change the 'add 3' in the term-to-term rule to 'add 5'.

4. a   Look at your answers to Questions **1** to **3**. See whether you can estimate to what value the sequence will get closer and closer when you change the 'add 3' in Question **1** to 'add 6'?

   b   Work out the sequence to see whether you were correct in part **a**.

5. Repeat Question **1** but change the 'divide by 2' to 'divide by 3'.

6. Repeat Question **5** but change the 'add 3' to 'add 4'.

7. Repeat Question **5** but change the 'add 3' to 'add 5'.

8. a   Look at your answers to Questions **5** to **7**. See whether you can estimate to what value the sequence will get closer and closer when you change the 'add 3' in Question **5** to 'add 6'?

   b   Work out the sequence to see whether you were correct in part **a**.

Extension **Work**

Continue the above investigation to see whether you can predict the limiting number that each sequence reaches from the term-to-term rule 'Divide by **A** and add **B**'.

LEVEL BOOSTER

5
I can predict the next terms in a linear sequence of numbers.

I can write down and recognise the sequence of square numbers.

I know the squares of all numbers up to 15^2 and the corresponding square roots.

I can find any term in a sequence given the first term, say 5, and the term-to-term rule such as 'goes up by 6 each time', that is, the 20th term is 119.

I can find any term in a sequence given the algebraic rule for the nth term, e.g. a sequence with an nth term of $6n - 5$ has a 10th term of 55.

6
I can find the nth term of a sequence in the form $an + b$; for example, the nth term of 3, 7, 11, 15, 19, ... is $4n - 1$.

7
I can find any term in a sequence given the algebraic rule for the nth term, where the nth term contains the tern n^2.

I can recognise and give the nth term of a sequence based on the square number sequence 1, 4, 9, 16, 25, ...

I can work out the inverse function of a function of the form $x \rightarrow ax + b$.

I can recognise and sketch graphs of real-life situations.

National Test questions

1 *2006 3–5 Paper 2*

    a   The following rules show how to get from one number to the next in these sequences.

        Use the rules to write the next **two** numbers in each sequence:

        Rule: **Add 8**

             4   12   ....

        Rule: **Multiply by 3**

             4   12   ....

        Rule: **Divide by 4 then add 11**

             4   12   ....

    b   A sequence of numbers starts like this:

          30   22   18

        Could the rule be **Subtract 8?**

        Explain your answer.

4

2 *2000 Paper 1*

Maria and Kay ran a 1500 metres race. The distance–time graph shows the race.

Use the graph to help you fill in the gaps in this report of the race.

Maria ——— Kay

> Just after the start of the race, Maria was in the lead.
>
> At 600 metres, Maria and Kay were level.
>
> Then Kay was in the lead for …… minutes. At …… metres, Maria and Kay were level again. …… won the race.
>
> Her time was …… minutes. …… finished …… minutes later.

3 *2007 6–8 Paper 1*

  a Match each *n*th term rule to its number sequence:

*n*th term	Number sequence
$4n$	4, 7, 12, 19, ……
$(n + 1)^2$	4, 8, 12, 16, ……
$n^2 + 3$	4, 9, 16, 25, ……
$n(n + 3)$	4, 10, 18, 28, ……

  b Write the first four terms of the number sequence using the *n*th term rule below:

$n^3 + 3 \rightarrow$ ……, ……, ……, ……

4 *2005 6–8 Paper 2*

  a The *n*th term of a sequence is $3n + 4$.

What is the **8th** term of this sequence?

  b The *n*th term of a different sequence is $\dfrac{n - 2}{n^2}$.

Write the first **three** terms of this sequence.

Mobile phone tariffs

Pick your plan

Mix & match plans		Inclusive UK minutes and texts	Free 3 to 3 minutes	Free voicemail	Free Instant Messaging	Free Skype
£12 a month	**£12 Promotional Tariff**	**100** Anytime any network minutes or texts or any mix of the two	**300** 3 to 3 minutes	✔	✔	✔
£15 a month	**Mix & match 300**	**300** Anytime any network minutes or texts or any mix of the two	**300** 3 to 3 minutes	✔	✔	✔
£18 a month	**Mix & match 500**	**500** Anytime any network minutes or texts or any mix of the two	**300** 3 to 3 minutes	✔	✔	✔
£21 a month	**Mix & match 700**	**700** Anytime any network minutes or texts or any mix of the two	**300** 3 to 3 minutes	✔	✔	✔
£24 a month	**Mix & match 900**	**900** Anytime any network minutes or texts or any mix of the two	**300** 3 to 3 minutes	✔	✔	✔
£27 a month	**Mix & match 1100**	**1100** Anytime any network minutes or texts or any mix of the two	**300** 3 to 3 minutes	✔	✔	✔

- Pay by voucher or direct debit
- If you pay by voucher, service is suspended once the monthly allowance is reached
- If you pay by direct debit, any minutes or texts over the allowance are charged at 15p per minute or 15p per text
- 10% discount if you pay by direct debit
- All tariffs do not include VAT which is charged at $17\frac{1}{2}\%$

Use the information on Mobile phone tariffs to help you answer these questions.

1 How many hours is 900 minutes?

2 How many hours and minutes is 700 minutes?

3 Janis has the '£12 promotional tariff'. She pays by voucher. She does not use her phone for voice calls. So far in a month she has sent 43 texts. How many more can she send that month before service is suspended?

4 Andy has the '£12 promotional' tariff. He pays by direct debit. How much will this cost per month after the 10% discount?

5 Ben has the 'Mix and match 300' tariff. Before any discounts or VAT how much would this cost for a 12-month contract?

6 Gordon has the '£12 promotional' tariff. So far he has used 24 minutes on voice calls and sent 19 texts. How many more minutes or texts can he send before he gets charged extra?

7 Ed has the 'Mix and match 700' tariff and pays by voucher each month.
  a How much does this cost a month before VAT is added?
  b How much does this cost a month when VAT at $17\frac{1}{2}\%$ is added?

8 Sandra has the 'Mix and match 500' tariff. She uses all of her any network minutes and all of her free '3 to 3' minutes. How many minutes did she talk in total? Give your answer in hours and minutes.

9 Mel has the 'Mix and match 500' tariff. She pays by direct debit. In one month she uses all of her allowed anytime, any network voice minutes and makes a further x minutes of voice calls. Her bill for the month before discount and VAT is £24. What is the value of x?

10 Phil has the 'Mix and match 700' tariff. He pays by direct debit. In one month He makes 550 anytime, any network voice minutes and sends y texts. His bill for the month before discount and VAT is £30. What is the value of y?

The table shows the tariffs for people who send a lot of texts

Pick your plan

Texter plans		Texts	Minutes	Free voicemail	One-Off Cost	Unlimited Skype
£15 a month	**£15 Texter**	**600**	**75** Anytime, any network			
£20 a month	**£20 Texter**	**1000**	**100** Anytime, any network			

- If you pay by direct debit, any extra voice minutes are charged at 15p per minute and extra texts are charged at 10p per text

- 10% discount if you pay by direct debit

- All tariffs do not include VAT which is charged at $17\frac{1}{2}\%$

11 Dave has the '£15 texter' tariff. He pays by direct debit. In one month he uses 750 texts and 100 minutes of voice calls.
What is his bill for that month?

12 Andy has the '£20 texter' tariff. He pays by direct debit. In one month he uses all of his 100 anytime, any network voice calls and makes x texts. His bill for the month before discount and VAT is £23. What is the value of x?

13 Lucy has the '£15 texter' tariff. She pays by direct debit. In one month she makes y minutes of voice calls and 540 texts. Her bill for the month before discount and VAT is £24.90. What is the value of y?

14 Coryn has a 'Mix and match 300' tariff. He pays by voucher. Coryn knows that his average voice calls per month are 220 minutes and he sends an average of 40 texts. He sees this advertisement.

> Special offer for existing customers
> 'Mix and match 250'
> 250 anytime any network minutes or texts or any mix of the two.
> Only £13.00 per month *including* VAT.
> Extra minutes or texts 15p.

If Coryn changes to the 'Mix and match 250' tariff, will he save money in an average month?
You must show your working to justify your answer.

Adding and subtracting fractions

You met the addition and subtraction of fractions in Year 8. This section will show you how to solve all types of problems involving the addition and subtraction of fractions.

Example 2.1

Work out the answer to each of these.

a $3\frac{1}{3} + 1\frac{2}{5}$ **b** $1\frac{3}{4} + 2\frac{5}{6}$

a When adding mixed numbers, you can convert them to improper (top-heavy) fractions and add them using a common denominator. If appropriate, cancel and/or convert the answer to a mixed number.

So, you have:

$$3\frac{1}{3} + 1\frac{2}{5} = \frac{10}{3} + \frac{7}{5}$$
$$= \frac{50}{15} + \frac{21}{15} = \frac{71}{15} = 4\frac{11}{15}$$

As this method involves large numbers, it is easy to make a mistake. A better method is to split up the problem:

$$3\frac{1}{3} + 1\frac{2}{5} = 3 + 1 + \frac{1}{3} + \frac{2}{5}$$

The whole-number part gives $3 + 1 = 4$, and the fraction part gives:

$$\frac{1}{3} + \frac{2}{5} = \frac{5}{15} + \frac{6}{15} = \frac{11}{15}$$

Hence, the total is:

$$4 + \frac{11}{15} = 4\frac{11}{15}$$

b Using the method of splitting up the calculation, you have:

$$1\frac{3}{4} + 2\frac{5}{6} = 1 + \frac{3}{4} + 2 + \frac{5}{6}$$
$$= 3 + \frac{9}{12} + \frac{10}{12}$$
$$= 3 + \frac{19}{12} = 3 + 1\frac{7}{12} = 4\frac{7}{12}$$

Example 2.2 ▶ Work out the answer to each of the following.

a $3\frac{5}{6} - 1\frac{1}{4}$ **b** $4\frac{3}{8} - 1\frac{2}{3}$

a When subtracting mixed numbers, you can convert them to improper (top-heavy) fractions and subtract them using a common denominator. If appropriate, cancel and/or convert the answer back to a mixed number.

So, you have:

$$3\frac{5}{6} - 1\frac{1}{4} = \frac{23}{6} - \frac{5}{4}$$
$$= \frac{46}{12} - \frac{15}{12} = \frac{31}{12} = 2\frac{7}{12}$$

As in Example 2.1, a better method is to split up the problem:

$$3 + \frac{5}{6} - 1 - \frac{1}{4} = 3 - 1 + \frac{5}{6} - \frac{1}{4}$$

The whole-number part gives $3 - 1 = 2$, and the fraction part gives:

$$\frac{5}{6} - \frac{1}{4} = \frac{10}{12} - \frac{3}{12} = \frac{7}{12}$$

Hence, the total is:

$$2 + \frac{7}{12} = 2\frac{7}{12}$$

b Again, using the method of splitting up the calculation, you have:

$$4\frac{3}{8} - 1\frac{2}{3} = 4 + \frac{3}{8} - 1 - \frac{2}{3}$$
$$= 4 - 1 + \frac{3}{8} - \frac{2}{3}$$
$$= 3 + \frac{9}{24} - \frac{16}{24}$$
$$= 3 - \frac{7}{24} = 2\frac{17}{24}$$

Exercise 2A

Convert each of the following pairs of fractions to a pair of equivalent fractions with a common denominator. Then work out the answer, cancelling down or writing as a mixed number if appropriate.

1 a $1\frac{2}{3} + 1\frac{1}{4}$ **b** $2\frac{2}{5} + 2\frac{1}{6}$ **c** $2\frac{1}{3} + 1\frac{2}{5}$ **d** $2\frac{1}{3} + 1\frac{1}{2}$

   e $4\frac{1}{5} + 1\frac{3}{4}$ **f** $5\frac{1}{2} + 1\frac{5}{6}$ **g** $6\frac{5}{6} + 2\frac{1}{9}$ **h** $7\frac{1}{6} + 3\frac{7}{8}$

2 a $3\frac{1}{3} - 1\frac{1}{4}$ **b** $4\frac{2}{5} - 1\frac{1}{6}$ **c** $2\frac{2}{5} - 1\frac{1}{3}$ **d** $3\frac{1}{2} - 1\frac{1}{3}$

   e $3\frac{2}{5} - 1\frac{3}{4}$ **f** $5\frac{1}{2} - 1\frac{5}{6}$ **g** $7\frac{5}{6} - 2\frac{8}{9}$ **h** $6\frac{5}{6} - 3\frac{7}{8}$

3 Find the lowest common multiple (LCM) of each of the following pairs of numbers. [*Hint:* Write out the tables of each number until you find the LCM. Start with the larger number.]

   a 4 and 14   **b** 9 and 21   **c** 12 and 21   **d** 18 and 24

4 Add or subtract each of the following pairs of fractions. Use the LCMs found in Question 3 as denominators.

   a $\frac{3}{4} + \frac{9}{14}$ **b** $\frac{2}{9} + \frac{4}{21}$ **c** $\frac{5}{12} - \frac{2}{21}$ **d** $\frac{13}{18} + \frac{11}{24}$

5 A rectangle measures $3\frac{5}{9}$ cm by $7\frac{5}{6}$ cm. Calculate its perimeter.

6 A knife has a total length of $13\frac{2}{3}$ cm. The handle is $6\frac{3}{4}$ cm. How long is the blade?

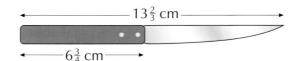

7 Work out each of the following.

   a $\frac{5}{16} + \frac{3}{20}$ **b** $\frac{11}{28} + \frac{9}{35}$ **c** $\frac{31}{48} - \frac{15}{32}$ **d** $\frac{19}{25} - \frac{7}{15}$

Extension Work

This is a fractional magic square.

What is the magic number?

Find the missing values in the cells.

$\frac{2}{15}$		
$\frac{7}{15}$	$\frac{1}{3}$	$\frac{1}{5}$

Multiplying and dividing fractions

So far, you have seen how to add and to subtract fractions. In this section, you will multiply and divide fractions.

Example 2.3 ▷   Jan's watering can is $\frac{3}{5}$ full. She waters her roses and uses half of this water. How full is her watering can now?

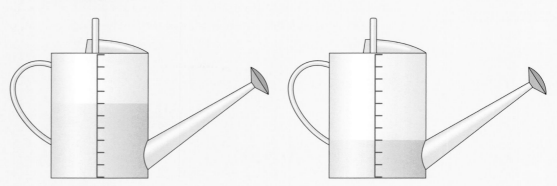

As you can see from the diagram, Jan's watering can is $\frac{3}{10}$ full after she has watered the roses. How can you calculate this result?

One half of $\frac{3}{5}$ is written as:

$$\frac{1}{2} \times \frac{3}{5} = \frac{1 \times 3}{2 \times 5} = \frac{3}{10}$$

This shows that when a fraction is multiplied by another fraction, the new numerator is found by multiplying together the two original numerators, and the new denominator by multiplying together the two original denominators.

Example 2.4 ▶   Work out each of these.

     a $\frac{3}{4} \times \frac{2}{9}$ **b** $2\frac{3}{7} \times 2\frac{4}{5}$

     a   Following Example 2.3, you can calculate mentally that the answer is $\frac{6}{36}$, which can be cancelled to $\frac{1}{6}$. However, this is an example of where it is easier to cancel before you complete the multiplication.

         When numerators and denominators have factors in common, you can cancel them. In this example, 3 and 9 will cancel, as do 2 and 4. The calculation is therefore given like this:

$$\frac{\cancel{3}^{1}}{\cancel{4}_{2}} \times \frac{\cancel{2}^{1}}{\cancel{9}_{3}} = \frac{1}{6}$$

         The remaining numbers are multiplied together to give the new numerator and the new denominator. When the fractions are cancelled properly, the final answer will not cancel.

     b   Convert the mixed numbers to improper (top-heavy) fractions and cancel when possible. Change the answer to a mixed number if appropriate.

         Hence, you have:

$$2\frac{3}{7} \times 2\frac{4}{5} = \frac{17}{\cancel{7}_{1}} \times \frac{\cancel{14}^{2}}{5}$$

$$= \frac{34}{5} = 6\frac{4}{5}$$

Example 2.5 ▶   Work out each of these.

     a $\frac{3}{5} \div \frac{1}{4}$ **b** $\frac{15}{24} \div \frac{9}{16}$ **c** $2\frac{2}{7} \div 1\frac{11}{21}$

     a   When you are dividing by a fraction, always use the following rule:
            Turn the dividing fraction upside down and multiply by it.

         So, you have:

$$\frac{3}{5} \div \frac{1}{4} = \frac{3}{5} \times \frac{4}{1} = \frac{3 \times 4}{5 \times 1} = \frac{12}{5} = 2\frac{2}{5}$$

     b   When possible, cancel during the multiplication.

$$\frac{15}{24} \div \frac{9}{16} = \frac{\cancel{15}^{5}}{\cancel{24}_{3}} \times \frac{\cancel{16}^{2}}{\cancel{9}_{3}} = \frac{5 \times 2}{3 \times 3} = \frac{10}{9} = 1\frac{1}{9}$$

     c   Convert the mixed numbers to improper (top-heavy) fractions. Turn the dividing fraction upside down, put in a multiplication sign and cancel if possible. Then change the result to a mixed number if appropriate.

$$2\frac{2}{7} \div 1\frac{11}{21} = \frac{16}{7} \div \frac{32}{21}$$

$$= \frac{\cancel{16}^{1}}{\cancel{7}_{1}} \times \frac{\cancel{21}^{3}}{\cancel{32}_{2}} = \frac{3}{2} = 1\frac{1}{2}$$

Exercise 2B

1. Work out each of the following. Cancel before multiplying when possible.

   a $\frac{1}{3} \times \frac{2}{5}$ **b** $\frac{3}{4} \times \frac{3}{4}$ **c** $\frac{2}{7} \times \frac{5}{8}$ **d** $\frac{3}{8} \times \frac{4}{9}$

   e $\frac{5}{8} \times \frac{12}{25}$ **f** $\frac{5}{6} \times \frac{3}{5}$ **g** $\frac{1}{2} \times \frac{6}{11}$ **h** $\frac{1}{4} \times \frac{8}{15}$

   i $\frac{3}{4} \times \frac{8}{9}$ **j** $\frac{3}{5} \times \frac{15}{22} \times \frac{11}{18}$

2. Work out each of the following. Write as improper (top-heavy) fractions and cancel before multiplying when possible.

   a $1\frac{3}{5} \times 2\frac{1}{8}$ **b** $2\frac{3}{4} \times 3\frac{1}{5}$ **c** $2\frac{1}{2} \times 1\frac{3}{5}$ **d** $1\frac{1}{4} \times 1\frac{4}{5}$

   e $2\frac{1}{5} \times \frac{10}{21}$ **f** $3\frac{1}{2} \times \frac{8}{35}$ **g** $\frac{1}{2} \times 3\frac{3}{5}$ **h** $2\frac{2}{7} \times 2\frac{4}{5}$

   i $1\frac{5}{6} \times 2\frac{2}{5}$ **j** $4\frac{1}{2} \times 2\frac{3}{5}$

3. Work out each of the following. Cancel at the multiplication stage when possible.

   a $\frac{1}{2} \div \frac{1}{8}$ **b** $\frac{2}{3} \div \frac{3}{5}$ **c** $\frac{5}{6} \div \frac{2}{3}$ **d** $\frac{1}{3} \div \frac{6}{7}$

   e $\frac{4}{5} \div \frac{3}{10}$ **f** $\frac{5}{8} \div \frac{15}{16}$ **g** $\frac{2}{7} \div \frac{7}{8}$ **h** $\frac{3}{4} \div \frac{9}{13}$

   i $\frac{1}{2} \div \frac{3}{5}$ **j** $\frac{1}{4} \div \frac{3}{8}$

4. Work out each of the following. Write as improper (top-heavy) fractions and cancel at the multiplication stage when possible.

   a $1\frac{1}{4} \div \frac{5}{8}$ **b** $3\frac{1}{2} \div 1\frac{3}{5}$ **c** $2\frac{1}{2} \div 1\frac{1}{4}$ **d** $1\frac{2}{3} \div 1\frac{3}{5}$

   e $2\frac{5}{6} \div 1\frac{7}{12}$ **f** $1\frac{1}{2} \div 2\frac{3}{8}$ **g** $4\frac{1}{2} \div \frac{3}{5}$ **h** $4\frac{1}{2} \div \frac{8}{9}$

   i $\frac{7}{8} \div 2\frac{3}{4}$ **j** $3\frac{1}{2} \div \frac{3}{4}$

5. A rectangle has sides of $\frac{3}{7}$ cm and $\frac{14}{27}$ cm. Calculate its area.

6. A rectangle has sides $5\frac{1}{4}$ cm and $4\frac{5}{8}$ cm. Calculate its area.

7. How many $\frac{2}{3}$ m lengths of cloth can be cut from a roll that is $3\frac{2}{9}$ m long?

8. A rectangle has an area of $7\frac{4}{5}$ m². Its length is $3\frac{1}{4}$ m. What is its width?

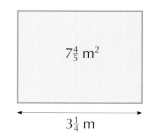

$7\frac{4}{5}$ m²

$3\frac{1}{4}$ m

Extension **Work**

The rules of BODMAS apply when working with fractions.
Work out each of these.

a $\frac{3}{4} \div \frac{7}{16} \times 1\frac{3}{4}$ **b** $(3\frac{3}{5} \div 2\frac{1}{4}) \div (4 - 1\frac{3}{5})$

c $\frac{11\frac{1}{4} \times 4\frac{2}{3}}{15}$ **d** $\frac{9}{5\frac{1}{3} \times 3\frac{3}{8}}$ **e** $(3\frac{1}{2})^2 \times \frac{8}{21}$

Percentages and compound interest

If you put £100 in a bank and it earns 5% interest each year, which graph do you think represents the way the amount of money in the bank changes as time passes – assuming you don't spend any of it!

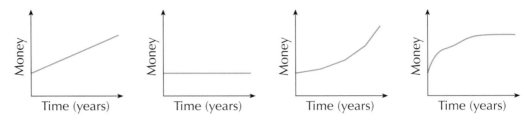

Example 2.6 ▷

Jenny puts £100 in a bank and it earns 5% interest per annum (Latin for 'each year'). How much will she have after 3 years ?

Making calculations such as this are sometimes called **compound interest** problems. There are two ways to solve such problems.

Method 1 *Increase and add on*

Calculate the amount of interest earned after each year and add it to the previous year's total, as shown below.

After first year: 5% of £100 = £5, which gives Jenny £100 + £5 = £105

After second year: 5% of £105 = £5.25, which gives Jenny £105 + £5.25
                                   = £110.25

After third year: 5% of £110.25 = £5.51, which gives Jenny £110.25 + £5.51
                                   = £115.76

The last amount of interest has been rounded to the nearest penny. As you can see, the increase gets bigger year by year.

Method 2 *Use a multiplier*

When dealing with percentage increase, the multiplier is found by adding the percentage increase expressed as a decimal to 1, which represents the original value. So, in this case, the multiplier is given by 1 + 0.05 = 1.05

(When dealing with a percentage decrease, the multiplier is found by subtracting the decrease from 1, which gives a value for the multiplier of less than 1.)

So, you have:

After first year: £100 × 1.05 = £105

After second year: £105 × 1.05 = £110.25

After third year: £110.25 × 1.05 = £115.76

This can also be done using the power key on the calculator as:
£100 × $(1.05)^3$ = £115.7625 ≈ £115.76

The second method is good if you use a calculator as you get the final answer very quickly. Make sure that you write down your calculation in case you make a mistake.

Example 2.7 ▷ A petri dish containing 200 000 bacteria is treated with a new drug. This reduces the number of bacteria by 16% each day.

a How many bacteria remain after 7 days?

b How long does it take to reduce the bacteria to below a safe level of 20 000?

a The method of calculating the decrease and subtracting it day by day will take too long. It is quicker to use a multiplier. For a 16% decrease, the multiplier is 0.84.

Key into your calculator:

> ⟦2⟧⟦0⟧⟦0⟧⟦0⟧⟦0⟧⟦0⟧⟦×⟧⟦(⟧⟦0⟧⟦.⟧⟦8⟧⟦4⟧⟦)⟧⟦$x^{\blacksquare}$⟧⟦7⟧⟦=⟧

You may not need the brackets and your power key may be different.

This gives an answer of 59 018.069 31, which can be rounded to 59 000 bacteria.

b Using trial and improvement to make this calculation, gives these rounded values:
> 168 000,   141 120,   118 541,   99 574,   83 642,   70 260,   59 018,
> 49 575,   41 643,   34 980,   29 383,   24 682,   20 733,   17 416

So, it takes 14 days to get below 20 000.

Check by calculating $200\,000 \times 0.84^{13}$ and $200\,000 \times 0.84^{14}$.

Compound interest does not only concern money. It can be applied to, for example, growth in population and increases in the body weight of animals. It can also involve reduction by a fixed percentage, such as decrease in the value of a car, pollution losses and water losses.

Exercise 2C

① Write down the multiplier which is equivalent to each of these.

a	12% increase	**b**	5% decrease	**c**	8% decrease
d	7% increase	**e**	4% decrease	**f**	2% increase
g	3.2% increase	**h**	$2\frac{1}{2}$% increase	**i**	15% decrease
j	6% increase	**k**	2.6% decrease	**l**	$\frac{1}{2}$% increase
m	24% decrease	**n**	7% decrease	**o**	$17\frac{1}{2}$% increase

You may want to check your answers, as they will help you with the rest of the questions.

For each part of questions 2–6 write down:

i the multiplier.   **ii** your calculation.   **iii** the answer to the question.

In questions 2 and 3, the first part has been done for you.

② How much money would you have in the bank if you invest:

a £200 at 2% interest per annum for 4 years?

    i Multiplier = 1 + 0.02 = 1.02

    ii Calculation: £200 × (1.02)^4

    iii Answer: £216.49 (to the nearest penny)

b £3000 at 3.2% interest per annum for 7 years?

c £120 at 6% interest per annum for 10 years?

d   £5000 at 7% interest per annum for 20 years?

e   £75 at $2\frac{1}{2}$% interest per annum for 3 years?

3   Investments (including stocks and shares) can decrease in value as well as increase. How much would your investments be worth in each of the following cases?

    a   You invested £3000 which lost 4% each year for 6 years.

        i   Multiplier = 1 − 0.04 = 0.96

        ii   Calculation: £3000 × $(0.96)^6$

        iii   Answer: £2348.27 (to the nearest penny)

    b   You invested £250 which lost 2.6% each year for 5 years.

    c   You invested £4000 which lost 24% each year for 4 years.

4   To decrease the rabbit population in Australia, the disease myxomatosis was introduced into rabbit colonies. In one colony, there were 45 000 rabbits. The disease decreased the population by 7% each month. How many rabbits were left in that colony after:

    a   4 months?   **b**   a year?

 5   Some Internet sales sites will decrease the price of a product by a certain percentage each day until someone buys it.

    Freda is interested in buying a computer. She has £1500 to spend. An Internet site has the computer Freda wants but it is £2000. The price is to be decreased by 5% per day. How many days will Freda have to wait until she can afford the computer?

 6   During a hot spell, a pond loses 8% of its water each day due to evaporation. It has 120 gallons in it at the start of the hot spell. How many days will it take before the pond's volume of water falls to 45 gallons?

Extension **Work**

 Jane started drinking a bottle of cola a day, which cost her £1.50.

Her brother Jack put £1.50 into a jar each day and took the money (£45) to the bank each month.

The bank paid Jack $\frac{1}{2}$% compound interest each month.

1   How much does Jane spend on cola in a year (365 days)?

2   The first £45 that Jack pays in earns 11 months of interest. How much does the first £45 increase to over the 11 months?

3   The second £45 that Jack pays in earns 10 months of interest. How much does the second £45 increase to over the 10 months?

4   Now work out the value of each £45 that Jack pays in. For example, the third £45 is in the bank for 9 months and the final £45 is paid in on the last day of the year, so gets no interest.

5   Add up the answers to parts **2**, **3** and **4** to find out how much Jack has in the bank at the end of the year.

A computer spreadsheet is useful for this activity.

Reverse percentages

In Britain, most prices in shops include VAT. In the USA, a sales tax (similar to VAT) has to be added to the displayed price.

Which camera is cheaper if the exchange rate is $1.56 to one pound?

Cost £175.25 (including 17½% VAT)

Cost $250.00 (not including 6% sales tax)

Example 2.8 ▶

After a 10% pay rise, John now gets £5.50 an hour. How much per hour did he get before the pay rise?

Making calculations such as this are sometimes called **reverse percentage** problems. There are two ways to solve such problems.

Method 1 *Unitary method*

A 10% pay rise means that he now gets 100% + 10% = 110%

   £5.50 represents 110%

   £0.05 represents 1% (dividing both sides by 110)

   £5.00 represents 100% (multiplying both sides by 100)

So, before his pay rise, John was paid £5.00 an hour.

Method 2 *Use a multiplier*

10% = 0.1

A 10% increase is represented by the multiplier 1 + 0.1 = 1.1

To work backwards to find John's hourly rate of pay before his pay rise, divide £5.50 by the multiplier.

This gives: £5.50 ÷ 1.1 = £5.00

Example 2.9 ▶

In a sale, the price of a coat is reduced by 20%. It now costs £40. How much did it cost before the sale?

Unitary method

In the sale, the price of the coat is 80% (100% − 20%) of the original cost.

So £40 represents 80%

0.50 represents 1% (dividing both sides by 80)

£50 represents 100% (multiplying both sides by 100)

So the price of the coat before the sale was £50.

Example 2.10 ▶

The number of fish in a pond was increased to 3750 in one year. This was a 25% increase. How many fish were in the pond originally?

Multiplier method

A 25% increase is represented by the multiplier 1 + 0.25 = 1.25

To work backwards to find the number of fish in the pond originally, divide 3750 by the multiplier.

This gives 3000.

Exercise 2D

Choose either the unitary method or the multiplier method to answer all the questions.

Set out your working using the following steps.

Unitary method	Multiplier method
Write down the percentage that the new amount represents (100% + % increase or 100% − % decrease)	Write down the multiplier (1 + the increase or 1 − the decrease) written as a decimal
Divide both sides by the percentage to get 1%	Divide the new amount by the multiplier to get the answer
Multiply both sides by 100 to get the answer	

1. The label on a packet of soap powder states it is 25% bigger. The packet now contains 1500 g. How much did it weigh before?

2. After a 10% price increase, a trombone now costs £286. How much was it before the increase?

 3. This table shows the cost of some goods after $17\frac{1}{2}$% VAT is added. Work out the cost of the goods before VAT is added.

Item	Cost (inc VAT)	Item	Cost (inc VAT)
Camera	£223.25	Dishwasher	£293.75
Heater	£70.50	Sofa	£528.75
Printer	£82.25	Computer	£2115.00

4. A suit is on sale at £96, which is 75% of its original price. What was the original price?

5. There was a 20% discount in a sale. Elle bought a pair of boots for £40 in the sale. What was the original price of the boots?

6. In the second year it was open, the attendance at the Magna exhibition went up by 30% to 1 230 000 visitors. How many visitors were there in the first year it was open?

7. I bought a CD in a sale and saved £2.25 off the normal price. This was a 15% reduction. What was the normal price of the CD?

FM

Credit card companies and loan companies quote the Annual Percentage Rate or APR. This is the equivalent over a year to the interest which they charge monthly.

For example, if 2% is charged each month on a loan of £1000, the amount owed after 12 months will be £1000 × $(1.02)^{12}$ = £1268, which is equivalent to 26.8% APR (because £1000 increased by 26.8% gives £1268).

1 Work out the APR for companies which charge an interest rate of:

   a 1.5% per month   **b** 0.9% per month

   c 1% per month   **d** 5% per month

2 Now work out the monthly interest rate for an APR of 30%. [*Hint:* Try trial and improvement.]

A computer spreadsheet is useful for this activity.

Ratio

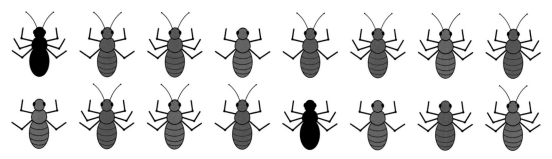

What is the ratio of blue to red to black bugs? What is the ratio of four legged to six legged bugs? What is the ratio of bugs with antennae to bugs without antennae?

You last had to deal with number ratios in Year 7. This section will give you the chance to revise ratios and to take the concept a step further.

Example 2.11 ▷

Simplify each of the following ratios.

  a 14 : 16   **b** 0.4 : 3   **c** 1.4 : 3.2

  a Cancel each number by the HCF (in this case 2), which gives:

     14 : 16 = 7 : 8

  b Ratios would not normally contain decimals but see Example 2.12. So, multiply by 5 to get rid of the decimal, which gives:

     0.4 : 3 = 2 : 15

  c In this case, it is easier to multiply by 10 to get rid of the decimals. Then cancel the resulting ratio. This gives:

     1.4 : 3.2 = 14 : 32 = 7 : 16

Example 2.12 ▷ Write each of the following in the form: **i** $1 : m$ **ii** $n : 1$

a $5 : 8$ **b** $7 : 10$

a **i** To obtain the form $1 : m$, divide by the first number, in this case 5, giving
$5 : 8 = 1 : 1.6$

ii To obtain the form $n : 1$, divide by the second number, in this case 8, giving
$5 : 8 = 0.625 : 1$

b **i** Divide by 7, which gives $7 : 10 = 1 : 1.43$ (rounded to two dp)

ii Divide by 10, which gives $7 : 10 = 0.7 : 1$

Example 2.13 ▷ Divide £750 in the ratio $7 : 8$.

The ratio $7 : 8$ means that £750 is first divided into $7 + 8 = 15$ equal parts. That is,
15 parts = £750, giving 1 part = £750 ÷ 15 = £50

Hence, you have:

  7 parts = $7 \times$ £50 = £350
  8 parts = $8 \times$ £50 = £400

which gives the ratio £350 : £400.

Exercise 2E

1 Cancel each of the following ratios to its simplest form.

  a $4 : 12$ **b** $10 : 16$ **c** $8 : 18$ **d** $9 : 15$ **e** $25 : 40$
  f $14 : 42$ **g** $15 : 50$ **h** $9 : 27$ **i** $6 : 15 : 21$ **j** $30 : 45 : 75$

2 Write each of the following ratios in the form $1 : n$.

  a $4 : 16$ **b** $5 : 16$ **c** $8 : 20$ **d** $6 : 15$ **e** $5 : 40$
  f $12 : 42$ **g** $15 : 50$ **h** $9 : 27$ **i** $24 : 72$ **j** $30 : 45$

3 Write each of the following ratios in the form $n : 1$.

  a $16 : 12$ **b** $10 : 16$ **c** $8 : 20$ **d** $9 : 25$ **e** $25 : 80$
  f $4 : 16$ **g** $15 : 50$ **h** $9 : 27$ **i** $6 : 15$ **j** $45 : 75$

4 The proportion of gold to base metals in two alloys used to make jewellery are
$16 : 25$ and $25 : 40$ respectively.

By writing the two ratios in the form $1 : n$, state which has the greater proportion
of gold.

5 In two sixth-form maths classes, the ratios of the total number of pupils in each class
to those with grade A at AS level are respectively $15 : 8$ and $13 : 7$. By writing the
ratios in the form $n : 1$, state which class has the greater proportion of grade As.

6 **a** Divide £320 in the ratio $3 : 5$. **b** Divide £210 in the ratio $3 : 11$.

  c Divide £800 in the ratio $1 : 0.6$. **d** Divide £450 in the ratio $2.125 : 1$.

7 A recipe for pastry uses two cups of flour to half a cup of margarine. How much flour will be needed to make 375 g of pastry?

8 A concrete mix is made from cement, gravel, sharp sand and builder's sand in the ratio 2 : 4 : 3 : 5.

How much cement will be needed to mix with 35 kg of builder's sand?

9 To make dark green paint, 2 parts of yellow paint are mixed with 5 parts of blue paint. I have 250 ml of yellow paint and 1 litre of blue paint. What is the maximum amount of dark green paint I can make?

10 When he was born, John weighed 2.7 kg. After 1 month, his weight had increased by 75%.

a What is the ratio of John's weight at birth to his weight after 1 month?

b Is any of the information in this question unnecessary?

Extension Work

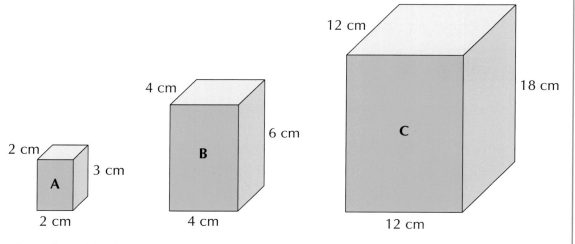

These three blocks are similar. That means that their shapes are the same but they are of different sizes. Work out the area of the front face of each block.

Next, work out each of the following ratios and write it in the form 1 : n.

1 a Length of block A to length of block B
  b Area of the front face of block A to area of the front face of block B
  c Volume of block A to volume of block B

2 a Length of block A to length of block C
  b Area of the front face of block A to area of the front face of block C
  c Volume of block A to volume of block C

3 a Length of block B to length of block C
  b Area of the front face of block B to area of the front face of block C
  c Volume of block B to volume of block C

Look at the answers to parts **1**, **2** and **3**. What do you notice?

Numbers between 0 and 1

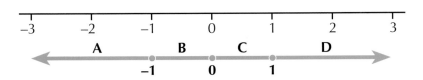

The special numbers −1, 0 and 1 divide the number line shown above into four sets of numbers: A, B, C and D.

A contains all the numbers less than −1. B contains all the numbers between −1 and 0. C contains all the numbers between 0 and 1 and D contains all the numbers greater than 1.

Example 2.14 ▷

a What happens when a number from set A is multiplied by a number from set D?

b What happens when a number from set B is divided by 1?

a Choose any number from set A, say −2. Choose any number from set D, say + 3. Multiply them together:

$$-2 \times +3 = -6$$

The answer belongs to set A.

Try other combinations of numbers from set A and set D. For example:

$$-4 \times +4 = -16 \quad -1.5 \times 5 = -7.5 \quad -5 \times 1.5 = -7.5$$

They all belong to set A. So, a number from set A multiplied by a number from set D always gives a number in set A.

b Pick numbers from set B and divide each one by 1. For example:

$$-0.4 \div 1 = -0.4 \quad -\tfrac{2}{3} \div 1 = -\tfrac{2}{3} \quad -0.03 \div 1 = -0.03$$

The answers are the same as the values from set B. So, they all give numbers in set B.

Exercise 2F

1 Copy and complete this table, which shows the result of multiplying the first number by the second number. The result from Example 2.14, part **a**, has been filled in along with some other results.

Second number

	×	Set A	−1	Set B	0	Set C	1	Set D
First number	Set A			C or D			Set A	
	−1						−1	
	Set B							
	0	0						
	Set C	A or B						
	1						1	
	Set D	Set A						

7

7

2) Copy and complete this table, which shows the result of dividing the first number by the second number. The result from Example 2.14, part **b**, has been filled in along with some other results. One thing you cannot do in maths is to divide by zero. So, this column has been deleted.

Second number

÷	Set A	−1	Set B	0	Set C	1	Set D
Set A	C or D						
−1						−1	
Set B			C or D		A or B		
0	0						
Set C							
1							
Set D							

First number

3) Use your tables to answer each of the following. Choose one answer.

a When any positive number is divided by a number between 0 and 1, the answer is:
- **i** the same.
- **ii** always bigger.
- **iii** always smaller.
- **iv** sometimes bigger, sometimes smaller.

b When any positive number is divided by a number bigger than 1, the answer is:
- **i** the same.
- **ii** always bigger.
- **iii** always smaller.
- **iv** sometimes bigger, sometimes smaller.

c When any positive number is multiplied by a number between 0 and 1, the answer is:
- **i** the same.
- **ii** always bigger.
- **iii** always smaller.
- **iv** sometimes bigger, sometimes smaller.

d When any positive number is multiplied by a number bigger than 1, the answer is:
- **i** the same.
- **ii** always bigger.
- **iii** always smaller.
- **iv** sometimes bigger, sometimes smaller.

4) In each case, give an example to show that the statement is not true. (Such an example is called a **counter-example**.)

a When you divide −1 by any number, the answer is always negative.

b When you multiply any number by a number less than −1, the answer is always bigger.

c Dividing any number by a number between −1 and 1 (except 0) always gives a bigger number.

d Multiplying any number by a number between −1 and 1 (except 0) always gives a smaller number.

Extension Work

Repeat Example 2.14 but this time add and subtract the numbers from each set. Can you reach any definite conclusion?

Order of operations

This section gives you more practice in working out mathematical operations in the correct order.

Do you remember BODMAS or BIDMAS?

B – Brackets	**B** – Brackets
O – pOwers	**I** – Indices
DM – Division and Multiplication	**DM** – Division and Multiplication
AS – Addition and Subtraction	**AS** – Addition and Subtraction

Example 2.15 ▷

Work out each of the following.

a $(2 + 3^2) \times 3 \div 5$ **b** $4 \times [3^2 - (4 + 2)]^2$

a The bracket is calculated first, and within the bracket the power or index is calculated first.

$$(2 + 3^2) \times 3 \div 5 = (2 + 9) \times 3 \div 5 = 11 \times 3 \div 5 = 33 \div 5 = 6.6$$

Note that when you get only multiplication and division in the problem, it is done from left to right.

b This has nested brackets. The inside (round) bracket is calculated first.

$$4 \times [3^2 - (4 + 2)]^2 = 4 \times [3^2 - 6]^2 = 4 \times [9 - 6]^2 = 4 \times 3^2 = 4 \times 9 = 36$$

Example 2.16 ▷

Work out each of these.

a $49 \div (11 - 4) - 5 + 2 \times (6 \div 3)^2$ **b** $\dfrac{(3 \times 7)^2}{6 \times 7}$

a $49 \div (11 - 4) - 5 + 2 \times (6 \div 3)^2 = 49 \div 7 - 5 + 2 \times 2^2$
$$= 49 \div 7 - 5 + 2 \times 4$$
$$= 7 - 5 + 2 \times 4$$
$$= 7 - 5 + 8 = 10$$

b Rather than work out the bracket, write the problem out in full and cancel.

$$\frac{(3 \times 7)^2}{6 \times 7} = \frac{\overset{1}{\cancel{3}} \times \overset{1}{\cancel{7}} \times 3 \times 7}{\underset{2}{\cancel{6}} \times \underset{1}{\cancel{7}}} = \frac{21}{2} = 10.5$$

Exercise 2G

Do not use a calculator to solve any of these problems.

1 Calculate each of the following. Show your working.

a $(2 + 3)^2 \times (4 - 2)$ **b** $(7^2 - 4) \div (2 + 1)^2$ **c** $(7 + 5^2) \div (2 \times 2^3)$

d $(2 + 4)^2 \div (3 - 1)^3$ **e** $(6^2 + 2^2) \div (6 + 2)^2$ **f** $(3 + 6)^2 \div (3^2 + 6^2)$

g $(4 + 4^2) \times (2 + 2^2)$ **h** $(6 + 3)^2 \div (2^3 + 1)$ **i** $(5^2 - 4) \div (3^2 - 2)$

2 Calculate each of the following.

a $45 \div (7 - 2) - 5 + 4(12 \div 6)^3$ **b** $(3 + 2) \times 5^2 - 6(3^2 - 4)$

c $(4 - 2) \times (3 + 2)^2 \div (4 + 4^2)$ **d** $63 \div (7 + 2) + 5 - 2(3^2 - 2^3)$

3 Put brackets into each of these problems to make it true.

a $5 - 1^2 \times 4 - 2 = 62$ **b** $5 - 1^2 \times 4 - 2 = -1$ **c** $5 - 1^2 \times 4 - 2 = 32$

d $3 + 2^2 + 4 \times 2 = 33$ **e** $3 + 2^2 + 4 \times 2 = 19$ **f** $3 + 2^2 + 4 \times 2 = 22$

4 Work out each of the following. Do the nested brackets first.

a $[3 + (2 + 1)^2] \div [5(4 - 2)^2]$ **b** $(8 - 2)^2 \div [(6 - 1) + (3^2 - 2)]$

c $[15 + (3 + 2)^2] \div [(5 - 3)^3 + 2]$ **d** $[(2 \times 3^2) \div (7 - 1)]^3 \times [(6 - 4) \times (7 - 2)]^2$

5 Work out each of these.

a $\dfrac{7 \times 6^2}{7 \times 3}$ **b** $\dfrac{(7 \times 6)^2}{7 \times 3}$ **c** $\dfrac{2 + 5^2}{7 - 2^2}$ **d** $\dfrac{(2 + 5)^2}{(7 - 2)^2}$

e $-6^2 + 5$ **f** $-(6 + 5)^2$ **g** $(-6)^2 + 5$ **h** $-6 + 5^2$

Extension **Work**

The opposite to BODMAS is SAMDOB.

This is the order in which operations are 'undone' or inverted when solving equations.

For example, to solve

$3x - 7 = 8$

ignore the right-hand side for the moment. On the left-hand side, you have '3 times' and 'subtract 7'. According to SAMDOB, you first undo the 'subtract 7' and then undo the '3 times'. To undo an operation, you perform the inverse operation, which is first add 7 and then divide by 3.

Now do this to the right-hand side. So, 8 add 7 = 15 and 15 divided by 3 is 5. Hence, $x = 5$.

Check: $3 \times 5 - 7 = 8$, which is correct.

To solve $\dfrac{x + 2}{3} = 8$, you must remember that the line acts as both a division operation and a bracket. So, by SAMDOB, you first undo 'divide by 3' and then undo the bracket 'plus 2'. The inverse operations are multiply by 3 and subtract 2, which give $8 \times 3 = 24$ and $24 - 2 = 22$. That is, $x = 22$.

Check: $\dfrac{22 + 2}{3} = 8$, which is correct.

For each of these equations, write down the order in which the left-hand side is undone, and then write down the inverse operations. Then apply these to the right-hand side to solve the equation.

a $5x + 8 = 18$ **b** $\dfrac{x - 3}{6} = 9$ **c** $3(x - 7) = 9$ **d** $\dfrac{x}{3} - 2 = 10$

Rounding and estimation

Example **2.17** Round each of the following numbers to one significant figure.

   a   582   b   0.0893   c   7341   d   23.42

When rounding to one significant figure, you need to find the nearest number which has just one digit followed or preceded by zeros. This gives:

   a $582 \approx 600$ (1 sf)   b $0.0893 \approx 0.09$ (1 sf)

   c $7341 \approx 7000$ (1 sf)   d $23.42 \approx 20$ (1 sf)

Example **2.18** By rounding the numbers to one significant figure, estimate the value of each of the following.

   a $(3124 \times 476) \div 283$ b $0.067 \times (0.82 - 0.57)$

   a   Round each number to one significant figure, then proceed with the calculation using the rules of operations.

$$(3124 \times 476) \div 283 \approx (3000 \times 500) \div 300$$
$$= 1\,500\,000 \div 300$$
$$= 150\,000 \div 30$$
$$= 15\,000 \div 3 = 5000$$

   b   Proceed as in part **a**.

$$0.067 \times (0.82 - 0.57) \approx 0.07 \times (0.8 - 0.6)$$
$$= 0.07 \times 0.2 = 0.014$$

Exercise 2H

1 Round each of the following numbers to one significant figure.

   a   598   b   312   c   6734   d   109
   e   32.7   f   0.092   g   345.8   h   0.378
   i   0.65   j   6098   k   888   l   98.52

2 Work out each of the following.

   a 200×400 b 300×5000 c 60×70 d 80×2000
   e 90×90 f 0.6×0.3 g 0.09×0.7 h 0.05×0.8
   i 2000×0.05 j 200×0.7 k 0.08×3000 l 0.6×700

3 Work out each of the following.

   a $300 \div 50$ b $600 \div 20$ c $2000 \div 400$ d $24000 \div 60$
   e $800 \div 20$ f $1500 \div 30$ g $200 \div 0.4$ h $300 \div 0.5$
   i $20 \div 0.05$ j $4 \div 0.08$ k $60 \div 0.15$ l $0.09 \div 0.3$

4 By rounding values to one significant figure, estimate the answer to each of the following. Show your working.

a 0.73×621	**b** $278 \div 47$
c $3127 \div 0.58$	**d** 0.062×0.21
e $(19 \times 4.9) + 598$	**f** $(3.7 + 5.8) \times (6.7 + 8.2)$
g $(211 \times 11.2) \times (775 \div 1.8)$	**h** $4.75 \times (3.36 - 0.41)$
i $4.8^2 \times 7.8 \div 0.19^2$	**j** $(19.7 \times 3.8) \div (1.98 + 0.46)$

Extension Work

You can round to any number of significant figures. For example, rounding to three significant figures is very common in trigonometry problems, which you will meet later.

Take, for example, 253.78, which has five significant figures.

$253.78 \approx 253.8 \text{ (4 sf)} \approx 254 \text{ (3 sf)} \approx 250 \text{ (2 sf)} \approx 300 \text{ (1 sf)}$

Now take as an example 0.098 54 which has four significant figures.

$0.098\,54 \approx 0.0985 \text{ (3 sf)} \approx 0.099 \text{ (2 sf)} \approx 0.1 \text{ (1 sf)}$

Round each of the following to the accuracy shown.

a 347 (2 sf)	**b** 4217 (3 sf)	**c** 4217 (2 sf)
d 0.6187 (3 sf)	**e** 0.6187 (2 sf)	**f** 302 (2 sf)
g 4698 (3 sf)	**h** 4698 (2 sf)	**i** 0.0785 (2 sf)
j 978.32 (4 sf)	**k** 978.32 (3 sf)	**l** 978.32 (2 sf)

LEVEL BOOSTER

5
I can work out lowest common multiples.
I can add and subtract simple fractions.
I can reduce a fraction to its simplest form by cancelling common factors.
I can solve simple ratio problems.

6
I can change fractions to decimals.
I can add and subtract fractions with different denominators.
I can solve problems involving ratio.
I can use percentages to solve real-life problems.
I can use brackets correctly.

7
I can multiply and divide by numbers between 0 and 1.
I can solve problems by multiplying and dividing with numbers of any size.
I can understand and use percentage change using multiplier methods.
I can follow a method to calculate reverse percentages.
I can round numbers to one significant figure.

5

1 *2002 Paper 2*

Screenwash is used to clean car windows. To use Screenwash, you mix it with water.

Winter mixture	Summer mixture
Mix 1 part Screenwash with 4 parts water.	Mix 1 part Screenwash with 9 parts water.

a In winter, how much water should I mix with 150 ml of Screenwash?

b In summer, how much Screenwash should I mix with 450 ml of water?

c Is this statement correct?

25% of winter mixture is Screenwash.

Explain your answer.

2 2000 Paper 2

Calculate

8% of £26.50 = £......

$12\frac{1}{2}$% of £98 = £......

3 *2006 5–7 Paper 2*

Three different kinds of woodpecker live in Britain.

The pictogram shows information about the numbers of each type.

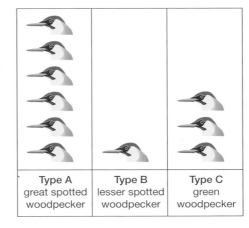

Type A great spotted woodpecker	Type B lesser spotted woodpecker	Type C green woodpecker

Key

 represents 10 000 woodpeckers

a Copy and complete the table below to show the **percentages** of each type of woodpecker:

Type A	Type B	Type C

b The ratio of **Type A : Type B** woodpeckers is 6 : 1.

What is the ratio of **Type B : Type C** woodpeckers?

4 *2007 5–7 Paper 1*

a In this design, the ratio of **grey to black** is **3 : 1**.

What percentage of the design is **black**?

b In this design, **60%** is **grey** and the rest is black.

What is the ratio of **grey to black?**

Write your ratio in its simplest form.

5 *2005 5–7 Paper 1*

a Look at this information:

Two numbers **multiply** to make zero.

One of the statements below is true. Which one?

● Both numbers must be zero.
● At least one number must be zero.
● Exactly one number must be zero.
● Neither number can be zero.

b Now look at this information:

Two numbers **add** to make zero.

If one number is zero, what is the other number?

If **neither** number is zero, give an example of what the numbers could be.

6 *2002 Paper 2*

a One calculation below gives the answer to the question:

What is 70 increased by 9%?

Choose the correct one.

70×0.9 70×1.9 70×0.09 70×1.09

Choose one of the other calculations. Write a question about percentages that this calculation represents.

Calculation chosen: ......

Question it represents: ......

Now do the same for one of the remaining two calculations:

Calculation chosen: ......

Question it represents: ......

b Fill in the missing decimal number.

To decrease by 14%, multiply by ......

7   *2006 5–7 Paper 1*

    a   Give an example to show the statement below is **not** correct:

> When you multiply a number by 2, the answer is always greater than 2.

    b   Now give an example to show the statement below is not correct:

> When you subtract a number from 2, the answer is always less than 2.

    c   Is the statement below correct for **all** numbers?

> The square of a number is greater than the number itself.

    Explain how you know.

8   *2004 5–7 Paper 1*

    a   Calculate $\frac{5}{6} \times \frac{3}{5}$.

    Show your working.

    Write your answer as a fraction in its **simplest form**.

    b   Four-fifths of the members of a club are female.
    Three-quarters of these females are over 20 years old.

    What fraction of the members of the club are females over 20 years old?

    Show your working.

The London Olympics 2012

Olympic village

Beds provided for 17 320 athletes and officials during Olympics.

Beds provided for 8756 athletes and officials during Paralympics.

The dining hall will cater for 5500 athletes at a time.

After the Games, the village will provide 4000 homes.

Tickets

Number of tickets for sale

- 8 million for the Olympics
- 1.6 million for the Paralympics

Tickets include free travel on London Transport.

Cost

75% of tickets will cost less than £50.

Organisers expect to sell 82% of all Olympic tickets and 63% of all Paralympics tickets.

Athletics

Ticket prices start from £15.

20 000 big screen tickets available for £10.

Travel

90% of venues will have three or more forms of public transport including:

- Docklands light railway
- 'Javelin' rail link from St Pancras to Olympic park
- London Underground
- New rail links
- Buses – The iBus: an automatic vehicle location system
- Cycle lanes and footpaths
- Two major park and ride sites off the M25 with a combined capacity of 12 000 cars

During the Games, up to 120 000 passengers will arrive and depart through Stratford station each day.

Use the information on the left to answer these questions.

1 How many beds are there for athletes and officials during the Olympics? Give your answer to one significant figure.

2 The Olympic stadium will have 80 000 seats.
If for an event the stadium is 85% full, how many seats will be empty?

3
a How many passengers will arrive and depart through Stratford station over the 17 days?

b 45% of all spectators visiting the games each day will arrive and depart through Stratford station.
How many spectators are expected each day?

4 Boccia is a Paralympic sport.

The aim of the game is to throw red or blue leather balls as close as possible to a white target ball.

At the end of every round, the competitor whose ball is closest to the target ball scores one point for every one of his balls that is closer than his opponent's.

a At the end of a game, the blue team has 8 points and the red team has 4 points. Write the number of points as a ratio in its simplest form.

b At the end of another game 15 points have been scored altogether. The points are divided between the blue team and the red team in the ratio 3 : 2.
How many points does each team have?

5 Here are some men's long jump world record distances and the years in which they occurred.

8.90 metres	8.95 metres	7.98 metres	8.13 metres	8.21 metres
1991	1968	1931	1960	1935

a Copy and complete the table by putting the distances and years in the correct order. Two of the answers have already been filled in.

Name	Year	World record
Mike Powell	1991	
Bob Beamon		
Ralph Boston		
Jesse Owens		
Chuhei Nambu		7.98 metres

b Ralph Boston broke Jesse Owens' world record.
For how long did Jesse Owens' world record stand before it was broken?

6
a How many tickets for the Olympics will cost less than £50?
b How many tickets for the Olympics that cost less than £50 do the organisers expect to sell?

This chapter is going to show you

- How to construct and solve different types of linear equation
- How to use trial and improvement
- How to solve problems involving direct proportion

What you should already know

- How to solve simple linear equations
- How to find the square root of a number

Equations, formulae and identities

Equations

An **equation** is formed when an expression is made equal to a number or another expression. As a general rule, an equation can be solved.

You will be expected to deal with equations which have only one **variable** or letter in them. For example:

$$3x + 2 = 7 \qquad x^2 = 24 \qquad y + 3 = 4y - 2$$

The **solution** to an equation is that value of the variable which makes the equation true. For example:

$$2x + 6 = 18$$

for which the solution is $x = 6$.

Always check that the answer makes the equation true. In this case:

$$2 \times 6 + 6 = 18$$

which is correct.

Example 3.1 ▷

Solve $4(2x - 3) = 3(x + 11)$.

Expand both brackets to obtain:

$$8x - 12 = 3x + 33$$

Subtract $3x$ from both sides, which gives:

$$5x - 12 = 33$$

Add 12 to both sides to obtain:

$$5x = 45$$

Dividing both sides by 5 gives the solution:

$$x = 9$$

Formulae

Although it may look like an equation, a formula states the connection between two or more quantities. Each quantity is represented by a different letter.

Every formula has a **subject**, which is the variable (letter) which stands on its own, usually on the left-hand side of the 'equals' sign. For example:

$$P = 2l + 2w \qquad A = lw$$

where P and A are the subjects.

Example 3.2 ▷

The formula for the volume of a cylinder is $V = \pi r^2 h$.

Calculate the volume when:

a $r = 5$ and $h = 8$. Give your answer in terms of π.

b $r = r$ and $h = 2r$. Give your answer in terms of π.

a $V = \pi \times 5^2 \times 8 = 200\pi$

b $V = \pi \times r^2 \times 2r = 2r^3\pi$

Identities

An identity is an algebraic equation or formula which is true for all values whether numerical or algebraic. It has a special sign $\equiv$.

Example 3.3 ▷

Show that $(a + b)^2 \equiv a^2 + 2ab + b^2$ is an identity by substituting:

a $a = 3$ and $b = 5$ **b** $a = x$ and $b = 2x$

a   Substitute into the left hand side:
$$(a + b)^2 = (3 + 5)^2 = 8^2 = 64$$

Substitute into the right hand side:
$$a^2 + 2ab + b^2 = 3^2 + 2 \times 3 \times 5 + 5^2 = 9 + 30 + 25 = 64$$

Both sides give the same value of 64.

b   Substitute into the left hand side:
$$(x + 2x)^2 = (3x)^2 = 9x^2$$

Substitute into the right hand side:
$$a^2 + 2ab + b^2 = x^2 + 2 \times x \times 2x + (2x)^2 = x^2 + 4x^2 + 4x^2 = 9x^2$$

Both sides give the same value of $9x^2$.

Exercise 3A

1 Solve each of the following equations.

    a $5(x - 1) = 4(x + 1)$ **b** $3(x - 2) = 2(x + 2)$ **c** $5(x + 3) = 3(x + 5)$

    d $3(2x + 1) = 2(4x + 3)$ **e** $4(3x - 2) = 5(2x + 3)$ **f** $6(2x - 1) = 4(2x + 5)$

2 Solve each of the following equations.

    a $3(m - 1) - 2(m + 4) = 0$ **b** $4(k + 3) - 3(k - 7) = 0$

    c $5(y + 2) - 4(y + 3) = 0$ **d** $2(5x - 4) - 3(2x + 5) = 1$

    e $4(3p - 2) - 2(5p + 3) = 0$ **f** $7(2w - 3) - 5(3w - 1) = 0$

3 a Look at each of the following statements

    A an equation

    B a formula

    C an identity

Note: None of the identities below carry a $\equiv$ sign.

Match either **A** or **B** or **C** to each of the following.

i $3x + 5 = x - 9$	**ii** $y = 4x + 3$	**iii** $t = u + st$
iv $p = 3d$	**v** $\sqrt{x} \times \sqrt{y} = \sqrt{xy}$	**vi** $m + 3 = 5m - 4$
vii $y = mx + c$	**viii** $ax + ay = a(x + y)$	**ix** $t = 3w + 5$

b Write a brief explanation about the difference between an equation, a formula and an identity.

4 The formula $A = 180(n - 2)$ is used to calculate the sum of the angles inside a polygon with n sides.

a Use the formula to calculate the sum of the angles for:

    i an octagon.   **ii** a dodecagon.

b A polygon has an angle sum of 1440°. How many sides does it have?

5 DJ Dave uses the following formula to work out how much to charge for his gigs:

$$C = £55 + £3N + £5T + £10E$$

where:

    N is the number of people attending the gig

    T is the number of hours worked before midnight

    E is the number of hours worked after midnight

Calculate the cost of each of the following gigs.

a A teenager's party with 25 people from 7 pm to 11 pm

b A wedding reception with 60 people from 9 pm to 2 am

6 Show that $2(a + b) = 2a + 2b$ is an identity by substituting the values below into both sides.

a $a = 5$ and $b = 4$ **b** $a = 5x$ and $b = 2x$

7 Show that $(a + b)(a - b) \equiv a^2 - b^2$ is an identity by substituting the values below into both sides:

a $a = 7$ and $b = 4$ **b** $a = 3x$ and $b = x$

Extension Work

1 The area of this rectangle is 6.4 cm². Find its perimeter.

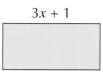

$3x + 1$

$8x$

Solving problems using equations

A problem can often be expressed by an equation which will allow you to solve that problem.

Example 3.4 ▷

Three friends have 200 game cards between them. Joe has 36 more cards than Chris. Kay has twice as many cards as Chris. How many cards does each friend have?

Let the number of cards which Chris has be x. This means that:

Joe has $x + 36$ cards

Kay has $2x$ cards

So, the total number of cards between them is:

$$x + x + 36 + 2x = 4x + 36$$

This gives:

$$4x + 36 = 200$$
$$4x = 200 - 36 = 164$$
$$x = 41$$

So, Chris has 41 cards, Joe has 77 cards and Kay has 82 cards.

Exercise 3B

In each of the following, use the information to set up an equation. Then solve the equation to answer the problem.

1 I think of a number, add 4, divide by 3, then multiply by 5. The final answer is 25. What is the number I am thinking about? Let the number be x.

2 If I double my age, add 4, divide by 5, then take away 2, I get the age at which I first voted (18). How old am I now? Let my age be x.

3 Uncle Jed had a sheep farm in New Zealand with 205 sheep ready to be sheared. I sheared a few sheep, my brother sheared 30 more than me, and Uncle Jed sheared 121 more than my brother. How many sheep did we each shear? Let the number I sheared be x.

4 Joy invited Nicola and Amy for a sleepover. They both took with them their favourite CDs. Joy added her CDs, giving them 64 CDs altogether. Nicola had nine more than Amy, and Amy had 14 more than Joy. How many CDs did each girl have at the sleepover? Let the number of CDs that Joy had be x.

5 The length of a rectangle is twice as long as its width. Its perimeter is 36 cm. What is the area of the rectangle? Let the width of the rectangle be x.

6 Multiplying a number by 3 and adding 4 is equal to subtracting the number from 28. What is the number? Let the number be x.

7 Catherine's age and her mother's age when added together make 63. Catherine's mother is twice as old as Catherine. How old are they both now? Let Catherine's age be x.

8 Helen and James had between them 160 CDs. Helen said to James, "If I had 5 more CDs, I would have twice as many as you". How many CDs do they have each? Let the number of CDs that James has be x.

9 If I double my age and subtract four, I get the same answer as if I add 48 to it. What is my age? Let my age be x.

10 Three data-entry workers were employed to enter 6660 items of data into a computer data bank.

Kathryn could enter twice as much data per hour as Lisa. Sally could enter 150 more items per hour than Lisa. Between them, they entered all the data in 6 hours. What were the number of items per hour that each worker could enter? Let the number of items Lisa enters per hour be x.

Extension Work

1 Charlie is a milkman. He takes ten fewer bottles out on a Tuesday than he does on a Monday. He takes 50 more bottles out on a Wednesday than a Tuesday. He takes two more bottles out on a Thursday than on a Monday. He takes ten less on a Friday than he does on a Monday. He takes out twice as many on a Saturday than he does on a Friday. In one week he will take out 800 bottles. How many does he take out each day? Let the number of bottles he takes out on Monday be x.

2 A, B and C are the three angles in a triangle. Angle A is twice the size of angle B. Angle B is 20° bigger than angle C. What is the size of each angle? Let Angle C be $x°$.

Equations involving fractions

When you have to solve an equation which involves a fraction, you have to use the rules for working out ordinary fractions.

For example, to solve $\frac{x}{3} = 5$, you first multiply both sides by 3 in order to remove the denominator:

$$\frac{x}{3} \times 3 = 5 \times 3$$

which gives:

$$x = 15$$

Follow through Examples 3.5 and 3.6, which show you how to remove the fractional part of equations.

Example 3.5 ▷

Solve $\frac{4x + 5}{3} = 7$.

First, multiply both sides by 3 to obtain:

$$4x + 5 = 21$$

Subtract 5 from both sides, which gives:

$$4x = 16$$

Dividing both sides by 4 gives the solution:

$$x = 4$$

Example 3.6 ▶

Solve $\dfrac{x-1}{2} = \dfrac{2x+8}{6}$.

The product of the two denominators is 12. So, multiply both sides by 12 which, after cancelling, gives:

$$6(x-1) = 2(2x+8)$$

Expand both sides to obtain:

$$6x - 6 = 4x + 16$$

which simplifies to:

$$2x = 22$$
$$x = 11$$

So, $x = 11$ is the solution.

Exercise 3C

1 Solve each of these equations.

   a $\dfrac{x}{6} = 5$ **b** $\dfrac{t}{7} = 3$ **c** $\dfrac{m}{8} = 5$ **d** $\dfrac{x}{2} = 9$ **e** $\dfrac{w}{3} = 6$

   f $\dfrac{g}{4} = 2$ **g** $\dfrac{x}{9} = 5$ **h** $\dfrac{x}{5} = 5$ **i** $\dfrac{x}{4} = 7$ **j** $\dfrac{x}{8} = 3$

2 Solve each of these equations.

   a $\dfrac{4x}{5} = 12$ **b** $\dfrac{2t}{5} = 6$ **c** $\dfrac{3m}{8} = 9$ **d** $\dfrac{2x}{3} = 8$ **e** $\dfrac{3w}{4} = 6$

   f $\dfrac{4y}{9} = 8$ **g** $\dfrac{4x}{7} = 8$ **h** $\dfrac{3x}{5} = 6$ **i** $\dfrac{3x}{4} = 9$ **j** $\dfrac{7x}{8} = 21$

3 Solve each of the following equations.

   a $\dfrac{x+1}{4} = 5$ **b** $\dfrac{x+5}{3} = 7$

   c $\dfrac{x+3}{2} = 5$ **d** $\dfrac{3x+1}{5} = 2$

   e $\dfrac{2x-1}{3} = 5$ **f** $\dfrac{5x+2}{3} = 4$

   g $\dfrac{4x-3}{5} = 5$ **h** $\dfrac{2x+1}{3} = 7$

4 Solve each of the following equations.

   a $\dfrac{(x-2)}{3} = \dfrac{(x+1)}{4}$ **b** $\dfrac{(x+3)}{2} = \dfrac{(x-3)}{5}$

   c $\dfrac{(x-3)}{4} = \dfrac{(x-5)}{2}$ **d** $\dfrac{(2x+1)}{5} = \dfrac{(x-4)}{2}$

   e $\dfrac{(3x-1)}{3} = \dfrac{(2x+3)}{4}$ **f** $\dfrac{(2x-3)}{2} = \dfrac{(3x-2)}{5}$

4

5

6

7

7

1. Solve each of the following equations.

   a $4(2t + 3) = 3(4t + 1) - 5(3t - 2)$ b $2(5h + 4) = 6(2h + 3) - 3(5h + 1)$

   c $5(3m + 1) = 4(5m - 2) - 4(2m - 3)$ d $7(8g - 5) = 5(6g + 4) - 2(3g + 4)$

   e $3(4k - 2) = 5(3k + 1) - 2(4k - 3)$ f $4(3x - 1) = 3(5x - 2) - 4(2x - 7)$

2. Solve each of the following equations.

   a $5(t + 0.3) = 2(t + 1.6) - 4(t - 0.2)$ b $2(h + 1.4) = 5(h + 3.1) + 3(h + 1.1)$

   c $6(m + 1.3) = 3(m - 0.2) - 3(m - 3.2)$ d $5(g - 0.5) = 4(g + 1.4) - 2(3g + 0.4)$

   e $4(4k - 0.2) = 4(k + 1.1) - 2(4k - 3.1)$ f $3(2x - 1.3) = 2(3x - 2.1) - 3(x - 0.7)$

3. Solve each of the following equations.

   a $\dfrac{4}{(x + 1)} = \dfrac{7}{(x + 4)}$ b $\dfrac{5}{(x + 3)} = \dfrac{4}{(x - 1)}$ c $\dfrac{3}{(x + 2)} = \dfrac{2}{(x - 5)}$

   d $\dfrac{7}{(x - 3)} = \dfrac{5}{(x + 4)}$ e $\dfrac{6}{(5x + 1)} = \dfrac{2}{(2x - 1)}$ f $\dfrac{2}{(4x + 3)} = \dfrac{3}{(5x - 1)}$

Equations involving x^2

When you have to solve an equation involving only x^2, try to get x^2 as the subject of the equation. That way you will simply need to find the square root of the other side. This will give two solutions, one positive and the other negative.

Example 3.7

Solve the equation $x^2 + 3 = 19$.

Subtract 3 from both sides to give:
$$x^2 = 19 - 3$$
$$x^2 = 16$$

Since the square root of 16 is 4, the two solutions will be:
$$x = 4 \quad \text{and} \quad x = -4$$

There will be equations for which the square root will need to be taken on both sides. Again, this will give two possible solutions, as Example 3.9 shows.

Example 3.8

Solve the equation $(x + 5)^2 = 81$.

Taking the square root of both sides gives two possibilities:
$$x + 5 = 9 \quad \text{and} \quad x + 5 = -9$$

Solve both of these equations as follows:
$$x + 5 = 9 \qquad \text{and} \qquad x + 5 = -9$$
$$x = 9 - 5 \qquad\qquad\qquad x = -9 - 5$$
$$= 4 \qquad\qquad\qquad\qquad = -14$$

So, the two solutions are $x = 4$ and $x = -14$.

Check out for yourself that both of these solutions work.

1 Solve each of these equations. Each has two solutions.

    a $x^2 = 25$ **b** $x^2 = 81$ **c** $m^2 = 49$ **d** $t^2 = 1.44$ **e** $t^2 = 400$

2 Solve each of these equations. Each has two solutions.

    a $x^2 + 4 = 40$ **b** $x^2 + 8 = 33$ **c** $m^2 + 13 = 62$

    d $t^2 + 23 = 104$ **e** $t^2 - 6 = 10$ **f** $x^2 - 12 = 52$

    g $8 + k^2 = 152$ **h** $12 + g^2 = 133$ **i** $21 + h^2 = 70$

    j $150 - t^2 = 101$ **k** $210 - n^2 = 146$ **l** $175 - y^2 = 94$

3 Solve each of these equations. Each has two solutions.

    a $(x + 3)^2 = 16$ **b** $(x + 5)^2 = 64$ **c** $(m + 1)^2 = 49$

    d $(t + 7)^2 = 900$ **e** $(t + 5)^2 = 400$ **f** $(k + 8)^2 = 144$

    g $(x - 2)^2 = 9$ **h** $(h - 4)^2 = 36$ **i** $(n - 7)^2 = 121$

4 Solve each of these equations. Each has two solutions.

    a $4 = \dfrac{100}{x^2}$ **b** $2 = \dfrac{72}{x^2}$ **c** $3 = \dfrac{48}{x^2}$

    d $5 = \dfrac{320}{x^2}$ **e** $7 = \dfrac{343}{x^2}$ **f** $6 = \dfrac{486}{x^2}$

5 I square a number, add 18 to the outcome and get 67. What are the two possible numbers I have squared?

6 I think of a number, subtract 5, square it and get the answer 169. What are the two possible numbers I am thinking of?

7 Alex thought of a number, squared it, then subtracted the result from 200 and got the answer 79. What two numbers might she have got if she had doubled her starting number instead of squaring it?

8 Joy and Amy both thought of the same number. Joy squared her number, then subtracted 12 to get 52. Amy doubled her number and added it to 12. What are the two possible final answers that Amy could get?

Extension Work

1   135 is a special number as $1^1 + 3^2 + 5^3 = 135$.

    a   Find the next highest number with this same property of powers.

    b   Use a spreadsheet to find another two such numbers.

2   The number 153 is equal to the sum of the cubes of its digits.

        $153 = 1^3 + 5^3 + 3^3 = 1 + 125 + 27 = 153$

     Find two numbers between 350 and 450 that have the same property.
     You may find a spreadsheet useful for this.

Trial and improvement

So far, most of the equations you have met have been **linear**. This means that they do not contain **powers** of the variable. Such an equation is solved by adding, subtracting, multiplying or dividing both sides of the equation by the same terms.

Equations which contain powers are called non-linear. Some non-linear equations cannot be solved exactly. However, a close approximation to the solution to such an equation can be found by the **trial-and-improvement** method.

The idea is to keep trying different values in the equation which will take it closer and closer to its 'true' solution. This step-by-step process is continued until a value is found which gives a solution to the required accuracy.

Example 3.9 ▶

Solve the equation $x^2 + x = 34$, giving the solution to one decimal place (dp).

The method involves finding two consecutive whole numbers between which x lies. This is done by intelligent guessing.

- Start with $x = 5$: the left-hand side (LHS) of the equation is $5^2 + 5 = 30$, which is too small.
- Try a larger integer, say $x = 6$: the LHS is $6^2 + 6 = 42$, which is too big.
- So, the solution lies between 5 and 6. Try the middle of this range, say $x = 5.5$: the LHS is $5.5^2 + 5.5 = 35.75$, which is too big. The next guess should be smaller.
- Try $x = 5.3$: the LHS is $5.3^2 + 5.3 = 33.39$, which is too small.
- Try $x = 5.4$: the LHS is $5.4^2 + 5.4 = 34.56$, which is too big.
- So, the solution lies between 5.3 and 5.4. Try the middle of this range, say $x = 5.35$: the LHS is $5.35^2 + 5.35 = 33.9725$, which is too small.
- So, the solution is bigger than 5.35 but smaller than 5.4. All of the numbers in this range round up to 5.4. Hence, the solution is $x = 5.4$ correct to 1 dp.

The table below summarises the calculations. You should always make a table for each equation you solve.

x	$x^2 + x$	Comment
5	$5^2 + 5 = 30$	Too small
6	$6^2 + 6 = 42$	Too big, so x lies between 5 and 6
5.5	$5.5^2 + 5.5 = 35.75$	Too big
5.3	$5.3^2 + 5.3 = 33.39$	Too small
5.4	$5.4^2 + 5.4 = 34.56$	Too big, so x lies between 5.3 and 5.4
5.35	$5.35^2 + 5.35 = 33.9725$	Too small, so x rounds up to 5.4

Example 3.10 ▶ Find a positive solution to the equation $x^3 + x = 52$ to 1 dp.

The solution can be followed in the table.

x	$x^3 + x$	Comment
4	$4^3 + 4 = 68$	Too big
3	$3^3 + 3 = 30$	Too small, so x lies between 3 and 4
3.5	$3.5^3 + 3.5 = 46.375$	Too small
3.7	$3.7^3 + 3.7 = 54.353$	Too big
3.6	$3.6^3 + 3.6 = 50.256$	Too smal, so x lies between 3.6 and 3.7
3.65	$3.65^3 + 3.65 = 52.277$	Too big, so x rounds down to 3.6

The solution is $x = 3.6$ to 1 dp.

Exercise 3E

1 The solutions of each of the following equations lie between two consecutive integers. In each case, make a table and find the integers.

   a $x^2 + x = 60$ **b** $x^2 - x = 40$ **c** $x^2 + x = 120$

   d $x^3 + x = 25$ **e** $x^3 - x = 75$ **f** $x^3 + x = 150$

2 The solutions of each of the following equations lie between two consecutive numbers with one decimal place. In each case, make a table and find the numbers.

   a $x^2 + x = 75$ **b** $x^2 - x = 17$ **c** $x^2 + x = 115$

   d $x^3 + x = 53$ **e** $x^3 - x = 76$ **f** $x^3 + x = 140$

3 Jess and Paul both solved the equation $x^3 + x = 74$ by trial and improvement. However, they used different methods, as shown in the tables.

Jess

x	$x^3 + x$	Comment
4	68.00	Too small
4.1	73.02	Too small
4.2	78.29	Too big
4.11	73.54	Too small
4.12	74.05	Too big
4.111	73.59	Too small
4.112	73.64	Too small
4.113	73.69	Too small
4.114	73.74	Too small
4.115	73.80	Too small
4.116	73.85	Too small
4.117	73.90	Too small
4.118	73.95	Too small
4.119	74.00	Spot on

The solution is $x = 4.119$

Paul

x	$x^3 + x$	Comment
4	68.00	Too small
5	130.00	Too big
4.5	95.63	Too big
4.2	78.29	Too big
4.1	73.02	Too small
4.15	75.62	Too big
4.12	74.05	Too big
4.11	73.54	Too small
4.115	73.80	Too small
4.118	73.95	Too small
4.119	74.00	It's there

The solution is $x = 4.119$

a Explain which of the two methods is more efficient for each of the following situations.

  i To find the solution to one decimal place

  ii To find the solution to two decimal places

  iii To find the solution to three decimal places

b Which method would you recommend and why?

Use a spreadsheet to find the solutions to the equation $x^3 - 10x^2 + 26x = 19$ to one decimal place. There are three positive solutions between 0 and 10.

Graphs showing direct proportion

When Mr Shah uses his car for business, he gets paid 80p per mile by his company.

The table below shows the amounts he claims for different lengths of journeys.

Length of journey (miles, M)	5	10	15	20	25	30
Claim (£, C)	4.00	8.00	12.00	16.00	20.00	24.00

The information can be graphed as shown below. Because the amount claimed is in direct proportion to the length of journey, the graph is a straight line.

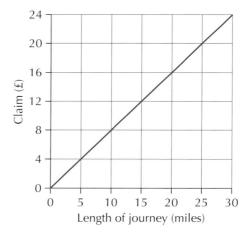

Note that the equation of the graph is $C = 0.8M$, where C is the amount claimed and M is the number of miles travelled. The gradient of the line, 0.8, is the amount paid per mile.

Straight-line graphs that pass through the origin show the relationship between two variables that are in direct proportion. This means that for every unit that one variable increases, the other variable increases by a fixed amount.

Not all graphs that show the relationship between two variables are in direct proportion.

For example, taxi fares have a fixed charge to start, then the rest of the cost of the journey is in direct proportion to the mileage travelled.

Example 3.11 ▶

Mr Evans wanted to convert the scores on a written French test to a standard percentage. All of his class already have 20 per cent on an oral test.

The table shows data he wants to use.

Written test score (F)	0	30	60
Final percentage (P)	20	60	100

a Create a graph which Mr Evans could use as a conversion graph from his French scores to percentage scores.

b What is the equation of this graph?

a Use the three points given above to draw a straight-line graph. Then use that graph to make a conversion graph.

b The gradient of the line is approximately 1.33, and the line starts at (0, 20) so the equation is $P = 20 + 1.33F$.

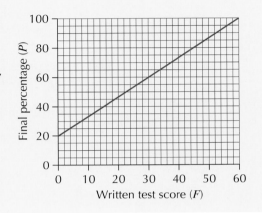

Exercise 3F

1 One morning in Scotland, Jenny recorded the temperature every hour from 8 am until noon. Her results are below.

Hours after 8 am	0	1	2	3	4
Temperature (°C)	4	5.5	7	8.5	10

a Plot the points on a graph and join them up with a suitable line.

b On this morning, are the temperature rises above 4°C directly proportional to the number of hours after 8 am?

c Write down the equation of the line showing the relationship between the time, t, and temperature, C.

d If the relationship held all day, what would be the temperature at 4 pm when $t = 8$?

2 Thousands of fans pour into a stadium ready to watch Joe King. A count is kept of the number of fans in the stadium after various time intervals.

Time after 1.30 pm	0	0.25	0.5	0.75
Number of fans	14 000	26 000	38 000	50 000

a Plot the points on a graph and join them up with a suitable line.

b For this hour, is the number of fans above 14 000 given directly proportional to the time after 1.30 pm?

c Write down the equation of the line showing the relationship between the time, t, and the number of fans, f.

d If the relationship held all evening, when did the first fan enter the stadium?

3 Given in the table below is the length of a stretched spring with each of a series of different weights hanging from it.

Weight (g)	0	200	400	600	800	1000
Length (cm)	10	12	14	16	18	20

a Plot the points on a graph and join them up with a suitable line.
b Is the extension directly proportional to the weight?
c Write down the equation of the line showing the relationship between hanging weight, w, and length, L.
d If the relationship continued to hold, what would be the hanging weight when the length of the spring is 27 cm?

4 Tea is served at a garden party between 3.00 pm and 5.30 pm. The number of cups of tea sold during the afternoon is shown in the table below.

Time after 3 pm	0	0.25	1	1.75	2	2.5
Cups of tea	0	13	52	91	104	130

a Plot the points on a graph and join them up with a suitable line.
b On this afternoon, is the number of cups of tea sold directly proportional to the time after 3.00 pm?
c Write down the equation of the line showing the relationship between the time, t, and the number of cups of tea sold, S.
d If the relationship held all day and the garden party continued, what is the value of S at 9.30 pm, when $t = 6.5$?

5 An experiment was done with a bouncing tennis ball. A tennis ball was dropped from different heights and the height of the first bounce was measured. The results are given in the table below.

Height of drop (cm)	25	50	75	100	125	150	175	200
Bounce (cm)	15	31	48	66	82	98	113	130

a Plot the points on a graph and join them up with a suitable line.
b Is the bounce directly proportional to the height of drop?
c Write down the equation of the line showing the relationship between height of drop, h, and bounce, b.
d If the relationship held, from what height would you need to drop the ball in order to have a bounce of 5 m?

Extension Work

Solve this problem by drawing a graph.

Two women are walking on the same long, straight road towards each other. One sets off at 9.00 am at a speed of 4 km/h. The other also sets off at 9.00 am, 15 km away, at a speed of 5 km/h. At 9.10 am, a butterfly leaves the shoulder of the quicker woman and flies to the other woman at 20 km/h. It continues to fly from one woman to the other until they both meet, and take a photograph of it.

a   At what time will the butterfly be photographed?

b   How many times will the butterfly have landed on the woman walking at 4 km/h?

LEVEL BOOSTER

6   I can expand and simplify expressions such as $2(3x + 5) + 2(x − 1) = 8x + 8$.

I can solve equations of the type $2(3x − 8) = 14$, for example, where the solution may be fractional or negative.

I can solve equations of the type $\frac{x+2}{5} = 3$, for example, where the solution may be negative.

I can use algebra to set up an equation to represent a practical situation.

I can solve equations of the type $x^2 = 49$ and $(x − 2)^2 = 25$, giving two possible solutions.

I can draw and interpret graphs that show direct proportion.

7   I can solve equations of the type $\frac{x+3}{2} = \frac{x+2}{5}$, for example, where the solution may be negative.

I can solve non-linear equations such as $x^3 + 2x = 60$ using trial and improvement.

5

1   *2007 3–5 Paper 1*

Look at this equation:

$$y = 2x + 10$$

a   When $x = 4$, what is the value of y?

b   When $x = -4$, what is the value of y?

c   Which of the equations below gives the **same** value for both $x = 4$ and $x = -4$?

$$y = 2x \qquad y = 2 + x \qquad y = x^2 \qquad y = \tfrac{x}{2}$$

7

2   *2000 Paper 2*

A class collected information about the number of children in each of their families.

The information was displayed in a frequency chart, but you cannot see all the information.

Call the number of families that have two children n.

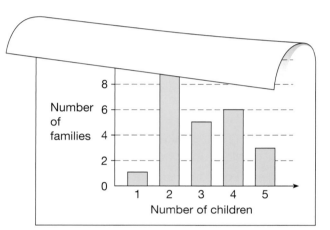

a   Show that the total number of children in all the families is $55 + 2n$.

b   Write an expression for the total number of families.

c   The mean number of children per familiy is 3.
What is the value of n? Show your working.

3   *2007 6–8 Paper 2*

Look at the equation below:

$$x + (x + 1) + (x + 2) = y$$

Use it to help you write the missing expressions **in terms of y**.

The first one is done for you.

a $5 + x + (x + 1) + (x + 2)$ $\qquad = y + 5$

b $(x + 5) + (x + 6) + (x + 7)$ $\qquad = \ldots\ldots$

c $2x + 2(x + 1) + 2(x + 2)$ $\qquad = \ldots\ldots$

d $(x + a) + (x + 1 + a) + (x + 2 + a) = \ldots\ldots$

This chapter is going to show you

- How to calculate the interior and exterior angles of polygons
- The names of the different parts of a circle
- How regular polygons tessellate
- How to construct right-angled triangles
- How to find the locus of a set of points
- How to distinguish between conventions, definitions and derived properties

What you should already know

- How to use the angles in parallel lines intersected by a straight line
- The sum of the interior angles of a triangle and of a quadrilateral
- The names of polygons
- How to draw a circle given its radius
- How to construct triangles from given information

Angles of polygons

Interior angles

The angles inside a **polygon** are known as **interior angles**.

For a triangle, the sum of the interior angles, a, b, and c, is 180°.

$$a + b + c = 180°$$

Example 4.1 ▷

Find the sum of the interior angles of a pentagon.

The diagram shows how a pentagon can be split into three triangles from one of its vertices. The sum of the interior angles for each triangle is 180°.

So, the sum of the interior angles of a pentagon is given by:

$$3 \times 180° = 540°$$

Exterior angles

If a side of a polygon is extended, the angle formed outside the polygon is known as an **exterior angle**.

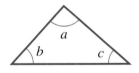

In the diagram, a is an exterior angle of the quadrilateral.

At any vertex of a polygon, the interior angle plus the exterior angle = 180° (angles on a straight line). Hence, in the diagram:

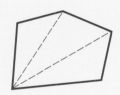

$$a + b = 180°$$

This is shown for a quadrilateral, but remember that it is true for any polygon.

Example 4.2 ▷

In the diagram on the right, all the sides of the pentagon have been extended to show all the exterior angles.

Imagine standing on each vertex of the pentagon and turning clockwise through all its exterior angles in turn. You can see that you will have turned through 360°.

This is true for all polygons.

The sum of the exterior angles for any polygon is 360°.

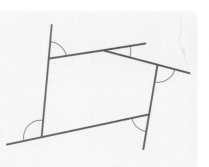

Exercise 4A

1 **a** By splitting each polygon into triangles, find the sum of the interior angles of:
 i a hexagon. **ii** an octagon.

 b Copy and complete the table below. The pentagon has been done for you. You should not draw the polygons.

Name of polygon	Number of sides	Number of triangles inside polygon	Sum of interior angles
Triangle			
Quadrilateral			
Pentagon	5	3	540°
Hexagon			
Heptagon			
Octagon			
n-sided polygon			

2 Calculate the unknown angle in each of the following polygons.

a

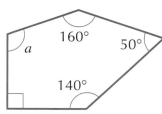

b

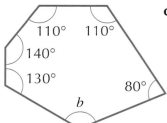

c

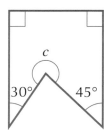

3 Calculate the unknown angle in each of the following diagrams.

a

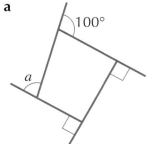

b

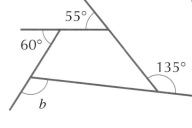

c

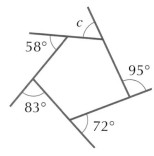

4 Find angle x in the pentagon on the right.

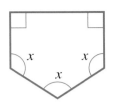

5 The four interior angles of a quadrilateral are $3x + 80°$, $5x + 10°$, $3x - 20°$ and $4x - 10°$. Calculate each interior angle of the quadrilateral.

6 Calculate each unknown angle in the diagrams below. For each angle, explain with a reason how you found the angle.

a

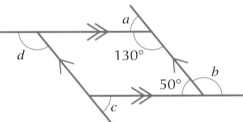

b

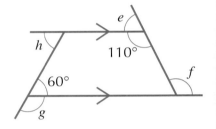

For each diagram, check that the sum of the exterior angles is 360°.

Interior angles in parallel lines

a and b are called **interior angles**:

$a + b = 180°$

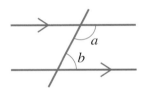

1 Calculate x in each of the following diagrams. You may need to set up and solve an equation.

a

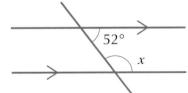

b

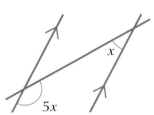

c

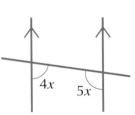

d

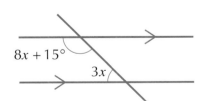

e

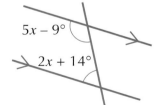

6

2   **Drawing parallel lines using a ruler and a set-square**

- Draw a line parallel to the line AB to pass through the point C.

A   B

- Place the ruler and the set square on the line, as shown below:

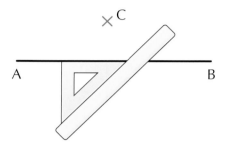

- Slide the set-square along the ruler until it touches C. Draw the line XY to pass through C. Then XY is parallel to AB.

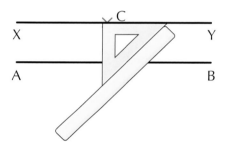

- Now draw a line AB and points X, Y and Z, as shown below. Draw lines parallel to AB which pass through the three points.

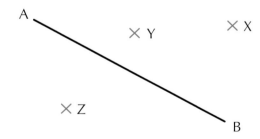

Angles of regular polygons

A polygon is regular when all its interior angles are equal and all its sides have the same length.

Example 4.3 shows how to find the interior and exterior angles of any regular polygon.

Example 4.3 ▷

Find the size of each exterior and each interior angle of a regular pentagon.

The regular pentagon has five equal exterior angles.

Let the size of each angle be x, as shown on the diagram.

Now, the sum of all the exterior angles is 360°. This gives:

$$5x = 360°$$
$$x = \frac{360°}{5} = 72°$$

The regular pentagon has five equal interior angles.

Let the size of each angle be y, as shown on the diagram.

Now, the sum of an interior angle and an exterior angle is 180°. This gives:

$$y + 72° = 180°$$
$$y = 180° - 72° = 108°$$

Exercise 4B

1 Copy and complete the table below for regular polygons. The regular pentagon has been done for you.

Regular polygon	Number of sides	Sum of exterior angles	Size of each exterior angle	Size of each interior angle
Equilateral triangle				
Square				
Regular pentagon	5	360°	72°	108°
Regular hexagon				
Regular octagon				
Regular decagon				
Regular n-sided polygon				

2 A regular dodecagon is a polygon whose 12 interior angles are all equal and whose 12 sides all have the same length.

   a Work out the size of each exterior angle.

   b Work out the size of each interior angle.

   c Calculate the sum of the interior angles.

6

3 ABCDE is a regular pentagon.

    a   What type of triangle is ADE?

    b   Calculate the size of ∠ DAE.

    c   Hence calculate the size of ∠ CAD.

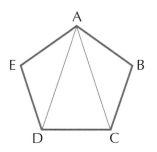

4 ABCDE is a regular pentagon. The sides BC and ED are extended to meet at X.

    Calculate the size of ∠ CXD.

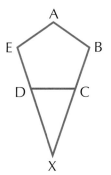

5 Two lines of symmetry are drawn on a regular hexagon, as shown on the diagram.

    Write down the size of each of the angles *a*, *b* and *c*.

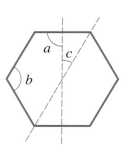

6 ABCDEFGH is a regular octagon. Copy the diagram and explain how to calculate the size of ∠AFB.

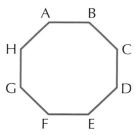

7 Each exterior angle of a regular polygon is 20°. How many sides does the polygon have?

8 Each interior angle of a regular polygon is 162°. How many sides does the polygon have?

Extension **Work**

1 Calculate each exterior and each interior angle of the following.

    a   A regular heptagon   **b**   A regular nonagon

    Give your answers to one decimal place where necessary.

2 Use computer software, such as Logo, to explain how a complete traverse of the sides of a polygon involves a total turn of 360°, and why this is equal to the sum of the exterior angles.

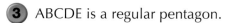

The circle and its parts

A circle is a set of points equidistant from a fixed point, called the **centre**, designated here by O.

You must learn all of the following terms for the different parts of a circle.

Circumference The length round a circle. It is a special name for the perimeter of a circle.

Arc One of the two parts between two points on a circumference.

Radius The distance from the centre of a circle to its circumference. The plural of the term is 'radii'.

Diameter The distance across a circle through its centre. The diameter d of a circle is twice its radius r so, $d = 2r$.

Chord A straight line which joins two points on the circumference of a circle.

Tangent A straight line that touches a circle at one point only on its circumference. This point is called the **point of contact**.

Segment The region of a circle enclosed by a chord and an arc. Any chord encloses two segments, which have different areas.

Sector A portion of a circle enclosed by two radii and one of the arcs between them.

Semicircle One half of a circle: either of the parts cut off by a diameter.

Exercise 4C

1. Measure the radius of each of the following circles, giving your answer in centimetres. Write down the diameter of each circle.

a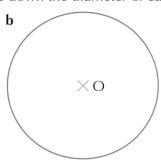

b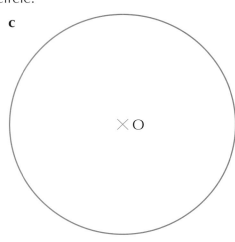

c

2. Draw circles with the following measurements.
   a Radius = 2.5 cm
   b Radius = 3.6 cm
   c Diameter = 8 cm
   d Diameter = 6.8 cm

3. Draw each of the following shapes accurately.

   a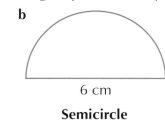

   3 cm
   4 cm

   Concentric circles

   b

   6 cm

   Semicircle

   c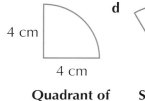

   4 cm
   4 cm

   Quadrant of a circle

   d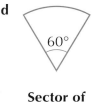

   60°

   Sector of a circle

4. Draw each of the following diagrams accurately.

   a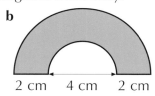

   4 cm

   4 cm

   b

   2 cm   4 cm   2 cm

   c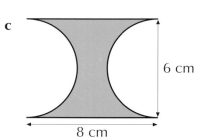

   6 cm

   8 cm

5. Draw a circle with centre O and with a radius of 4 cm. Draw six radii that are 60° apart, as shown in the diagram on the right. Join the points on the circumference to make an inscribed regular hexagon.

   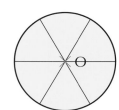

   a Explain why the radii must be 60° apart.
   b Use this method to draw each of these.
      i An inscribed regular pentagon
      ii An inscribed regular octagon

To find the centre of a circle

Draw a circle around a circular object so that the centre is not known.

Draw any two chords on the circle, as shown on the diagram. Then draw the perpendicular bisector for each chord.

The two perpendicular bisectors will intersect at the centre of the circle.

Repeat for different circles.

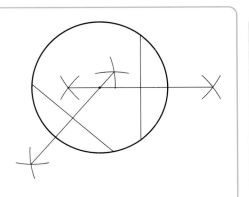

Tessellations and regular polygons

A **tessellation** is a repeating pattern made on a plane (flat) surface with identical shapes which fit together exactly, leaving no gaps.

This section will show you how some of the regular polygons tessellate.

Note: To show how a shape tessellates, draw up to about ten repeating shapes.

Example 4.4 ▷ The diagrams below show how equilateral triangles and squares tessellate.

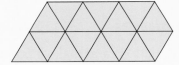 

Exercise 4D

1 On an isometric grid, show how a regular hexagon tessellates.

2 Trace this regular pentagon onto card and cut it out to make a template.

    a Use your template to show that a regular pentagon does not tessellate.

    b Explain why a regular pentagon does not tessellate.

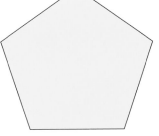

3 Trace this regular octagon onto card and cut it out to make a template.

    a Use your template to show that a regular octagon does not tessellate.

    b Explain why a regular octagon does not tessellate.

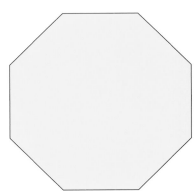

 4 **a** Copy and complete the table below for regular polygons.

b Use the table to explain why only some of the regular polygons tessellate.

c Do you think that a regular nonagon tessellates? Explain your reasoning.

Regular polygon	Size of each interior angle	Does this polygon tessellate?
Equilateral triangle		
Square		
Regular pentagon		
Regular hexagon		
Regular octagon		

Extension **Work**

Polygons can be combined together to form a **semi tessellation**. Two examples are shown below.

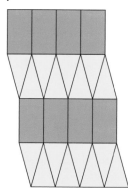

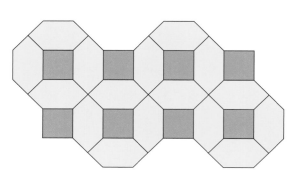

Rectangles and isosceles triangles   **Squares and hexagons**

Invent your own semi tessellations and make a poster to display in your classroom.

Constructing right-angled triangles

You already know how to construct triangles from given information, using a ruler, protractor and compasses. Hence, you should be able to construct any triangle given.

- Two sides and the included angle (SAS)

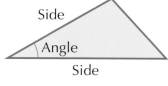

- Two angles and the included side (ASA)

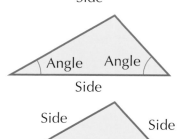

- Three sides (SSS)

Example 4.5 shows you how to construct a triangle, given a right angle, the **hypotenuse** (the longest side) and another side (RHS).

You will need a sharp pencil, a ruler and compasses for this construction. Remember to leave all your construction lines on the diagram.

Example 4.5 ▷

Construct the right-angled triangle ABC, where the hypotenuse AC is 5 cm, BC is 4 cm and the angle at B is 90°.

- First, draw line BC 4 cm long. Label its ends.

- Next, construct the perpendicular from B by first extending CB to a point D.

- Then, with centre at B, draw arcs to intersect CD at X and Y.

- Setting your compasses to a larger radius, draw arcs with centres at X and Y to intersect at Z above B.

- Join BZ to make a right angle at B.

- Set your compasses to a radius of 5 cm and, with its centre at C, draw an arc to intersect the perpendicular from B.

- The intersection of the arc with the perpendicular is A.

- Finally, join AC to complete the triangle.

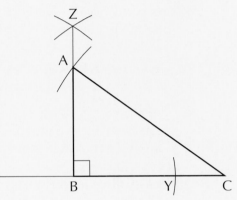

Exercise 4E

1. Using only a ruler and compasses, construct each of the following right-angled triangles. Show all of your construction lines. Remember to label all the sides.

   a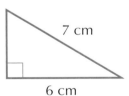

   b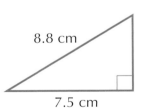

   c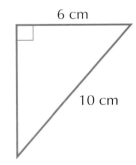

2. A 10 m ladder leans against a wall with its foot on the ground, 3 m from the wall.
   a Use a scale of 1 cm to 1 m to construct an accurate scale drawing. Only a ruler and compasses may be used. Leave all of your construction lines on the diagram.
   b Find how far up the wall the ladder actually reaches.
   c Find the angle the ladder makes with the ground.

3 The diagram shows the position of three towns, X, Y and Z.

Town Y is due east of town X and town Z is due south of town X.

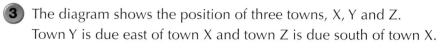

a Use a scale of 1 cm to 5 km to construct an accurate scale drawing which shows the position of the three towns. Use only a ruler and compasses. Show all of your construction lines.

b Find the direct distance of town X from town Z, giving your answer to the nearest kilometre.

c Find the bearing of town Y from town Z, giving your answer to the nearest degree.

Extension Work

1 To construct the circumscribed circle of a triangle

Draw a triangle ABC with sides of any length. Construct the perpendicular bisector for each of the three sides. The three perpendicular bisectors will meet at a point O. Using O as the centre, draw a circle to touch the three vertices of the triangle.

The circle is known as the **circumcircle** of the triangle, and O is known as the **circumcentre**.

2 This is a revision exercise in constructing triangles.

Construct each of the following triangles ABC from the given information. Two are impossible to construct. Give a reason to explain why they cannot be constructed.

You will need a sharp pencil, a ruler, compasses and a protractor.

Leave all your construction lines on the diagrams.

a AB = 4 cm, AC = 5 cm, BC = 6 cm
b AB = 4 cm, BC = 6 cm, ∠B = 50°
c ∠A = 40°, ∠B = 60°, ∠C = 80°
d BC = 6 cm, ∠B = 45°, ∠C = 65°
e AB = 5 cm, BC = 7 cm, ∠C = 60°
f BC = 2.5 cm, AC = 6.5 cm, ∠C = 90°

Loci

A **locus** (plural 'loci') is the movement of a point according to a given set of conditions or a rule.

In Year 8, you met two important constructions, which can now be stated to be loci.

Example 4.6 ▷

● The locus of a point which is always equidistant from each of two fixed points, A and B, is the perpendicular bisector of the line joining the two points.

● The locus of a point which is equidistant from two fixed lines AB and BC, which meet at B, is the bisector of the angle ABC.

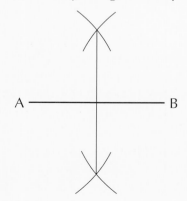

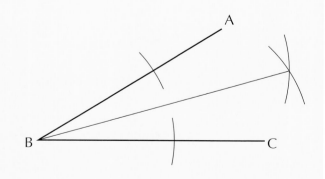

A locus can sometimes be a region.

Example 4.7 ▷

- A point which moves so that it is always 5 cm from a fixed point X has a locus which is a circle of radius 5 cm, with its centre at X.

- The locus of a set of points which are 5 cm or less from a fixed point X is a region inside a circle of radius 5 cm, with its centre at X.

  Note that the region is usually shaded.

- The locus of a set of points which are less than 5 cm from a fixed point X is a region inside a circle of radius 5 cm, with its centre at X.

  Note that the boundary usually is drawn as a dashed line to show that the points which are exactly 5 cm from X are not to be included.

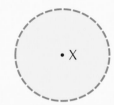

Exercise 4F

1 Using a ruler and compasses, construct the perpendicular bisector of each of the following lines.

a

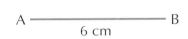

b

2 Using a ruler and compasses, construct the bisector of each of the following angles.

a

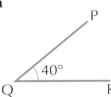

b

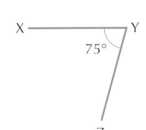

c

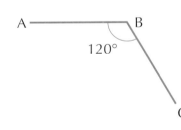

3 X is a fixed point. Draw diagrams to show the following.

a The locus of a point which is always 3 cm from X

b The locus of a point which is always 3 cm or less from X

c The locus of a point which is always less than 3 cm from X

4 A and B are two points, 6 cm apart. Draw a diagram to show the region which is 4 cm or less from A and 3 cm or less from B.

5 Make a copy of Treasure Island, as shown on the right. The treasure is buried at a point X on the island.

X is equidistant from A and D and is also equidistant from B and C. Mark the position of the treasure on your map.

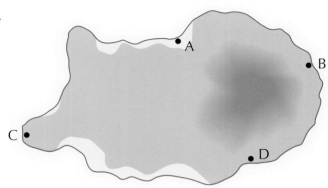

6 The diagram shows two perpendicular fences, PQ and QR. Bob wants to plant a tree so that it is equidistant from both fences and equidistant from P and R.

On a copy of the diagram, mark, with a cross, the position where Bob plants the tree.

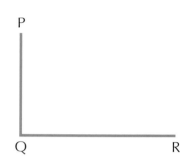

7 A radar station at X has a range of 100 km, and a radar station at Y has a range of 80 km. The direct distance from X to Y is 140 km.

Using a scale of 1 cm to 20 km, make a scale drawing to show the region where an aircraft can be picked up by both radar stations.

8 The line AB is 6 cm long.

A ———————————————— B

Draw the line AB. Then draw an accurate diagram to show all the points which are 3 cm or less from AB.

9 The diagram is a plan of a yard with part of a building in it. The building is shown in grey. A guard dog is tethered to the base of the wall of the building, at the point marked ✕. The guard dog's chain is 3 m long.

Draw a scale diagram to show the area of the yard where the dog can patrol. Use a scale of 1 cm to 1 m.

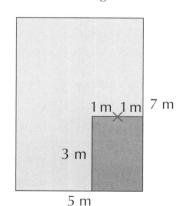

1 X is a point on the circumference of a circle. Draw the locus of X as the circle rolls along the line AB.

To help you draw the locus, use a coin and a ruler. Put a mark on the coin and as it rolls along the edge of the ruler, make marks on your paper for different positions of the coin, as on the diagram below. Join the marks with a curve to show the locus of X.

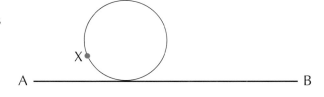

 2 The diagram on the right shows a 6 m ladder leaning against the wall of a house. The ground is slippery and the ladder slides down the wall until it lies flat on the ground.

Make a scale drawing to show the locus of the middle point of the ladder as the ladder slides down the wall. Use a scale of 1 cm to 1m.

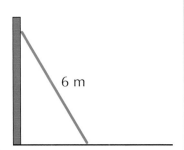

3 If you have access to ICT facilities, find how to draw the locus for more complex rules.

Geometrical reasoning

In geometry it is important that everyone agrees with all the facts that are used so that everyone arrives at the same conclusions when solving problems. The following examples illustrate the use of three terms which are fundamental to mathematical reasoning. You must know and understand these terms.

Example 4.8 The end-points of a straight line are labelled with capital letters. Any pair of different letters may be used. This is a **convention**, which is an agreed way of describing something mathematical.

A ─ ─ ─ ─ ─ ─ ─ B

Example 4.9 The definition of a square is a quadrilateral whose angles are all right angles and whose sides are equal in length.

It is not sufficient to define a square as a quadrilateral whose sides are equal in length, as this could also apply to a rhombus.

Hence, a **definition** is an exact description of something by its basic properties.

Example 4.10 The area of a square is equal to the square of its sides. This is a **derived property** which follows from the definition of a square.

Exercise 4G

1 Which of the following statements are conventions?

   a   Unknown angles are indicated on diagrams by lower-case letters.

   b   The letter Q is used to designate the origin of coordinate axes.

   c   Arrows are used to indicate straight lines which are parallel.

   d   Part of a square is used to show a 90° angle.

   e   A star symbol is used as a unit for the value of an angle.

2 Which of the following statements are definitions?

   a   A polygon is an enclosed shape with straight sides.

   b   Supplementary angles add up 180°.

   c   A parallelogram is a quadrilateral whose opposite sides are equal and parallel.

   d   Shapes are congruent when all their sides are the same length.

   e   The base angles of an isosceles triangle are equal.

3 Which of the following statements are derived properties?

   a   The angles of a triangle add up to 180°.

   b   A rectangle has rotational symmetry of order 2.

   c   A square has diagonals which are equal in length.

   d   An acute angle is less than 90°.

   e   Points on a mirror line reflect on to themselves.

4 The shape on the right is a parallelogram. Copy the shape and label it using the correct conventions.

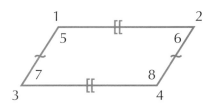

5 Write down the definition for each of the following geometrical terms.

   a   Parallel lines   **b**   Regular polygon   **c**   Tessellation

   d   Equilateral triangle   **e**   Cube

6 Write down as many derived properties for a square as you can.

Extension **Work**

Practical demonstrations

In Year 8, you found how to prove that the angles of a triangle add up to 180°. This can be demonstrated practically by cutting out a triangle, tearing off its vertices and placing them together to form a straight line.

Describe how you would give a practical demonstration to show the following geometrical properties.

1 The corresponding angles in a pair of parallel lines crossed by a straight line are equal.

2 The exterior angles of a polygon add up to 360°.

3 An exterior angle of a triangle is equal to the sum of the opposite interior angles.

4 Regular hexagons tessellate.

5 A rectangle has only two lines of symmetry.

5
I know the sum of the interior angles of a triangle and of a quadrilateral.
I can draw shapes which involve circles.
I know how to tessellate shapes.

6
I can find and use interior and exterior angles of polygons.
I know how to construct a right-angled triangle from given data.
I understand the difference between a convention, a definition and a derived property.
I know how to construct the perpendicular of a straight line.
I know how to construct the bisector of an angle.

7
I know how to find the locus of a point.
I can solve problems using the locus of a set of points which defines a region.

National Test questions

1 *1997 Paper 2*

Here is a rough sketch of a sector of a circle.

Make an accurate, full size drawing of this sector.

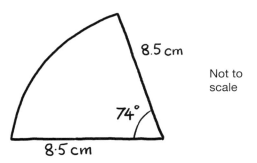

8.5 cm

74°

8·5 cm

Not to scale

2 *2000 Paper 2*

a Any quadrilateral can be split into two triangles.

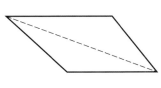

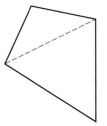

Explain how you know that the angles inside a quadrilateral add up to 360°.

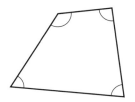

b What do the angles inside a pentagon add up to?

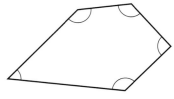

c What do the angles inside a heptagon (seven-sided shape) add up to?

Show your working.

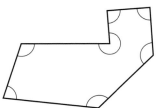

3 *2002 Paper 1*

The diagram shows a rectangle which just touches an equilateral triangle.

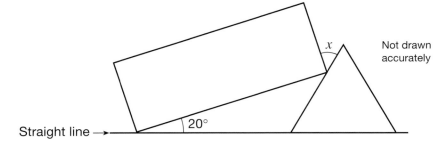

a Find the size of the angle marked x. Show your working.

b Now the rectangle just touches the equilateral triangle so that ABC is a straight line.

Show that triangle BDE is isosceles.

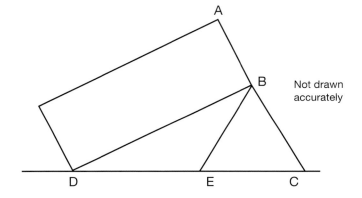

4 *2000 Paper 1*

The plan shows the position of three towns, each marked with a ✕. The scale of the plan is 1 cm to 10 km.

The towns need a new radio mast. The new radio mast must be nearer to Ashby than Ceewater, and less than 45 km from Beaton.

Show on a copy of the plan the region where the new radio mast can be placed. Leave in your construction lines.

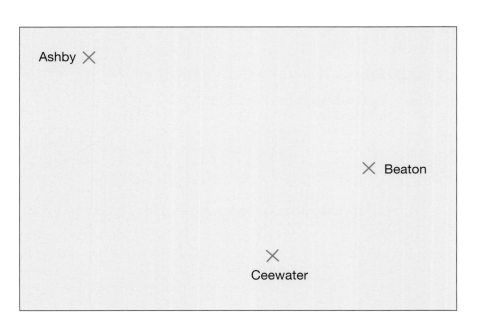

5 *2001 Paper 2*

A gardener wants to plant a tree.

She wants it to be more than 8 m away from the vegetable plot.

She wants it to be more than 18 m away from the greenhouse.

The plan below shows part of the garden. The scale is 1 cm to 4 m.

Show accurately on a copy of the plan the region of the garden where she can plant the tree. Label this region R.

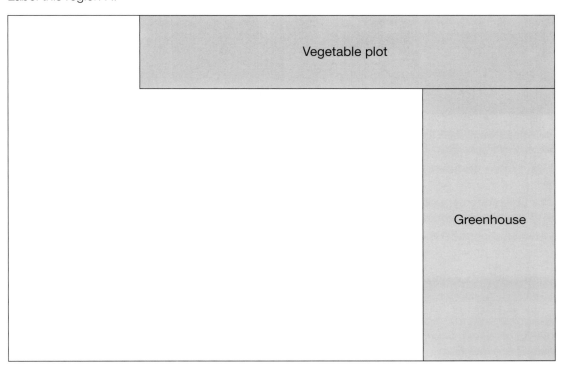

Garden design

Greg has just moved house and is designing his new garden.

To work out the questions related to Greg's garden, you will need a copy of the Activity Worksheet on page 247.

1 Greg wants a flower bed that is in the shape of a right-angled triangle.

His rough sketch is shown here on the right.

Draw the flowerbed accurately on a copy of the activity worksheet.

Leave in your construction lines.

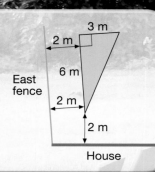

2 The hexagonal seat that goes around the tree is to be made from planks of wood. Each of the six sections are identical.

Work out the angles, (shown in the diagram), that each section needs to be cut at.

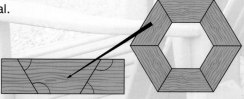

3 Gravel is to be put on the ground up to 2 m away from the centre of the tree. A length of thick rope will be used to stop the gravel spilling onto the lawn.

Draw the line that shows where the rope will go.

4 A 1 m wide path will be laid around the BBQ area. The path will be made using square paving slabs which are 50 cm by 50 cm.

  a Draw the path on the activity worksheet.

  b What is the area of the path?

  c How many paving slabs will be needed?

5 A large semi-circular table will be placed in front of the BBQ area, as shown here.

Draw the table accurately on the activity worksheet.

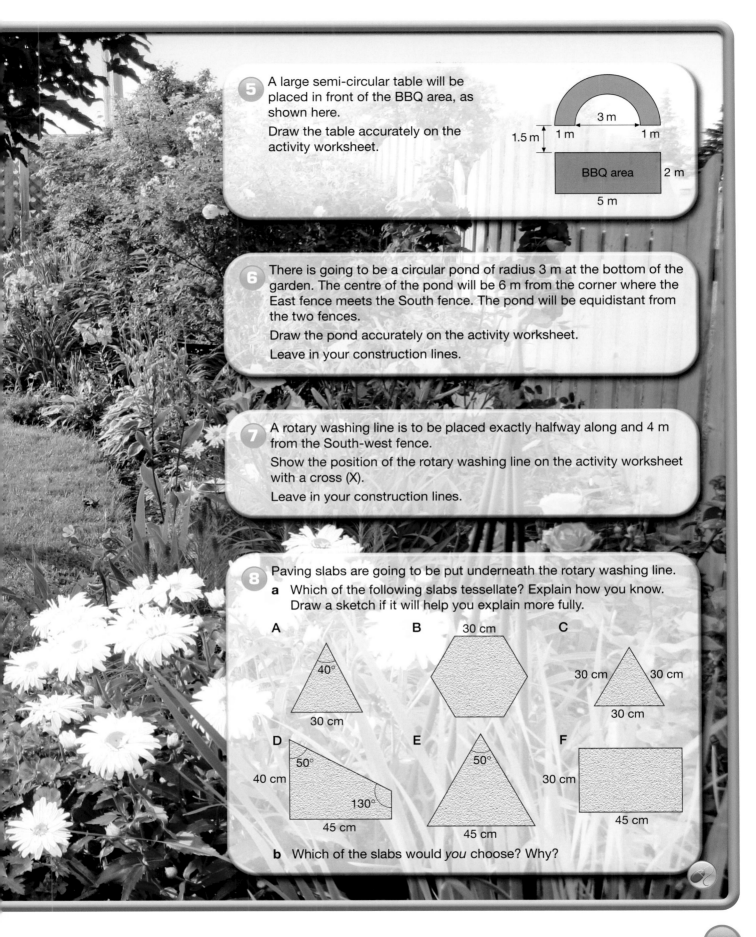

6 There is going to be a circular pond of radius 3 m at the bottom of the garden. The centre of the pond will be 6 m from the corner where the East fence meets the South fence. The pond will be equidistant from the two fences.

Draw the pond accurately on the activity worksheet.

Leave in your construction lines.

7 A rotary washing line is to be placed exactly halfway along and 4 m from the South-west fence.

Show the position of the rotary washing line on the activity worksheet with a cross (X).

Leave in your construction lines.

8 Paving slabs are going to be put underneath the rotary washing line.

a Which of the following slabs tessellate? Explain how you know. Draw a sketch if it will help you explain more fully.

A B 30 cm C

40° 30 cm / 30 cm

30 cm 30 cm

D E F

50° 50°

40 cm 30 cm

130°

45 cm 45 cm 45 cm

b Which of the slabs would *you* choose? Why?

CHAPTER 5 Statistics 1

This chapter is going to show you

- How to interpret correlation from two scatter graphs
- How to interpret time series graphs
- How to construct and interpret two-way tables
- How to compare two sets of data from statistical diagrams
- How to plan a statistical investigation

What you should already know

- How to calculate statistics
- How to collect data using a suitable method
- How to draw and interpret graphs for discrete data
- How to compare two sets of data using mode, median, mean or range

Scatter graphs and correlation

The maximum temperature, rainfall and hours of sunshine were recorded each day in a town on the south coast of England.

Look at the two scatter graphs below, which were plotted from this data. Is it possible to work out the relationship between rainfall and hours of sunshine?

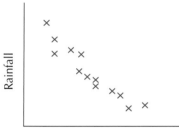

The graph on the left shows **negative correlation**. In this case, it means that the higher the temperature, the less rainfall there is.

The graph on the right shows **positive correlation**. In this case, it means that the higher the temperature, the more hours of sunshine there are.

Looking at both graphs together, what do they tell you about the effects of changes in temperature?

From the graph on the left, high rainfall means low temperature. From the graph on the right, low temperature means little sunshine. So, you can deduce that high rainfall means little sunshine. That is, rainfall and sunshine are negatively correlated. The graph opposite illustrates this.

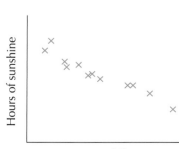

The graph on the right shows **no correlation** between the temperature and the number of fish caught daily off Rhyl – as you might expect.

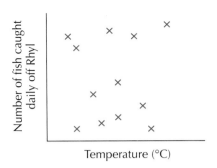

Here is a table which gives you the rules for combining two scatter graphs, which have a common axis, to obtain the resulting correlation.

	Positive correlation	No correlation	Negative correlation
Positive correlation	Positive	No correlation	Negative
No correlation	No correlation	*Cannot tell*	No correlation
Negative correlation	Negative	No correlation	Positive

As you may see from the table, the new graph can have its axes in either order, as this does not affect the correlation.

To remember these rules, think of the rules for multiplying together positive and negative numbers. See below.

Multiply (×)	+	0	−
+	+	0	−
0	0	*The exception*	0
−	−	0	+

1 A competition has three different games.

a Ryan plays two games.

	Game A	Game B	Game C
Score	62	53	

To win, Ryan needs a mean score of 60.
How many points does he need to score in Game C? Show your working.

b Ian and Nina play the three games.

	Game A	Game B	Game C
Ian's scores	40		
Nina's scores	35	40	45

Their scores have the same mean.
The range of Ian's scores is twice the range of Nina's scores. Copy the table above and fill in the missing scores.

c The scatter diagrams below show the scores of everyone who plays all three games.

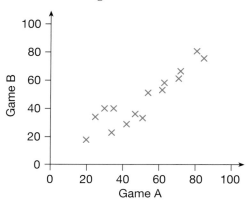 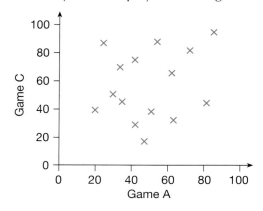

Look at the scatter diagrams and describe the relationship between the games.

i Game A and Game B

ii Game A and Game C

iii Game B and Game C

2 A post office compares the cost of postage with the weight of each parcel and also the cost of postage with the size of each parcel. The results are shown on the scatter graphs below.

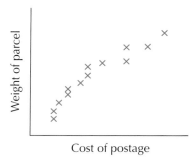 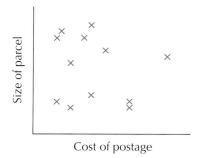

a Describe the type of correlation between the weight of parcels and the cost of postage.

b Describe the type of correlation between the size of parcels and the cost of postage.

c Describe the relationship between the weight of parcels and the size of parcels.

d Draw a scatter graph to show the correlation between the weight of parcels and the size of parcels. (Plot about ten points for your graph.)

3 A pupil compared the ages of a group of men with the length of their hair and also with their weights. His results are shown on the two scatter graphs.

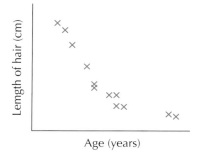 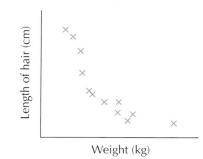

a Describe the type of correlation between the length of hair and age.

b Describe the type of correlation between the length of hair and weight.

c Describe the relationship between age and weight.

d Draw a scatter graph to show the correlation between age and weight. (Plot about ten points for your graph.)

Collect test marks for ten pupils in three different subjects: for example, mathematics, science and art. Draw the scatter graphs for mathematics/science, mathematics/art and science/art. Comment on your results. You may wish to use a table to show the test marks.

	Pupil 1	Pupil 2	Pupil 3	Pupil 4	Pupil 5	Pupil 6	Pupil 7	Pupil 8	Pupil 9	Pupil 10
Maths										
Science										
Art										

Time series graphs

A time series graph is any graph which has a time scale.

Look at the graphs below to see whether you can match each graph to one of the statements listed after graph 5.

Graph 1: Mean temperature difference from normal for UK in 2002

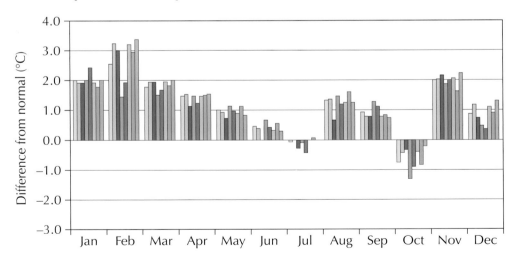

Graph 2: Average annual temperatures of Central England 1659–2001

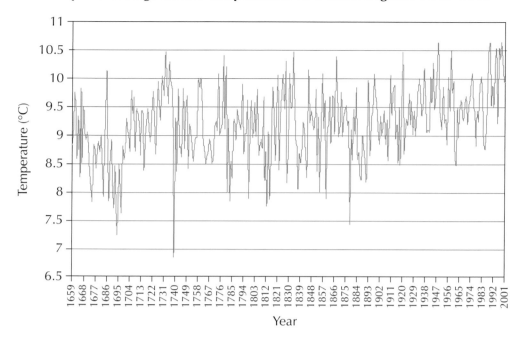

Graph 3: Monthly rainfall data for Perth, Australia

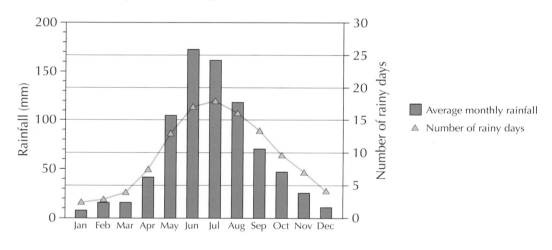

Graph 4: Monthly rainfall data for Brisbane, Australia

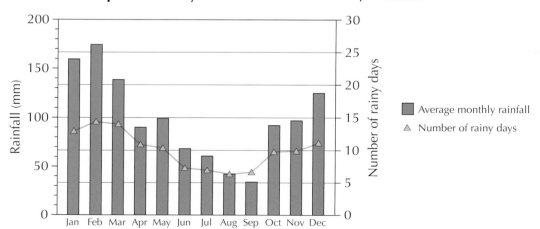

Graph 5: Monthly temperature data for Perth, Australia

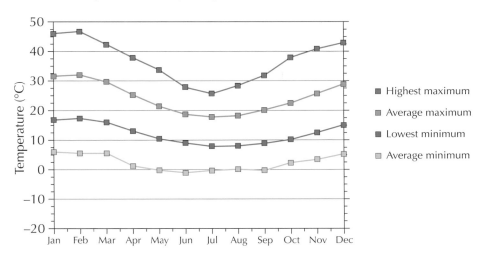

Statement A: February is the hottest month here.

Statement B: October was colder than normal.

Statement C: September is a fairly dry month in Australia.

Statement D: This country is gradually getting warmer.

Statement E: The difference between the lowest and highest temperatures is least in July.

Exercise 5B

 1 The Highway Code states the minimum distance there should be between cars. There are different distances for bad weather and good weather. The graph on the right shows this.

a The weather is bad. A car is travelling at 40 miles per hour.

What is the minimum distance it should be from the car in front?

b The weather is good. A car is travelling at 55 miles per hour.

What is the minimum distance it should be from the car in front?

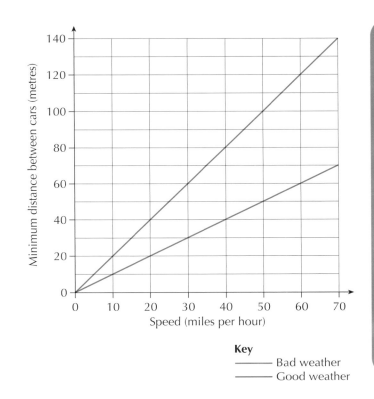

Key
— Bad weather
— Good weather

2 The time series graph shows the height to which a ball bounces against the time taken to reach that height.

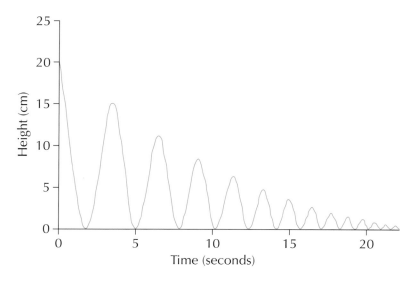

- **a** Write a comment stating what happens to the length of time for which the ball is in the air after each bounce.
- **b** This ball always bounces to a fixed fraction of its previous height. What fraction is this?
- **c** After how many bounces does this ball bounce to less than half of the greatest height?
- **d** In theory, how many bounces does the ball make before it comes to rest?

 3 Look again at the graph showing the mean temperature changes in the UK for 2002.
- **a** Which months were colder than normal?
- **b** Which month was much warmer than normal?
- **c** In a short sentence, describe what the graph shows about the UK in 2002.

 4 Look again at the graphs showing the rainfall for Perth and Brisbane.
- **a** Which month has the greatest rainfall in Perth?
- **b** Which month has the least rainfall in Brisbane?
- **c** Explain how you can tell that Perth and Brisbane are not in the same region.
- **d** Which place, Perth or Brisbane, has more days of rainfall over the year? Show how you work it out.

Extension Work

Use an atlas, encyclopaedia or the Internet to find a graph on whose coordinates, shape and trend you would be able to comment.

Two-way tables

Example 5.1 ▷ An Internet company charges delivery for goods based on the type of delivery – normal delivery (taking 3 to 5 days) or next-day delivery – and also on the cost of the order. The table shows how it is calculated.

Cost of order	Normal delivery (3 to 5 days)	Next-day delivery
0–£10	£1.95	£4.95
£10.01–£30	£2.95	£4.95
£30.01–£50	£3.95	£6.95
£50.01–£75	£2.95	£4.95
Over £75	Free	£3.00

a Comment on the difference in delivery charges for normal and next-day delivery.

b Two items cost £5 and £29. How much would you save by ordering them together: **i** using normal delivery? **ii** using next-day delivery?

a It always costs more using next-day delivery but for goods costing between £10.01 and £30, or between £50.01 and £75, it is only £2 more. It is £3 more for all other orders.

b Using normal delivery and ordering the items separately, it would cost £1.95 + £2.95 = £4.90, but ordering them together would cost £3.95. The saving would be £4.90 − £3.95 = 95p.

Using next-day delivery and ordering the items separately, it would cost £4.95 + £4.95 = £9.90, but ordering them together would cost £6.95. The saving would be £9.90 − £6.95 = £2.95.

Exercise 5C

1 Look at this two-way table. If a car is chosen at random, what is the probability that it is one of the following?

a Peugeot   **b** Red   **c** Red Peugeot
d Not blue   **e** Not a Ford

		Colour of cars				
		Red	**White**	**Blue**	**Black**	**Other**
	Peugeot	8	1	4	1	4
	Ford	11	2	4	2	6
Make of cars	**Vauxhall**	5	4	0	0	2
	Citroen	1	2	2	0	3
	Other	6	3	3	4	2

2 The table shows the percentage of boys and girls by age group who have a mobile phone.

a Comment on any differences between boys and girls.

b Comment on any other trends that you notice.

Age	Boys	Girls
10	18%	14%
11	21%	18%
12	42%	39%
13	53%	56%
14	56%	59%
15	62%	64%

 3 The cost of a set of old toys depends on whether the toys are still in the original boxes and also on the condition of the toys. The table shows the percentage value of a toy compared with its value if it is in perfect condition and boxed.

Condition	Boxed	Not boxed
Excellent	100%	60%
Very good	80%	50%
Good	60%	40%
Average	40%	25%
Poor	20%	10%

a Copy and complete the table.

Condition	Difference between boxed and not boxed
Excellent	100% – 60% = 40%
Very good	
Good	
Average	
Poor	

b Explain the effect of the set being boxed compared with the condition of the toys.

 4 The heights of 70 Year 9 pupils are recorded. Here are the results given to the nearest centimetre.

Height (cm)	Boys	Girls
130–139	3	3
140–149	2	4
150–159	10	12
160–169	14	11
170–179	6	5

Use the results to examine the claim that boys are taller than girls in Year 9. You may use a frequency diagram to help you.

A school analyses the information on the month of birth for 1000 pupils. The results are shown in the table.

Month	Jan	Feb	Mar	Apr	May	Jun	Jul	Aug	Sep	Oct	Nov	Dec
Boys	34	36	43	39	47	50	44	39	55	53	42	35
Girls	37	31	36	35	44	43	36	40	52	49	43	37

a On the same grid, plot both sets of values to give a time series graph for the boys and another for the girls.

b Use the graphs to examine the claim that more children are born in the summer than in the winter.

Comparing two or more sets of data

Two cars, A and B, each cost £20 000 when they were new.

The graphs show how the values of the cars fell over eight years.

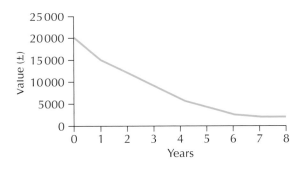

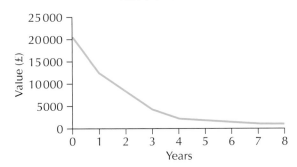

Which car's value fell more? How can you tell?

Example 5.2 ▷ A teacher is comparing the reasons for the absence of pupils who have had time off school. The charts show the reasons for absence of two different year groups.

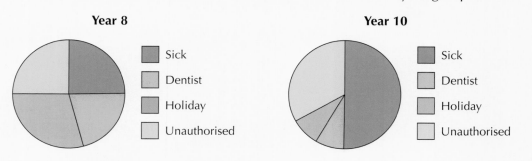

Year 8   **Year 10**

Sick
Dentist
Holiday
Unauthorised

One hundred pupils in Year 8 had time off school, and 40 pupils in Year 10.

The teacher says: 'The charts show that more pupils were off sick in Year 10'. Explain why the charts do not show this.

In Year 8, the number of pupils off sick was a quarter of 100, which is 25.

In Year 10, the number of pupils off sick was a half of 40, which is 20. So fewer pupils were off sick in Year 10.

Exercise 5D

FM **1** The graph shows the attendance at two concerts, a classical concert and a rock concert.

Comment on the proportion of children attending each concert.

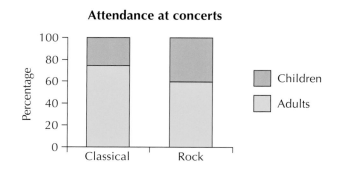

Attendance at concerts

Children
Adults

FM **2** One hundred pupils took two tests: a science test and a maths test. The results are shown on the graph.

Which test did the pupils find more difficult? Explain your answer.

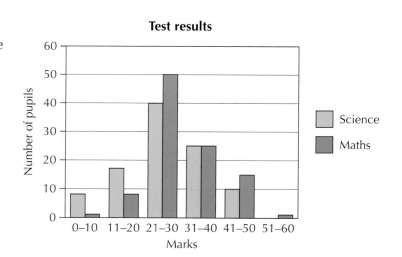

Test results

Science
Maths

3 The chart shows the percentage of trains that were on time and late during one day.

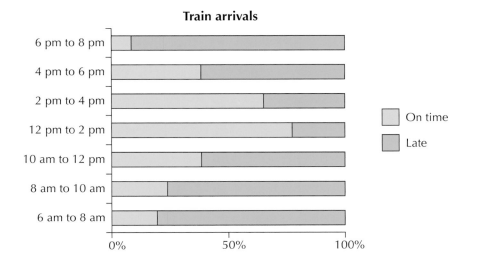

Train arrivals

6 pm to 8 pm
4 pm to 6 pm
2 pm to 4 pm
12 pm to 2 pm
10 am to 12 pm
8 am to 10 am
6 am to 8 am

0%   50%   100%

☐ On time
☐ Late

a Compare the lateness for different parts of the day.

b Comment on what you would expect to happen between 8 pm and 10 pm.

Extension Work

 Here are two sets of weights of a sample of two different makes of 400 g chocolate bars.

Chucky Bar (g)	Choctastic (g)
401	391
407	410
405	407
404	402
403	413
404	395

a Calculate the mean and range of the data for each sample.

b Draw charts to compare the two makes of chocolate.

c Comment on which one you would buy.

Statistical investigations

Investigating a problem will involve several steps. Three examples will be studied from different subjects alongside an overall plan.

Step	Example 1 PE	Example 2 Science	Example 3 Geography
1 Decide which general topic to study	How to improve pupil performance in sport	Effect of engine size on a car's acceleration	Life expectancy versus cost of housing
2 Specify in more detail	A throwing event	A particular make of car	Compare house prices in Yorkshire with those in South-east England
3 Consider questions which you could investigate	How much further do pupils throw using a run up? Is a Year 9 pupil able to throw as far as a Year 11 pupil of the same height?	Does a bigger engine always mean that a car can accelerate faster?	Do people who live in expensive housing tend to live longer?
4 State your hypotheses (Your guesses at what could happen)	Distance thrown will improve using a run up. Year 11 pupils of the same height may be physically stronger and would therefore throw further	In general, more powerful engines produce the greater acceleration. More powerful engines tend to be in heavier cars and therefore the acceleration will not be affected. Larger engines in the same model of car will improve acceleration	People in expensive housing have greater incomes and also may have a longer life expectancy
5 Sources of information required	Survey of distance thrown with different lengths of run-up	Magazines and/or books with information on engine sizes and acceleration times for 0–60 mph	Library or the Internet for census data for each area

Step	Example 1 PE	Example 2 Science	Example 3 Geography
6 Relevant data	Choose pupils from different age groups with a range of heights Make sure that there is an equal number of boys and girls Choose pupils from the full range of ability	Make of car, engine size and acceleration **Note:** The government requires car manufacturers to publish the time taken to accelerate from 0–60 mph	Average cost of housing for each area Data about life expectancy for each area
7 Possible problems	Avoid bias when choosing your sample or carrying out your survey	Petrol engines must be compared with other petrol engines not with diesel engines	
8 Data collection	Make sure that you can record all the factors which may affect the distance thrown: for example, age or height	Make sure that you can record all the information which you need, such as engine size and weight of car. Remember to quote sources of data	Extract relevant data from sources. Remember to quote sources of data
9 Decide on the level of accuracy required	Decide how accurate your data needs to be: for example, nearest 10 cm	Round any published engine sizes to the nearest 100 cm^3 (usually given as 'cc' in the car trade), which is 0.1 litre For example, a 1905 cc engine has a capacity of approximately 1.9 litres	
10 Determine sample size	Remember that collecting too much information may slow down the experiment		
11 Construct tables for large sets of raw data in order to make work manageable	Group distances thrown into intervals of 5 metres Use two-way tables to highlight differences between boys' and girls' data		Group population data in age groups of, for example, 10 year intervals
12 Decide which statistics are most suitable	When the distances thrown are close together, use the mean. When there are a few extreme values, use the median		Sample should be sufficiently large to be able to use the mean

Exercise 5E

Look at the three examples presented above and investigate either one of the problems given or a problem of your own choice. You should follow the steps given here, including your own ideas.

7

Extension **Work**

Think of a problem related to a piece of work, such as a foreign language essay or a history project. See whether you can use the step-by-step plan to carry out a statistical investigation.

For example, you may wish to compare the word length of an English and a French piece of writing, or you may wish to compare data about two wars.

LEVEL BOOSTER

5 I know how to interpret graphs and charts, and how to draw conclusions.
I know how to compare two simple distributions.

6 I know how to draw conclusions from scatter graphs, and I have a basic understanding of correlation.
I know how to identify all the outcomes using diagrams, tables or other forms of communication when dealing with a combination of two experiments.

7 I know how to generate a detailed solution to a problem.
I know how to compare distributions and comment on what I find.
I know how to use measures of average and range to compare distributions and make inferences.

National Test questions

1 *2007 5–7 Paper 1*

The line on the graph below represents a speed of 60 km/hour.

a Copy the graph and draw on it a line to represent a speed of **30 km/hour**.

Label the line by writing '30 km/hour'.

b Now draw a line on the graph to represent a speed of **120 km/hour**.

Label the line by writing '120 km/hour'.

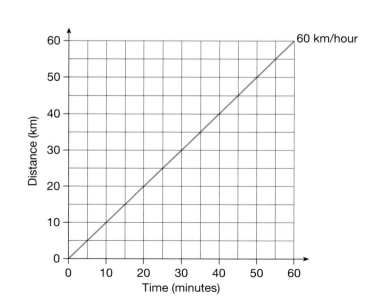

2 *2002 Paper 2*

A newspaper wrote an article about public libraries in England and Wales. It published this diagram.

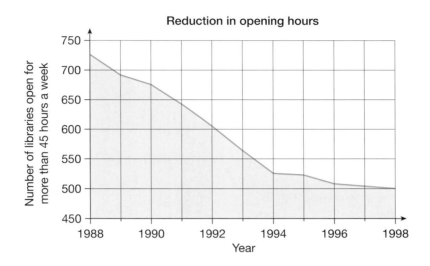

Reduction in opening hours

Use the diagram to decide whether each statement below is true or false, or whether you cannot be certain.

a The number of libraries open for more than 45 hours per week fell by more than half from 1988 to 1998.

☐ True ☐ False ☐ Cannot be certain

Explain your answer.

b In 2004 there will be about 450 libraries open in England and Wales for more than 45 hours a week.

☐ True ☐ False ☐ Cannot be certain

Explain your answer.

3 *2006 5–7 Paper 2*

The graph below shows information about the diameters and heights of a sample of three types of tomato.

The dotted lines on the graph can be used to decide which types of tomato each point is likely to represent.

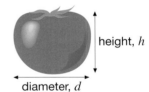

height, h

diameter, d

a The diameter of a tomato of **type C** is **11 cm**.

What would you expect its height to be?

b The diameter of a different tomato is 3.2 cm.
Its height is 5.8 cm.

Which of the three types of tomato is it most likely to be?

Explain your answer.

c Which type of tomato is most nearly **spherical** in shape?

Explain your answer.

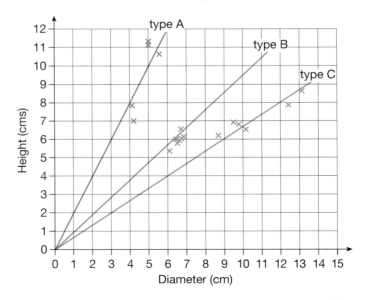

d You can find the approximate volume of a tomato by using this formula:

$$V = \frac{1}{6}\pi d^2 h$$

Key:
V is the volume
d is the diameter
h is the height

The diameter and the height of a tomato are both **3.5 cm**.

What is the approximate volume of this tomato?

4 *2006 5–7 Paper 1*

A pupil investigated whether students who study more watch less television.

The scatter graph shows his results. The line of best fit is also shown.

a What type of correlation does the graph show?

b The pupil says the equation of the line of best fit is $y = x + 40$.

Explain how you can tell that this equation is **wrong**.

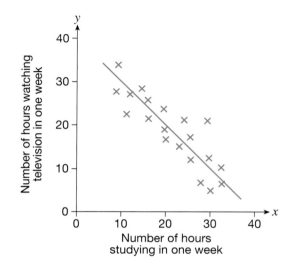

5 *2005 5–7 Paper 1*

Car tyres are checked for safety by measuring their tread.

The tread on a tyre and the distance travelled by that tyre were recorded for a sample of tyres. The scatter graph shows the results:

Tyres with a tread of **less than 1.6 mm** are illegal.

Suppose the government changes this rule to **less than 2.5 mm**.

a How many of these tyres would now be illegal?

b About **how many fewer kilometres** would you expect a tyre to last before it became illegal?

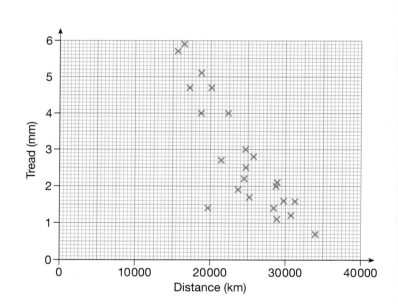

6 *2002 Paper 1*

Three types of mice might come into our homes.

Some mice are more likely to be found in homes far from woodland. Others are more likely to be found in homes close to woodland.

The bar charts show the percentages of mice that are of each type.

Use the bar charts to answer these questions.

(a) About what percentage of mice in homes close to woodland are wood mice?

(b) About what percentage of mice in homes far from woodland are not wood mice?

(c) The brown bars show the percentages for house mice. One of the brown bars is taller than the other.

Does that mean there must be more house mice in homes far from woodland than in homes close to woodland?

Explain your answer.

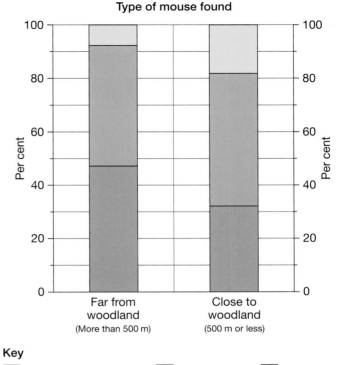

Type of mouse found

Key

☐ Yellow-necked mice ☐ Wood mice ☐ House mice

Rainforest deforestation

Since 1970, over 600 000 km² of Amazon rainforest have been destroyed. This is an area larger than Spain.

Between the years 2000 and 2005, Brazil lost over 132 000 km² of forest – an area about the same size as Greece.

The table below shows how much of the rainforests in Brazil have been lost each year since 1988.

Deforestation figure

Year	Deforestation (sq km)
1988	21 000
1989	18 000
1990	14 000
1991	11 000
1992	14 000
1993	15 000
1994	15 000
1995	29 000
1996	18 000
1997	13 000
1998	17 000
1999	17 000
2000	18 000
2001	18 000
2002	21 000
2003	25 000
2004	27 000
2005	19 000
2006	14 000
2007	10 000

Use the information on the left to answer these questions.

1 From 1988–1991, Brazil had an economic slowdown. What was happening to the rate of deforestation during that time?

2 From 1992–1995, Brazil had economic growth. What was happening to the rate of deforestation during that time?

3 What do think was happening to Brazil's economy:
   a from 1998–2004?
   b from 2005–7?

4 What does the chart and the information given in questions 1 and 2 suggest about the link between deforestation in Brazil and the economy?

5 Draw a cumulative graph, showing the total deforestation since 1988, year by year.

6 If the rate of deforestation from 2005–7 continued at the same rate, estimate when the deforestation would be 4000 km^2.

The pie chart below shows the three main reasons for deforestation in the Amazon from 2000–5.

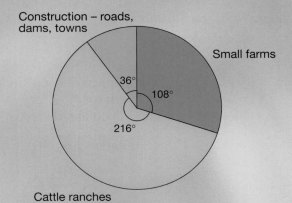

Construction – roads, dams, towns

Small farms

36°

108°

216°

Cattle ranches

7 What percentage of the deforestation was caused by each reason?

8 It was suggested that over the next two years:
   - the same amount of deforestation would take place.
   - the amount of construction work would actually double.
   - the number of small farms would halve.
   - the number of cattle ranches would increase.

Draw a new pie chart reflecting the reasons for deforestation suggested for 2007.

<table>
<tr><th>This chapter is going to show you</th><th>What you should already know</th></tr>
</table>

This chapter is going to show you

- How to use the formulae for calculating the circumference and the area of a circle
- How to convert from one metric unit to another for area and volume
- How to calculate the surface area and the volume of prisms

What you should already know

- The definition of a circle and the names of its parts
- The metric units for area and volume
- How to calculate areas of 2-D shapes
- How to calculate the surface area and volume of a cuboid

Circumference of a circle

This section will show you how to find the circumference of a circle. You have already met its formula in your Year 8 Pupil Book.

How can you measure exactly the **circumference** of a circle?

Is there a relation between the length of the diameter and the circumference?

Exercise 6A will show you.

Exercise 6A

You will need compasses, a 30 cm ruler and a piece of fine, high-quality string at least 40 cm long.

Copy the following table and draw circles with the given radii.

Measure the circumference of each circle by tracing the string round the circumference as shown. Mark the length on the string with a pencil. Measure this length with a ruler and complete the table. Calculate the last column to one decimal place.

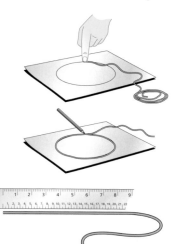

Radius r (cm)	Diameter d (cm)	Circumference C (cm)	$C \div d$
1			
1.5			
2			
2.5			
3			
3.5			
4			
4.5			
5			
5.5			
6			

What do you notice about the last column?

Can you say how the circumference is related to the diameter?

Write down in your book what you have found out.

Draw a circle on paper and cut it out. Draw a narrow sector on the circle and cut it out. Make a cone with the remaining, larger sector.

What happens as you increase the size of the removed sector?

Formula for the circumference of a circle

In Exercise 6A, you should have found that the **circumference**, C, of a circle with **diameter** d is given approximately by the formula $C = 3d$.

In fact, the number by which you have to multiply the diameter to get a more accurate value for the circumference is slightly larger than 3.

This special number is represented by the Greek letter π (pronounced *pi*). The value of π cannot be written down exactly as a fraction or a terminating decimal, so approximate values are used. The most common of these are:

$\pi = \frac{22}{7}$ (as a fraction)

$\pi = 3.14$ (as a decimal rounded to two decimal places)

$\pi = 3.1416$ (as a decimal rounded to four decimal places)

$\pi = 3.141\,592\,654$ (on a scientific calculator)

π has been calculated to millions of decimal places, using computers. So far, no repeating pattern has ever been found.

Look for the $\boxed{\pi}$ key on your calculator.

So, the formula for calculating the circumference, C, of a circle with diameter d is written as:

$C = \pi d$

As the diameter is twice the **radius**, r, the circumference is also given by:

$C = \pi d = \pi \times 2r = 2\pi r$

Example 6.1 ▷ Calculate the circumference of each of the following circles. Give each answer to one decimal place.

a
6 cm

b
3.4 m

a The diameter, $d = 6$ cm, which gives:
$C = \pi d = \pi \times 6 = 18.8$ cm (to 1 dp)

b The radius, $r = 3.4$ m, so $d = 6.8$ m. This gives:
$C = \pi d = \pi \times 6.8 = 21.4$ m (to 1 dp)

Exercise 6B

In this exercise, take π = 3.14 or use the [π] key on your calculator.

1 Calculate the circumference of each of the following circles. Give each answer to one decimal place.

a 7 cm b 11 mm c 21 mm d 2.4 m e 1.4 cm

2 Take a 2p coin and measure its diameter to the nearest millimetre. Calculate the circumference of the coin, giving your answer to the nearest millimetre.

3 The Big Wheel at a theme park has a diameter of 5 m. How far would you travel in one complete revolution of the wheel? Give your answer to the nearest metre.

4 The diagram shows the dimensions of a running track at a sports centre. The bends are semicircles.

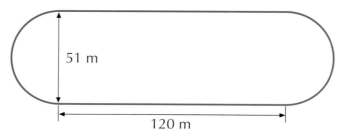

51 m

120 m

Calculate the distance round the track. Give your answer to the nearest metre.

5 The Earth's orbit can be taken to be a circle with a radius of approximately 150 million km.

Calculate the distance the Earth travels in one orbit of the Sun. Give your answer to the nearest million kilometres.

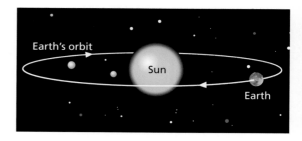

Earth's orbit

Sun

Earth

6 By measuring the diameter, calculate the perimeter of this semicircular shape. Give your answer to one decimal place.

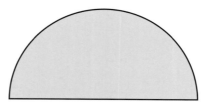

Extension Work

1 a 'How I wish I could calculate pi exactly'. This is a mnemonic to remember π to seven decimal places. (A mnemonic is an aid to remember facts.) Can you see how this one works?

Look on the Internet to find other mnemonics for π, or make one up yourself.

b Look on the Internet to find the world record, so far, for the greatest number of decimal places to which π has been calculated.

2 In each of the following shapes, all the curves are semicircles.

Calculate the perimeter of each shape as follows.

i Use a calculator and give your answer to one decimal place.

ii Use $\pi = \frac{22}{7}$ and give your answer as a mixed number.

a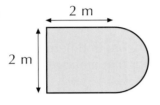

2 m

2 m

b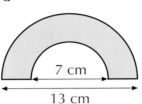

7 cm

13 cm

c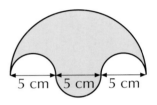

5 cm 5 cm 5 cm

3 The distance round a circular running track is 200 m. Calculate the radius of the track, giving your answer to the nearest metre.

Formula for the area of a circle

The circle shown has been split into 16 equal sectors. These have been placed together to form a shape which is roughly a rectangle.

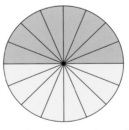
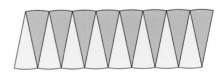

As the circle is split into more and more sectors which are placed together, the resulting shape eventually becomes a rectangle. The area of this rectangle will be the same as the area of the circle.

The length of the rectangle is half the circumference, C, of the circle and its width is the radius, r, of the circle. So, the area of the rectangle is given by:

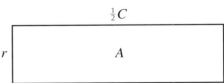

$\frac{1}{2}C$

r A

$A = \frac{1}{2}C \times r$

$= \frac{1}{2} \times 2 \times \pi \times r \times r$

$= \pi \times r \times r$

$= \pi r^2$

Hence, the formula for the area, A, of a circle of radius r is:

$A = \pi r^2$

Example 6.2

Calculate the area of each of the following circles. Give each answer to one decimal place.

a

3 cm

b

3.4 m

a   The radius, $r = 3$ cm, which gives:
$$A = \pi r^2 = \pi \times 3^2$$
$$= 9\pi = 28.3 \text{ cm}^2 \text{ (to 1 dp)}$$

b   The diameter, $d = 3.4$ m, so $r = 1.7$ m. This gives:
$$A = \pi r^2 = \pi \times 1.7^2$$
$$= 2.89\pi = 9.1 \text{ m}^2 \text{ (to 1 dp)}$$

Note: Different makes of calculators work in different ways. For example, the following may be the calculator keys needed for part **a** above:

Other makes may require the x^2 key to be used first.

Note also that when appropriate, answers may be left in terms of π. For example, this may be necessary when the use of a calculator is not allowed. This would give 9π and 2.89π as the answers above.

Exercise 6C

In this exercise, take $\pi = 3.14$ or use the π key on your calculator.

1 Calculate the area of each of the following circles. Give each answer to one decimal place.

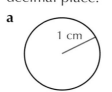   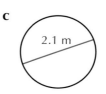   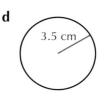   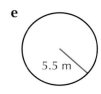

a 1 cm   **b** 14 mm   **c** 2.1 m   **d** 3.5 cm   **e** 5.5 m

2 Calculate the area of a circular tablemat with a diameter of 21 cm. Give your answer to the nearest square centimetre.

3 Measure the diameter of a 1p coin to the nearest millimetre. Calculate the area of one face of the coin, giving your answer to the nearest square millimetre.

4 Calculate the area of the sports ground shown. The bends are semicircles. Give your answer to the nearest square metre.

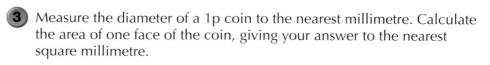

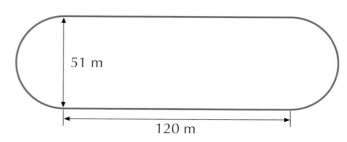

51 m

120 m

5 The minute hand on a clock has a length of 13 cm. Calculate the area swept by the minute hand in one hour. Give your answer in terms of π.

6 Calculate the area of one face of the semicircular protractor shown. Give your answer to one decimal place.

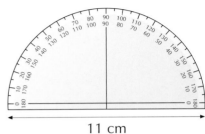

11 cm

Extension Work

1 Calculate the area of each of the following shapes. Give your answers to one decimal place.

a

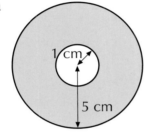

1 cm

5 cm

b

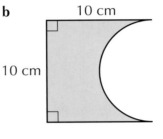

10 cm

10 cm

c

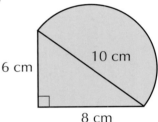

6 cm

10 cm

8 cm

2 A circular lawn has an area of 200 m². Calculate the radius of the lawn, giving your answer to one decimal place.

3 A circular disc has a circumference of 15 cm. Calculate the area of one face of the disc, giving your answer to one decimal place.

4 Show that the formula for the area, A, of a circle with diameter d can also be written as:

$$A = \frac{\pi d^2}{4}$$

Metric units for area and volume

The following are the metric units for area, volume and capacity which you need to know. Also given are the conversions between these units.

Area	Volume	Capacity
10 000 m² = 1 hectare (ha) 10 000 cm² = 1 m² 1 m² = 1 000 000 mm² 100 mm² = 1 cm²	1 000 000 cm³ = 1 m³ 1000 mm³ = 1 cm³	1 m³ = 1000 litres (l) 1000 cm³ = 1 litre 1 cm³ = 1 millilitre (ml) 10 millilitres = 1 centilitre (cl) 1000 millilitres = 100 centilitres = 1 litre

The unit symbol for litres is the letter l. To avoid confusion with the digit 1 (one), the full unit name may be used instead of the symbol.

Note:
To change **large** units to **smaller** units, **always multiply** by the conversion factor.
To change **small** units to **larger** units, **always divide** by the conversion factor.

Example 6.3 ▷

Convert each of the following as indicated.

a $72\,000$ cm^2 to m^2 **b** 0.3 cm^3 to mm^3 **c** 4500 cm^3 to litres

a $72\,000$ cm^2 = $72\,000 \div 10\,000 = 7.2$ m^2

b 0.3 cm^3 = $0.3 \times 1000 = 300$ mm^3

c 4500 cm^3 = $4500 \div 1000 = 4.5$ litres

Exercise 6D

1 Express each of the following in cm^2.

a 4 m^2 **b** 7 m^2 **c** 20 m^2 **d** 3.5 m^2 **e** 0.8 m^2

2 Express each of the following in mm^2.

a 2 cm^2 **b** 5 cm^2 **c** 8.5 cm^2 **d** 36 cm^2 **e** 0.4 cm^2

3 Express each of the following in cm^2.

a 800 mm^2 **b** 2500 mm^2 **c** 7830 mm^2 **d** 540 mm^2 **e** 60 mm^2

4 Express each of the following in m^2.

a 20 000 cm^2 **b** 85 000 cm^2 **c** 270 000 cm^2 **d** 18 600 cm^2
e 3480 cm^2

5 Express each of the following in mm^3.

a 3 cm^3 **b** 10 cm^3 **c** 6.8 cm^3 **d** 0.3 cm^3 **e** 0.48 cm^3

6 Express each of the following in m^3.

a 5 000 000 cm^3 **b** 7 500 000 cm^3 **c** 12 000 000 cm^3 **d** 650 00 cm^3
e 2000 cm^3

7 Express each of the following in litres.

a 8000 cm^3 **b** 17 000 cm^3 **c** 500 cm^3 **d** 3 m^3 **e** 7.2 m^3

8 Express each of the following as indicated.

a 85 ml in cl   **b** 1.2 litres in cl   **c** 8.4 cl in ml
d 4500 ml in litres   **e** 2.4 litres in ml

9 How many square paving slabs, each of side 50 cm, are needed to cover a rectangular yard measuring 8 m by 5 m?

10 A football pitch measures 120 m by 90 m. Find the area of the pitch in the following units.

a m^2 **b** Hectares

11 A fish tank is 1.5 m long, 40 cm wide and 25 cm high. How many litres of water will it hold if it is filled to the top?

12 The volume of the cough medicine bottle is 240 cm³. How many days will the cough medicine last?

13 How many lead cubes of side 2 cm can be cast from 4 litres of molten lead?

Extension Work

1 A farmer has 100 m of fencing to enclose his sheep. He uses the wall for one side of the rectangular sheep-pen. If each sheep requires 5 m² of grass inside the pen, what is the greatest number of sheep that the pen can hold?

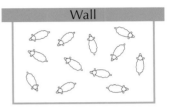

2

| 12 inches = 1 foot |
| 3 feet = 1 yard |

Use this information to find:

a the number of square inches in one square yard.

b the number of cubic inches in one cubic yard.

3 What is an acre? Use reference books or the Internet to find out.

Volume and surface area of prisms

A **prism** is a three-dimensional (3-D) shape which has exactly the same two-dimensional (2-D) shape running all the way through it.

This 2-D shape is called the **cross-section** of the prism.

The shape of the cross-section depends on the type of prism, but it is always the same for a particular prism.

The volume, *V*, of a prism is found by multiplying the area, *A*, of its cross-section by the length, *l*, of the prism (or its height if it stands on one end).

$$V = Al$$

The surface area of a prism is found by calculating the sum of the areas of its faces. For example, in the prism shown here, its surface area is composed of the two end pentagons plus five rectangles.

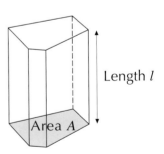

Length *l*

Area *A*

Example 6.4 ▷

For the triangular prism shown, calculate:
a the total surface area.   **b** the volume.

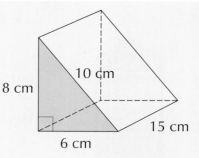

a   The total surface area is composed of two equal right-angled triangles and three different rectangles.

The area of one triangle is:

$$\frac{8 \times 6}{2} = 24 \text{ cm}^2$$

So, the area of two triangles is 48 cm².

The sum of the areas of the three rectangles is:

$$(6 \times 15) + (8 \times 15) + (10 \times 15) = 360 \text{ cm}^2$$

So, the total surface area is:

$$48 + 360 = 408 \text{ cm}^2$$

b   The cross-section is a right-angled triangle with an area of 24 cm².

Hence, the volume is given by:

Area of cross-section × Length = 24 × 15 = 360 cm³

Exercise 6E

1 For each of the following prisms, calculate: **i** the total surface area.   **ii** the volume.

a

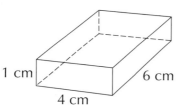

b

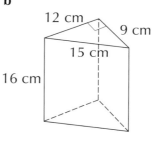

c

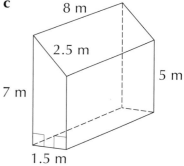

2 The section of pencil shown is a hexagonal prism with a cross-sectional area of 50 mm² and a length of 160 mm.

   a   Calculate the volume of the pencil in cubic millimetres.
   b   Write down the volume of the pencil in cubic centimetres.

3 The biscuit tin shown is an octagonal prism with a cross-sectional area of 350 cm² and a height of 9 cm. Calculate the volume of the tin.

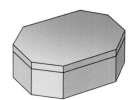

4 The diagram shows the cross-section of a swimming pool along its length. The pool is 15 m wide.

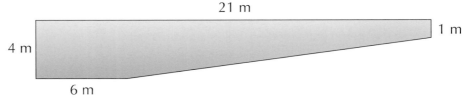

    a Calculate the area of the cross-section of the pool.

    b Find the volume of the pool.

    c How many litres of water does the pool hold when it is full?

5 Andy is making a solid concrete ramp for wheelchair-access to his house. The dimensions of the ramp are shown on the diagram.

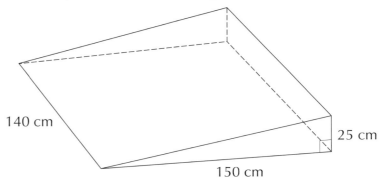

    a Calculate the volume of the ramp, giving your answer in cubic centimetres.

    b What volume of concrete does Andy use? Give your answer in cubic metres.

Extension Work

Volume of a cylinder

Note that some pupils may wish to see a range of cylindrical objects before embarking on this work. (See also Question **2**.)

The cross-section of a cylinder is a circle of radius r.

The area of the cross-section is $A = \pi r^2$.

If the height of the cylinder is h, then the volume, V, of the cylinder is given by:

$$V = \pi r^2 \times h = \pi r^2 h$$

1 Calculate the volume of each of the following cylinders, giving each answer to three significant figures.

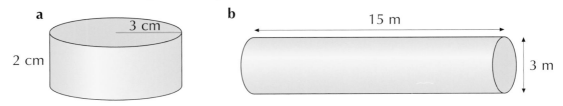

    a   **b**

2 Ask your teacher for some cylindrical objects. Calculate the volume of each, using the most appropriate units.

LEVEL BOOSTER

5 I know the metric units for area, volume and capacity.

6 I can use the formulae for calculating the circumference and the area of a circle.
I can solve problems using metric units.

7 I can calculate the surface area and the volume of a prism.

National Test questions

1 *2003 5–7 Paper 2*

An adult needs about **1.8 litres** of water each day to stay healthy.

How many glasses is that?

225 ml

2 *2001 Paper 2*

A trundle wheel is used to measure distances.

Imran makes a trundle wheel, of diameter 50 cm.

a Calculate the circumference of Imran's trundle wheel. Show your working.

b Imran uses his trundle wheel to measure the length of the school car park.

His trundle wheel rotates 87 times. What is the length of the car park, to the nearest metre?

3 *2004 5–7 Paper 2*

a The cross-section of a cylindrical cotton reel is a circle.

The **diameter** of this circle is **3 cm**.

What is the **circumference** of this circle?

3 cm

b **91 metres** of cotton goes around the cotton reel.

About how many times does the cotton go around the reel?

Show your working and give your answer to the **nearest ten**.

3 cm

4   *2005 5–7 Paper 2*

The diagram shows two circles and a square, ABCD.

A and B are the centres of the circles.

The radius of each circle is **5 cm**.

Calculate the area of the **shaded part** of the square.

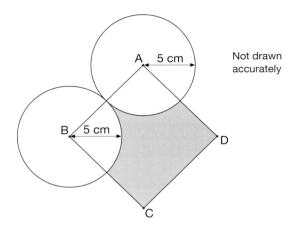

Not drawn accurately

5   *2007 5–7 Paper 2*

a   Look at the triangular prism.

Work out the volume of the prism.

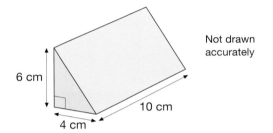

Not drawn accurately

b   One face of a prism is made from 5 squares.

Each square has side length 3 cm.

Work out the volume of the prism.

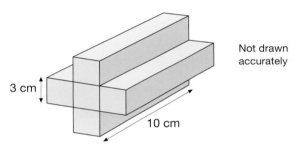

Not drawn accurately

Athletics stadium

An athletics stadium is having a 'face-lift'.

1 The shot-put circle is going to be resurfaced.
   a What is the perimeter of the circle?
   b What is the area of the circle?
   c The circle is resurfaced with a sand and cement mix which is 25 mm thick.
   What is the volume of the sand and cement mix that is needed to resurface the shot-put circle?

2.135 m

2 The high jump zone is also going to be resurfaced.
   a What is the area of the high jump zone?
   b Resurfacing costs £57.50 per square metre.
   What is the cost to resurface the high jump zone?

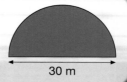

30 m

3 The running track is going to be repainted.
   This diagram shows the dimensions of the inside line of the track.
   a What is the total distance of the inside line?

   One litre of paint is mixed with 2 litres of water.
   The paint is bought in large 20-litre tins.
   Each tin costs £52.70.
   b How much water do you need to mix with 50 tins of paint?
   c What is the cost of 50 tins of paint?

73 m

85 m

4 A new winners' podium is going to be built.
   This sketch shows the dimensions.
   a Work out the volume of each cylinder.
   b What is the total volume of the podium?

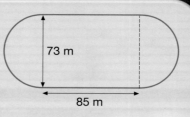

20 cm   3rd   1st   2nd   40 cm   60 cm

90 cm   90 cm   90 cm

5 This sketch shows the dimensions of the sandpit for the long jump.

40 cm

3 m

8 m

  a How many cubic metres of sand does the sandpit hold when full?

  b 0.6 m³ of sand weighs 1 tonne.

    How many tonnes of sand are needed to fill the sandpit?

6 A ramp for wheelchair access into the stadium is going to be built.

30 cm

2 m

3 m

  a What is the area of the triangular cross-section of the ramp?

  b What volume of concrete will be needed to make the ramp?

  c Concrete costs £48 per cubic metre.

    How much does it cost to make the ramp?

CHAPTER **7** Number **2**

This chapter is going to show you

- How to extend your ability to work with powers of 10
- How to round numbers and use rounded numbers to estimate the results of calculations
- How to use your calculator efficiently

What you should already know

- How to multiply and divide by 10, 100, 0.1 and 0.01
- Basic column methods for addition, subtraction, multiplication and division

Powers of 10

You have met powers of 10 before. This section will remind you how to use them to solve problems. The following table shows you some powers of 10.

Power	10^{-4}	10^{-3}	10^{-2}	10^{-1}	10^{0}	10^{1}	10^{2}	10^{3}	10^{4}
Value	0.0001	0.001	0.01	0.1	1	10	100	1000	10 000

Example 7.1 ▷

Multiply and divide each of the following by: **i** 10^2 and **ii** 10^4

  a   0.752   **b**   1.508   **c**   0.0371

You have $10^2 = 100$ and $10^4 = 10\,000$. Hence, multiplying and dividing by each of them gives:

  a   **i** $0.752 \times 10^2 = 75.2$; $0.752 \div 10^2 = 0.00752$
        ii $0.752 \times 10^4 = 7520$; $0.752 \div 10^4 = 0.000\,0752$

  b   **i** $1.508 \times 10^2 = 150.8$; $1.508 \div 10^2 = 0.015\,08$
        ii $1.508 \times 10^4 = 15\,080$; $1.508 \div 10^4 = 0.000\,1508$

  c   **i** $0.0371 \times 10^2 = 3.71$; $0.0371 \div 10^2 = 0.000\,371$
        ii $0.0371 \times 10^4 = 371$; $0.0371 \div 10^4 = 0.000\,003\,71$

Example 7.2 ▷

Multiply and divide each of the following by: **i** 10^{-1} and **ii** 10^{-2}

  a   3.45   **b**   0.089   **c**   7632

You have $10^{-1} = 0.1$ and $10^{-2} = 0.01$. Hence, multiplying and dividing by each of them give:

  a   **i** $3.45 \times 0.1 = 0.345$; $3.45 \div 0.1 = 34.5$
        ii $3.45 \times 0.01 = 0.0345$; $3.45 \div 0.01 = 345$

  b   **i** $0.089 \times 0.1 = 0.0089$; $0.089 \div 0.1 = 0.89$
        ii $0.089 \times 0.01 = 0.000\,89$; $0.089 \div 0.01 = 8.9$

  c   **i** $7632 \times 0.1 = 763.2$; $7632 \div 0.1 = 76\,320$
        ii $7632 \times 0.01 = 76.32$; $7632 \div 0.01 = 763\,200$

1 Calculate each of these.

a	6.34×100	**b**	$47.3 \div 100$	**c**	66×1000
d	$2.7 \div 1000$	**e**	$3076 \times 10\ 000$	**f**	$7193 \div 10\ 000$
g	9.2×0.1	**h**	$0.64 \div 0.1$	**i**	0.84×0.01
j	$8.71 \div 0.01$				

2 Multiply each of the following numbers by: **i** 10^3 and **ii** 10^4

    a 8.7   **b** 0.32   **c** 103.5   **d** 0.09   **e** 23.06

3 Divide each of the following numbers by: **i** 10^3 and **ii** 10^4

    a 8.7   **b** 0.32   **c** 103.5   **d** 0.09   **e** 23.06

4 Divide each of the following numbers by: **i** 0.01 and **ii** 0.001

    a 2.7   **b** 0.45   **c** 207   **d** 0.08   **e** 41.7

5 Multiply each of the following numbers by: **i** 0.01 and **ii** 0.001

    a 2.7   **b** 0.45   **c** 207   **d** 0.08   **e** 41.7

6 Calculate each of these.

a	3.76×10^2	**b**	$2.3 \div 10^3$	**c**	0.09×10^5
d	$3.09 \div 10^3$	**e**	2.35×10^2	**f**	$0.01 \div 10^4$

7 a Use the table on page 110 to write down each of these numbers in full.

    i 10^{-1} = ...   **ii** 10^{-2} = ...   **iii** 10^{-3} = ...   **iv** 10^{-4} = ...

    b Use the answers to part **a** to work out each of the following.

        i 9.2×10^{-1} **ii** 0.71×10^{-3} **iii** 45.6×10^{-2}

        iv $4.2 \div 10^{-1}$ **v** $0.98 \div 10^{-2}$ **vi** $2.14 \div 10^{-3}$

Extension Work

You have already met three terms, called prefixes, which may be used to make decimal multiples of units. They are kilo-, as in kilogram (1000 grams), centi-, as in centilitre (one hundredth of a litre) and milli-, as in millimetre (one thousandth of a metre).

The table below gives the main prefixes and their equivalent multiples given as powers of 10.

Prefix	giga	mega	kilo	centi	milli	micro	nano	pico
Power	10^9	10^6	10^3	10^{-2}	10^{-3}	10^{-6}	10^{-9}	10^{-12}

For example, 7 000 000 000 grams could be given as 7 gigagrams, or – which is more likely – as 7 kilotonnes.

a Write each of the following quantities in a simpler form using words.

    i 0.004 grams   **ii** 8 000 000 watts   **iii** 0.75 litres

b Use the Internet or a reference book to find out the common abbreviations for these units. For example, kilo is k, as in 6 kg.

c Use the Internet or a reference book to find out how far light travels in 1 nanosecond.

Rounding

There are two main uses of rounding, both of which you have met before. One is to give an answer to a sensible degree of accuracy. The other is to enable you to make an estimate of the answer to a problem.

Example 7.3 ▶

Round each of the following numbers to: **i** one decimal place.
ii two decimal places.

a 7.356 **b** 13.978 **c** 0.2387

a 7.356 = 7.4 to one decimal place; 7.356 = 7.36 to two decimal places

b 13.978 = 14.0 to one decimal place; 13.978 = 13.98 to two decimal places

c 0.2387 = 0.2 to one decimal place; 0.2387 = 0.24 to two decimal places

Example 7.4 ▶

Round the following numbers to one significant figure.

a 18.67 **b** 0.037 61 **c** 7.95

a 18.67 = 20 to one significant figure

b 0.037 61 = 0.04 to one significant figure

c 7.95 = 8 to one significant figure

Example 7.5 ▶

Estimate the answer to each of the following.

a 21% of £598 **b** $\dfrac{23.7 + 69.3}{3.1 \times 5.2}$ **c** $3.9^2 \div 0.0378$

The method is to round the numbers to one significant figure, which gives:

a 21% of £598 ≈ 20% of £600 = £120

b $\dfrac{23.7 + 69.3}{3.1 \times 5.2} \approx \dfrac{20 + 70}{3 \times 5} = \dfrac{90}{15} = 6$

c $3.9^2 \div 0.0378 \approx 4^2 \div 0.04 = 16 \div 0.04 = 160 \div 0.4 = 1600 \div 4 = 400$

Example 7.6 ▶

Which of each of the following is the most sensible answer?

a The distance from my house to the local post office: **i** 721.4 m **ii** 721 m or **iii** 700 m

b The time in which an athlete runs a 100 m race: **i** 10.14 seconds **ii** 10.1 seconds or **iii** 10 seconds

a Distances are usually rounded to one or two significant figures. Hence, 700 m is the sensible answer.

b 100-metre times need to be accurate to the nearest hundredth of a second. Hence, 10.14 s is the sensible answer.

[**Note:** An answer cannot be 'more accurate' than the accuracy of the numbers in the question.]

① Round each of the following numbers to: **i** one decimal place.
ii two decimal places.

a	2.367	**b**	13.0813	**c**	8.907	**d**	20.029
e	0.999	**f**	4.0599	**g**	0.853	**h**	3.14159

② Round each of the following numbers to one significant figure.

a	4560	**b**	0.0941	**c**	3.098	**d**	42.611
e	0.999	**f**	5.0598	**g**	3.472	**h**	3.14159

③ Write each of the following to one significant figure.

a **i** 19% **ii** £278   **b** **i** 23.2 **ii** 0.018

c **i** 12.3 **ii** 0.058   **d** **i** 23.1 **ii** 57.3 **iii** 16.5 **iv** 7.3

④ Use your answers to question 3 to estimate the answer to each of the following.

a 19% of £278   **b** 23.2 ÷ 0.018   **c** $12.3^2 \times 0.058$ **d** $\dfrac{23.1 + 57.3}{16.5 + 7.3}$

⑤ Estimate the answer to each of the following. Where appropriate, round each answer to a sensible degree of accuracy.

a $\dfrac{0.245 \times 0.03}{1.89 \times 3.14}$ **b** $\dfrac{45.9 \times 83.2}{26.7 - 9.8}$ **c** 14% of 450 kg

d $59.5 \div 0.13^2$ **e** $(3.95 \times 0.68)^2$ **f** 28% of 621 km

g 4% of £812   **h** 0.068×0.032

⑥ Round each of the following quantities to a sensible degree of accuracy.

a Average speed of a journey: 63.7 mph

b Size of an angle in a right-angled triangle: 23.478°

c Weight of a sack of potatoes: 46.89 kg

d Time taken to boil an egg: 4 minutes 3.7 seconds

e Time to run a marathon: 2 hours 32 minutes and 44 seconds

f World record for running 100 m: 9.78 seconds

⑦ Use a calculator to work out each of the following, and then round each result to an appropriate degree of accuracy.

a $\dfrac{56.2 + 48.9}{17.8 - 12.5}$ **b** $\dfrac{12.7 \times 13.9}{8.9 \times 4.3}$ **c** 1 ÷ 32

d 0.58^2 **e** 1 ÷ 45   **f** 23.478 ÷ 0.123

Extension Work

Below are four calculator displays rounded to one decimal place, four ordinary numbers and four standard form numbers which are rounded to three significant figures.

Match them up.

3.8×10^4 7.2×10^{-3} 3.8×10^{-4} 7.2×10^3

37 842	7234	0.000 3784	0.007 234
7.23×10^{-3}	3.78×10^4	3.78×10^{-4}	7.23×10^3

Multiplying decimals

This section will give you more practice in multiplying integers and decimals.

Example 7.7 ▷ Find each of the following.

    a 0.03×0.05 **b** 900×0.004 **c** $50 \times 0.04 \times 0.008$

    a There are four decimal places in the multiplication, so there are four in the answer. Therefore, you have:

        $0.03 \times 0.05 = 0.0015$

    b Rewrite as equivalent products. That is:

        $900 \times 0.004 = 90 \times 0.04 = 9 \times 0.4 = 3.6$

    c Calculate this in two parts. First:

        $50 \times 0.04 = 5 \times 0.4 = 2$

    Then rewrite 2×0.008 as $2 \times 8 = 16$ but with three decimal places in the answer. This gives:

        $50 \times 0.04 \times 0.008 = 0.016$

Example 7.8 ▷ Without using a calculator, work out 13.4×0.63.

There are several ways to do this. Three (a column method and two box methods) are shown. Whichever method you use, you should first estimate the answer:

    $13.4 \times 0.63 \approx 13 \times 0.6 = 1.3 \times 6 = 7.8$

Remember also that there are three decimal places in the product, so there will be three in the answer.

In the first two methods, the decimal points are ignored in the multiplication and then placed in the answer.

Column method

```
    134
×    63
    402
   8040
   8442
```

Box method 1

	100	30	4	Total
60	6000	1800	240	8040
3	300	90	12	402
			Total	8442

Box method 2

	10	3	0.4	Total
0.6	6	1.8	0.24	8.04
0.03	0.3	0.09	0.012	0.402
			Total	8.442

By all three methods the answer is 8.442.

Exercise 7C

Do not use a calculator to answer any of these questions.

(1) Work out each of these. Show your working.

a	400×0.5	**b**	0.07×200	**c**	0.3×400	**d**	0.06×500
e	0.07×400	**f**	0.008×200	**g**	0.005×700	**h**	0.003×4000
i	0.004×7000	**j**	300×0.009	**k**	900×0.01	**l**	900×0.04
m	600×0.1	**n**	700×0.01	**o**	800×0.001	**p**	900×0.0001

2 Work out each of these. Show your working.

a $0.002 \times 500 \times 300$ **b** $0.03 \times 0.04 \times 60\,000$

c $0.4 \times 0.02 \times 800$ **d** $400 \times 600 \times 0.05$

e $40 \times 0.006 \times 20$ **f** $0.3 \times 0.08 \times 4000$

3 Work out the answer to each of the following. Use any method you are happy with. Show your working.

a 73×9.4 **b** 5.82×4.5

c 12.3×2.7 **d** 1.24×10.3

e 2.78×0.51 **f** 12.6×0.15

g 2.63×6.5 **h** 0.68×0.42

4 A rectangle is 2.46 m by 0.67 m. What is the area of the rectangle? Show your working.

Extension Work

1 Work out each of the following.

a 1.2^2 **b** 1.7^2 **c** $1.7^2 - 1.2^2$ **d** 0.5×2.9

2 Work out each of the following.

a 1.5^2 **b** 2.1^2 **c** $2.1^2 - 1.5^2$ **d** 0.6×3.6

3 Look for a connection between the calculations in parts **c** and **d** of Questions **1** and **2**. Then *write down* the answer to $3.1^2 - 2.1^2$. Check your answer with a calculator.

Dividing decimals

This section will give you more practice in dividing integers and decimals.

Example 7.9 ▷   Work out each of these.

a $0.12 \div 0.03$ **b** $600 \div 0.15$

a Simplify the division by rewriting it as equivalent divisions. In this case, keep multiplying both numbers by 10 until the divisor (0.03) becomes a simple whole number (3). This is equivalent to shifting the digits in both numbers to the left by the same amount. So you have:

$$0.12 \div 0.03 = 1.2 \div 0.3$$
$$= 12 \div 3 = 4$$

b Rewriting as equivalent divisions gives:

$$600 \div 0.15 = 6000 \div 1.5$$
$$= 60\,000 \div 15 = 4000$$

Example 7.10 ▷

Work out each of these.

a $32.8 \div 40$ **b** $7.6 \div 800$

a   Simplify the division by rewriting it as equivalent divisions. In this case, keep dividing both numbers by 10 until the divisor (40) becomes a simple whole number (4). This is equivalent to shifting the digits in both numbers to the right by the same amount. So, you have:

$$32.8 \div 40 = 3.28 \div 4 = 0.82$$

which can be worked out as a short division:

$$\frac{0.82}{4\overline{)3.28}}$$

b   Rewriting as equivalent divisions gives:

$$7.6 \div 800 = 0.76 \div 80$$
$$= 0.076 \div 8 = 0.0095$$

which can be worked out as a short division:

$$\frac{0.0095}{8\overline{)0.076\,^40}}$$

Example 7.11 ▷

Work out $4.32 \div 1.2$.

First estimate the answer:

$$4.32 \div 1.2 \approx 4 \div 1 = 4$$

Write the problem as an equivalent problem without its decimal points ($432 \div 12$) and use repeated subtraction (chunking). This gives:

$$
\begin{array}{rl}
432 & \\
-\,360 & (30 \times 12) \\
\hline
72 & \\
-\,72 & (6 \times 12) \\
\hline
0 & (36 \times 12)
\end{array}
$$

Insert the decimal point in the quotient (36), which gives $4.32 \div 1.2 = 3.6$.

Exercise 7D

Do not use a calculator to answer any of these questions.

1 Work out each of the following. Show your working.

   a $0.36 \div 0.02$ **b** $0.48 \div 0.5$ **c** $0.45 \div 0.02$ **d** $0.18 \div 0.03$

   e $0.24 \div 0.02$ **f** $0.48 \div 0.3$ **g** $0.39 \div 0.3$ **h** $0.24 \div 0.05$

2 Work out each of the following. Show your working.

   a $600 \div 0.4$ **b** $500 \div 0.25$ **c** $300 \div 0.08$ **d** $300 \div 0.02$

   e $60 \div 0.015$ **f** $60 \div 0.25$ **g** $500 \div 0.02$ **h** $40 \div 0.25$

3 Work out each of the following. Show your working.

   a $3.2 \div 40$ **b** $2.8 \div 400$ **c** $24 \div 400$ **d** $36 \div 90$

   e $4.8 \div 80$ **f** $4.8 \div 200$ **g** $3.5 \div 700$ **h** $0.16 \div 400$

4 Work out each of the following. Use any method you are happy with.

    a $3.36 \div 1.4$ **b** $1.56 \div 2.4$ **c** $5.688 \div 3.6$ **d** $20.28 \div 5.2$

    e $22.23 \div 6.5$ **f** $2.89 \div 3.4$ **g** $5.75 \div 23$ **h** $2.304 \div 0.24$

5 A rectangle has an area of 3.915 cm^2. The length is 2.7 cm. Calculate the width.

Extension **Work**

1 Given that $46 \times 34 = 1564$, work out each of these.

    a 4.6×17 **b** 2.3×1.7 **c** $1564 \div 0.34$ **d** $15.64 \div 0.23$

2 Given that $39 \times 32 = 1248$, work out each of these.

    a 3.9×16 **b** 0.13×32 **c** 3900×0.08 **d** 0.0039×32

3 Given that $2.8 \times 0.55 = 1.540$, work out each of these.

    a 14×55 **b** $154 \div 11$ **c** $15.4 \div 0.28$ **d** 0.014×5500

Efficient use of calculators

  It is important that you know how to use your calculator. You should be able to use the basic functions ($\times$, $\div$, $+$, $-$) and the square, square root and brackets keys. You have also met the memory and sign-change keys. This exercise introduces the fraction and power keys.

Example 7.12

Use a calculator to work out:

a $\left(1\frac{1}{2} - \frac{3}{4}\right) \times \frac{2}{3}$ **b** $\dfrac{\frac{1}{5} + 1\frac{3}{4}}{1\frac{1}{2} - \frac{3}{10}}$

a Using the fraction button, key in the calculation as:

$$(\;\; \text{SHIFT} \;\; \boxed{\tfrac{\blacksquare}{\square}} \;\; 1 \;\; \blacktriangleright \;\; 1 \;\; \blacktriangledown \;\; 2 \;\; \blacktriangleright \;\; - \;\; \boxed{\tfrac{\blacksquare}{\square}} \;\; 3 \;\; \blacktriangledown \;\; 4 \;\;) \;\; \times \;\; \boxed{\tfrac{\blacksquare}{\square}} \;\; 2 \;\; \blacktriangledown \;\; 3 \;\; =$$

The display should show $\frac{1}{2}$. Note that the way this is keyed in may be different on your calculator.

b Using brackets and the fraction buttons gives an answer of $1\frac{5}{8}$.

(Shown in some displays as $\;\; 1 \lrcorner 5 \lrcorner 8 \;\;$.)

Example 7.13

Use a calculator to work out:

a 3^7 **b** $\sqrt[3]{125}$ **c** $\sqrt{6.5^2 - 2.5^2}$

a Using the power key, which may look like $x^{\blacksquare}$, the answer should be 2187.

b This can be keyed in as $\boxed{1}\;\boxed{2}\;\boxed{5}\;\text{SHIFT}\;\boxed{\sqrt{\blacksquare}}\;\boxed{=}$ or $\text{SHIFT}\;\boxed{\sqrt{\blacksquare}}\;\boxed{1}\;\boxed{2}\;\boxed{5}\;\boxed{=}$

The answer is 5. Make sure you can use your calculator to find this answer.

c Using the square root, bracket and square keys, the answer should be 6. For example, the following are two ways to key the problem into the calculator:

$$\boxed{\sqrt{}}\;\boxed{(}\;\boxed{6}\;\boxed{.}\;\boxed{5}\;\boxed{x^2}\;\boxed{-}\;\boxed{2}\;\boxed{.}\;\boxed{5}\;\boxed{x^2}\;\boxed{)}\;\boxed{=}$$

or $$\boxed{(}\;\boxed{6}\;\boxed{.}\;\boxed{5}\;\boxed{x^2}\;\boxed{-}\;\boxed{2}\;\boxed{.}\;\boxed{5}\;\boxed{x^2}\;\boxed{)}\;\boxed{\sqrt{}}\;\boxed{=}$$

7

Use your calculator to work out each of these questions.

1 **a** $\dfrac{22.7 - 7.1}{2.72 + 2.48}$ **b** $\sqrt{6.1^2 - 1.1^2}$ **c** $5.75 \div (4.6 - 2.1)$

2 Give each answer as a mixed number or a fraction in its simplest form, as appropriate.

a $\frac{1}{8} + \frac{1}{3} + \frac{5}{6}$ **b** $2\frac{2}{5} + 2\frac{3}{10}$ **c** $\frac{2}{3} \times \frac{9}{14}$

d $(2\frac{1}{2} + 2\frac{3}{4}) \times \frac{4}{5}$ **e** $\dfrac{1\frac{1}{5} - \frac{3}{4}}{\frac{1}{2} + \frac{1}{10}}$ **f** $\dfrac{2\frac{1}{3} - 1\frac{1}{4}}{1\frac{3}{8} - \frac{5}{6}}$

g $(\frac{3}{8})^2$ **h** $\sqrt{3\frac{1}{9} - 1\frac{1}{3}}$ **i** $(1\frac{1}{4} + \frac{7}{8}) \div \frac{5}{8}$

3 Where necessary, round the answers to two decimal places.

a 3^5 **b** 3.2^2 **c** $\sqrt[3]{2197}$

d $\sqrt{2^5 + 5^2}$ **e** 4^5 **f** $3 \times (2.12)^3$

g 4×1.8^2 **h** $(4 \times 1.8)^2$ **i** $\sqrt{5.3^2 - 2.3^2}$

4 **a** Add 3 hours and 15 minutes to 2 hours and 50 minutes.

b Subtract 1 hour and 55 minutes from 3 hours and 25 minutes.

c Multiply 1 hour and 20 minutes by 4.

Extension Work

Choose a number between 1 and 2, say 1.5. Key it into the calculator display.

Perform the following sequence of key presses:

$$\boxed{+} \;\; \boxed{1} \;\; \boxed{=} \;\; \boxed{1/x} \;\; \boxed{=}$$

Note: The $\boxed{1/x}$ key may be in the form $\boxed{x^{-1}}$. This is called the **reciprocal** key.

After the sequence has been performed, the display should show 0.4.

Repeat the above sequence of key presses. The display should now show 0.714 … .

Keep repeating the above sequence of key presses until the first three decimal places of the number in the display starts to repeat.

Solving problems

Example 7.14 Which jar of jam offers the better value?

The smaller jar gives
454 ÷ 89 = 5.1 grams/penny.

The larger jar gives
2000 ÷ 400 = 5 grams/penny.

So, the smaller jar offers the better value.

Example 7.15 ▷ A bag of identical marbles weighs 375 g. Seven marbles are taken out. The bag then weighs 270 g. How many marbles were in the bag to start with?

The difference in weights is 375 – 270 = 105 g. This is the weight of seven marbles, so one marble weighs:

105 ÷ 7 = 15 g

Hence, the number of marbles originally in the bag is given by:

375 ÷ 15 = 25

Exercise 7F

1 Two families went to the cinema. It cost the Ahmed family of one adult and two children £11.50. It cost the Smith family of two adults and two children £16. What is the cost of an adult's ticket and a child's ticket?

2 This is the charge for hiring a car.
   a How much will it cost to hire the car for 5 days?
   b John pays £137.00 for car hire. For how many days did he hire the car?

> **CAR HIRE**
> **£25 plus**
> **£16.00 per day**

3 Leisureways sell Kayenno trainers for £69.99 but give 10% discount for Running Club members. All Sports sell the same trainers for £75 but are having a sale for which everything is reduced by 15%. In which shop are the trainers cheaper?

4 A supermarket sells crisps in different sized packets. An ordinary bag contains 30 g and costs 28p. A large bag contains 100 g and costs 90p. A jumbo bag contains 250 g and costs £2.30. Which bag is the best value? You must show all your working.

5 A cash-and-carry sells crisps in boxes. A 12-packet box costs £3.00. An 18-packet box costs £5.00. A 30-packet box costs £8.00. Which box gives the best value?

6 A box of chocolate has three soft-centred chocolates for every two hard-centred chocolates. There are 40 chocolates altogether in the box. How many of them are soft-centred?

7 Davy is twice as old as Arnie. The sum of their ages is 36 years. How old are they?

8 A recipe for marmalade uses 65 g of oranges for every 100 g of marmalade. Mary has 10 kg of fruit. How many 454-gram jars of marmalade can Mary make?

9 Fibonacci sequences are formed by adding the previous two numbers to get the next number. For example:

     1, 1, 2, 3, 5, 8, 13, 21, 34, 55, …

   a Write down the next three terms of the Fibonacci sequence that starts 2, 2, 4, 6, 10, 16, … .
   b Work out the missing values of this sequence: 2, 4, 6, …, 16, …, …, 68… .
   c Work out the first three terms of this sequence: …, …, …, 0, 1, 1, 2, 3, 5, 8, … .

10 What fraction is halfway between $\frac{3}{5}$ and $\frac{9}{10}$?

Choose a two-digit number such as 18.

Multiply the units digit by 3 and add the tens digit, which give:

$3 \times 8 + 1 = 25$

Repeat with the new number:

$3 \times 5 + 2 = 17$

Keep repeating the procedure until the numbers start repeating, namely:

$17 \rightarrow 22 \rightarrow 8 \rightarrow 24 \rightarrow \dots$

Show the chains on a poster. For example:

LEVEL BOOSTER

5
I can multiply and divide by simple powers of 10.
I can round numbers to one decimal place.
I can use the brackets, square and square root keys on my calculator.

6
I can round numbers to two or more decimal places.
I can use the power and roots buttons on my calculator.

7
I can use my calculator efficiently to solve more complex calculations.
I can round numbers to one significant figure.
I can solve best value problems.

1 *2002 Paper 1*

a Peter's height is 0.9 m. Lucy is 0.3 m taller than Peter. What is Lucy's height?

b Lee's height is 1.45 m. Misha is 0.3 m shorter than Lee. What is Misha's height?

c Zita's height is 1.7 m. What is Zita's height in centimetres?

2 *2002 Paper 1*

Some people use yards to measure length.

The diagram shows one way to change yards to metres.

Number of yards — × 36 — × 2.54 — ÷ 100 — Number of metres

a Change 100 yards to metres.

b Change 100 metres to yards.

Show your working

3 *2006 5–7 Paper 1*

a Show that **9 × 28 is 252**.

b What is **27 × 28**?

You can use part **a** to help you.

4 *2006 5–7 Paper 2*

A shop sells toilet rolls.

You can buy them in packs of 9 or packs of 6.

Which pack gives you better value for money?

You **must** show your working.

Pack of 9 toilet rolls
£3.90

Pack of 6 toilet rolls
£2.50

5 *2002 Paper 1*

a The number 6 is halfway between 4.5 and 7.5.
What are the missing numbers below?

The number 6 is halfway between 2.8 and …

The number 6 is halfway between –12 and …

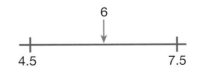

b Work out the number that is halfway between 27 × 38 and 33 × 38.

6 *2002 Paper 2*

A company sells and processes films of two different sizes. The tables show how much the company charges.

Film size: 24 photos	
Cost of each film	£2.15
Postage	Free
Cost to print film	£0.99
Postage of each film	60p

Film size: 36 photos	
Cost of each film	£2.65
Postage	Free
Cost to print film	£2.89
Postage of each film	60p

I want to take 360 photos. I need to buy the film, pay for the film to be printed and pay for the postage.

a Is it cheaper to use all films of 24 photos or all films of 36 photos?

b How much cheaper is it?

7 *2007 5–7 Paper 2*

The value of π correct to 7 decimal places is **3.1415927**.

a Write the value of π correct to **4 decimal places**.

b Which value below is closest to the value of π?

$\frac{179}{57}$ $3\frac{1}{7}$ $(\frac{16}{9})^2$ $\frac{355}{113}$

8 *2006 5–7 Paper 1*

a Put these values in order of size with the **smallest first**:

5^2 3^2 3^3 2^4

b Look at this information:

5^5 is 3125

What is 5^7?

9 *2007 5–7 Paper 1*

Here is the rule to find the **geometric mean** of two numbers:

Multiply the two numbers together, then find the **square root** of the result.

Example: geometric mean of 4 and 9 $= \sqrt{4 \times 9}$
$= \sqrt{36}$
$= 6$

a For the two numbers **10** and x, the geometric mean is **30**.

What is the value of x?

b Reena says:

"For the two numbers **–2** and **8** it is **impossible** to find the geometric mean."

Is Reena correct?

Explain your answer.

Copy these multiplication grids and write in the missing numbers:

×	8	
9	72	
−6		30

×	0.2	
3		1.2
		6

Paper

Paper sizes

Standard paper sizes are called A0, A1, A2 and so on.
A0 is approximately 1188 mm by 840 mm.
The next size A1 is found by cutting A0 in half.

Here is a diagram of a piece of paper of size A0.

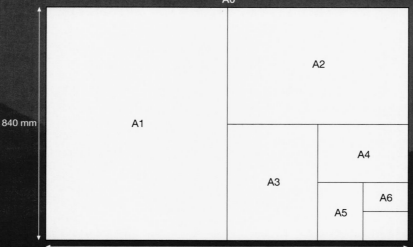

Paper for sale

1 ream = 500 sheets

Reams of Paper – Special offer

Grade of paper	Prices		
	1 ream	5–9 reams	10+ reams
Standard	£2.10	SAVE $\frac{1}{3}$ per ream	EXTRA 10% discount
Special	£1.80		
Quality	£3.00		
Photo	£3.60		

Example for Standard paper:

1 ream costs £2.10
5 reams at full price = 5 × £2.10 = £10.50
Saving = $\frac{1}{3}$ of £10.50 = £3.50
Cost of 5 reams = £7.00
10 reams with $\frac{1}{3}$ off = 2 × £7.00 = £14.00
Extra 10% discount = £1.40
Cost of 10 reams = £12.60

Buy 5 reams
You save
£3.50

Buy 10 reams
You save
£8.40

1 How many sheets of paper are there in 40 reams of paper?

2 The thickness of a piece of paper is 0.12 mm.
How high would 4 reams (2000 sheets) of this paper be?
Give your answer in centimetres.

3 Here is a table of paper sizes.

Paper size	A0	A1	A2	A3	A4	A5
Length (mm)	1188	840	594			
Width (mm)	840	594				

Copy and complete the table.
Check your result for A4 paper by measuring.

4 How many pieces of A5 paper would be needed to make a piece of A1 paper?

5 Look at the special offers and work out the cost of:
  a 3 reams of Special grade paper.
  b 5 reams of Quality grade paper.
  c 10 reams of Photo grade paper.

6 Work out the saving if you buy 20 reams of Quality paper using the offers.

Factorisation

When a number can be broken down into a pair of numbers which, when multiplied together, give that number, this is called **factorisation**. For example:

$24 = 3 \times 8$ Both 3 and 8 are called **factors**.

Common factors

24 and 18 both have factors which are common to them: for example, 2, 3 and 6. These are called **common factors**, and the **highest common factor** is abbreviated to **HCF**. Here, the HCF is 6.

Example 8.1 ▷

Write down the HCF of 60 and 36.

Start with the smaller number. The factors of 36 are:

1   2   3   4   6   9   12   18   36

Compare these with the factors of 60:

1   2   3   4   5   6   10   12   15   20   30   60

The comparison shows that the HCF of 60 and 36 is 12.

Algebraic expressions also have factors, as shown in Example 8.2.

Example 8.2 ▷

Write down all the common factors of $4ab$ and $6bc$.

Both $4ab$ and $6bc$ can be broken down into factors, as follows.

Take $4ab$:

Factors of 4: 1, 2, 4
Factors involving letters only: a, b, ab
Factors involving numbers and letters: $2a$, $2b$, $4a$, $4b$, $2ab$, $4ab$

Now take $6bc$:

Factors of 6: 1, 2, 3, 6
Factors involving letters only: b, c, bc
Factors involving numbers and letters: $2b$, $2c$, $2bc$, $3b$, $3c$, $3bc$, $6b$, $6c$, $6bc$

Comparing both sets of factors shows that the common factors of $4ab$ and $6bc$ are 1, 2, b and $2b$.

To find the HCF of two algebraic expressions, do the following.

- Find the HCF of their numbers.
- Then find all the letters they have in common.
- Finally, multiply together the two answers.

Example 8.3 ▷

Find the HCF of $6pq$ and $8pr$.

The HCF of 6 and 8 is 2.

There is only one letter in common: p.

So, the HCF of $6pq$ and $8pr$ is $2p$.

Example 8.4 ▷

Find the HCF of $12x^2y$ and $18x^2y^2$.

$12x^2y$ can be written as $12xxy$.

$18x^2y^2$ can be written as $18xxyy$.

The HCF of 12 and 18 is 6.

The letters common to $12x^2y$ and $18x^2y^2$ are xxy.

So, the HCF of $12x^2y$ and $18x^2y^2$ is $6xxy$ or $6x^2y$.

Note: The method set out in Example 8.4 can be extended to more complex problems, for example, $24a^3b^2c$ and $20a^2bc^2d$.

Exercise 8A

1 Write down all the common factors of each of these pairs of numbers.

   a   2 and 6   **b**   6 and 9   **c**   10 and 15   **d**   12 and 22

2 Find the HCF of the numerator and denominator in order to cancel down each of the following fractions. The first one has been done for you.

   a $\dfrac{9}{15} = \dfrac{3 \times 3}{3 \times 5}$ Now divide top and bottom by 3 which gives $\dfrac{3}{5}$.

   b $\dfrac{16}{28}$ **c** $\dfrac{32}{48}$ **d** $\dfrac{27}{45}$ **e** $\dfrac{18}{42}$

3 Write down the HCF of each of the following pairs of numbers.

   a   8 and 10   **b**   16 and 24   **c**   32 and 48   **d**   56 and 84

4 For each pair of expressions below, write down: **i**   all the common factors.
   ii   the HCF.

   a $3ab$ and $2ab$ **b** $5cd$ and $10c$ **c** $4gh$ and $6h$

   d $6ab$ and $8ac$ **e** $8pr$ and $12pt$ **f** $10mnp$ and $15mp$

5 For each pair of expressions below, write down: **i**   all the common factors.
   ii   the HCF.

   a $3a^2$ and $4a$ **b** $5b^2$ and $3ab$ **c** $4a^2b$ and $6ab^2$

   d $6b^2c^2$ and $8bc$ **e** $9mn^2$ and $15mn$ **f** $12p^2q$ and $16pq^2$

5

6

6 Write down the HCF of each of the following pairs of expressions.

    a $4a^2$ and $6ab$ **b** $6ab^2$ and $9ab$ **c** $6a^2b$ and $15ab^2$

    d $5bc^2$ and $7bc$ **e** $12m^2n^2$ and $9mn$ **f** $2p^2q$ and $8pq^2$

Extension Work

The Lowest Common Multiple (LCM) of a pair of numbers is the smallest number in both times tables.

So, for example, the LCM of 24 and 60 is 120 as $5 \times 24 = 120$ and $2 \times 60 = 120$.

The LCM of $6pq$ and $8pr$ is worked out as follows:

The LCM of 6 and 8 is 24, the LCM of p and p is p, the LCM of q is q, the LCM of r is r, so the LCM of $6pq$ and $8pr$ is $24pqr$.

Find the LCM of all the pairs of expressions in questions 4, 5 and 6 of Exercise 8A.

Index notation with algebra

Time can be saved by writing $5 \times 5 \times 5$ as 5^3. That is, using the index notation to form **powers** of numbers. Variables can be treated in the same way. For example, $m \times m \times m$ can be written as m^3.

Look at each of the following examples of **multiplying** one power by another power of the same variable:

$$m^2 \times m^3 = (m \times m) \times (m \times m \times m) = m \times m \times m \times m \times m = m^5$$
$$t^1 \times t^2 = t \times (t \times t) = t \times t \times t = t^3$$
$$k^3 \times k^4 = (k \times k \times k) \times (k \times k \times k \times k) = k \times k \times k \times k \times k \times k \times k = k^7$$

Notice that, in each case, the indices are *added*:

$$m^2 \times m^3 = m^{2+3} = m^5$$
$$t^1 \times t^2 = t^{1+2} = t^3$$
$$k^3 \times k^4 = k^{3+4} = k^7$$

Hence, when multiplying powers of the same variable, *add the indices*:

$$x^A \times x^B = x^{A+B}$$

Now look at the following examples of **dividing** one power by another power of the same variable:

$$m^6 \div m^2 = \frac{m^6}{m^2} = \frac{m \times m \times m \times m \times m \times m}{m \times m} = m^4$$

$$t^4 \div t = \frac{t^4}{t} = \frac{t \times t \times t \times t}{t} = t^3$$

Notice that, in each case, the indices are subtracted:

$$m^6 \div m^2 = m^{6-2} = m^4$$
$$t^4 \div t = t^{4-1} = t^3$$

Hence, when dividing powers of the same variable, *subtract the indices*:

$$x^A \div x^B = \frac{x^A}{x^B} = x^{A-B}$$

Example 8.5 ▶

Simplify each of these.

a $x \times x$ **b** $4m \times 3m$ **c** $a^3 \times a^4$

a $x \times x = x^2$

b $4m \times 3m = 12mm = 12m^2$

c $a^3 \times a^4 = a^{3+4} = a^7$

Example 8.6 ▶

Simplify each of these.

a $2m^3 \times 5m$ **b** $m^5 \div m^3$ **c** $8t^7 \div 4t^2$

a $2m^3 \times 5m = 2 \times 5 \times m^3 \times m = 10m^{3+1} = 10m^4$

b $m^5 \div m^3 = \dfrac{m^5}{m^3} = m^{5-3} = m^2$

c $8t^7 \div 4t^2 = \dfrac{8t^7}{4t^2} = 2t^{7-2} = 2t^5$

Exercise 8B

1 Calculate each of the following powers. Use a calculator if necessary.

    a 2^5 **b** 3^4 **c** 5^3 **d** 4^4

    e 13^3 **f** 15^4 **g** 18^3 **h** 21^2

2 Write down each of the following in index form.

    a $t \times t \times t$ **b** $m \times m \times m \times m$ **c** $p \times p$ **d** $q \times q$

3 Simplify each of these.

    a $3m \times 2m$ **b** $5a \times 3a$ **c** $3x \times 3x \times 2x$

    d $(3y)^2$ **e** $4z \times 2z$ **f** $2w \times 3w \times 5w$

    g $2m^2 \times 4m$ **h** $3x^2 \times 2x^2$ **i** $3y^2 \times 4y^2 \times y$

4 Given that $10^{-1} = 0.1$ and $10^{-2} = 0.01$, write down the decimal value of each of these.

    a 10^{-3} **b** 10^{-4} **c** 10^{-5} **d** 10^{-6}

    e 10^{-7} **f** 10^{-8} **g** 10^{-9}

5 Write down the answer to each of the following in index form.

    a $3^2 \times 3^3$ **b** $5^3 \times 5^4$ **c** $8^3 \times 8^2$ **d** $7^2 \times 7^4$

    e $4^3 \times 4^3$ **f** $6^4 \times 6^3$ **g** $a^2 \times a^3$ **h** $m^3 \times m^4$

    i $p^3 \times p^2$ **j** $d^2 \times d^4$ **k** $t^3 \times t^3$ **l** $k^4 \times k^3$

6 Write down the answer to each of the following in index form.

    a $3^5 \div 3^2$ **b** $5^9 \div 5^3$ **c** $8^6 \div 8^2$ **d** $7^{10} \div 7^5$

    e $4^9 \div 4^3$ **f** $6^8 \div 6^2$ **g** $a^5 \div a^2$ **h** $m^9 \div m^3$

    i $p^7 \div p^3$ **j** $d^8 \div d^3$ **k** $t^3 \div t^2$ **l** $k^{12} \div k^4$

5

7

7 Simplify each of these.

    a $6m \div 2m$ **b** $15a^2 \div 3a$ **c** $12x^6 \div 2x^2$

    d $8y^8 \div 4y^3$ **e** $8z^5y^4 \div 2zy$ **f** $3w^2 \times 4w^7 \div 2w^4$

    g $12m^2 \div 4m$ **h** $10x^2y^7 \div 2x^2y^2$ **i** $4xy^2 \times 9xy^2 \div 12xy$

Extension Work

1   Find some values of x which meet each of the following conditions.

    a x^2 is always larger than x.

    b x^2 is always smaller than x.

    c $x^2 = x$

2   Find some values of x which meet each of the following conditions.

    a x^2 is always larger than $5x$.

    b x^2 is always smaller than $5x$.

    c $x^2 = 5x$

Square roots and cube roots

The **square root** of a given number is that number which, when multiplied by itself, produces the given number.

For example, the square root of 36 is 6, since $6 \times 6 = 36$. A square root is represented by the symbol $\sqrt{}$. For example, $\sqrt{36} = 6$.

Example 8.7 ▷

> Solve $x^2 = 49$
>
> Taking the square root of both sides gives $x = 7$ and -7
>
> The negative value of x is also a solution, because $-7 \times -7 = 49$
>
> Note that all square roots have two solutions: a positive value and its negative.

The **cube root** of a given number is that number which, when multiplied by itself twice, produces the given number.

For example, the cube root of 64 is 4, since $4 \times 4 \times 4 = 64$. A cube root is represented by the symbol $\sqrt[3]{}$. For example, $\sqrt[3]{64} = 4$.

Example 8.8 ▷

> Solve $y^3 = 216$
>
> Taking the cube root of both sides gives $y = 6$
>
> Note that the sign (+ or –) of the value is the *same* as the sign of the original number, because here $+ \times + \times + = +$. If the original number had been –216, the solution would have been –6 (because $- \times - \times - = -$).

You should be familiar with the following square roots and cube roots.

$\sqrt{1}$	$\sqrt{4}$	$\sqrt{9}$	$\sqrt{16}$	$\sqrt{25}$	$\sqrt{36}$	$\sqrt{49}$	$\sqrt{64}$	$\sqrt{81}$	$\sqrt{100}$	$\sqrt{121}$	$\sqrt{144}$	$\sqrt{169}$	$\sqrt{196}$	$\sqrt{225}$
±1	±2	±3	±4	±5	±6	±7	±8	±9	±10	±11	±12	±13	±14	±15

$\sqrt[3]{1}$	$\sqrt[3]{8}$	$\sqrt[3]{27}$	$\sqrt[3]{64}$	$\sqrt[3]{125}$	$\sqrt[3]{216}$	$\sqrt[3]{343}$	$\sqrt[3]{512}$	$\sqrt[3]{729}$	$\sqrt[3]{1000}$
1	2	3	4	5	6	7	8	9	10

Often a calculator will be needed to find a square root or a cube root. So, do make sure you know how to use the power key and root key on your calculator.

When decimal numbers are involved, solutions are usually rounded to one decimal place. For example: $\sqrt[3]{250} = 6.3$, $\sqrt{153} = 12.4$

Exercise 8C

1 Write down each of the following values.

     a $\sqrt{16}$ **b** $\sqrt{25}$ **c** $\sqrt{64}$ **d** $\sqrt{100}$ **e** $\sqrt{225}$

2 Jack has done his homework incorrectly. Find on which line he has gone wrong and correct the homework from there.

     a   Solve the equation $2x^2 = 50$.   **b**   Solve the equation $4x^2 = 36$.

           $x^2 = 2 \times 50 = 100$ $4x = \sqrt{36} = 6$ and -6

           $x = 10$ and -10 $x = \frac{6}{4}$ and $-\frac{6}{4}$

                                                  $x = 1\frac{1}{2}$ and $-1\frac{1}{2}$

3 Use a calculator to find the positive root of each of the following to one decimal place.

     a $\sqrt{26}$ **b** $\sqrt{55}$ **c** $\sqrt{94}$ **d** $\sqrt{109}$ **e** $\sqrt{275}$

4 Without using a calculator, state the cube root of each of the following numbers.

     a   8   **b**   1   **c**   125   **d**   27   **e**   1000

     f -64 **g** -1 **h** -1000 **i**   0.001   **j**   0.008

5 Use a calculator to find the cube root of each of the following to one decimal place.

     a   86   **b**   100   **c**   45   **d**   267   **e**   2000

6 State which of each pair of numbers is larger. You can use a calculator.

     a $\sqrt{10}$, $\sqrt[3]{50}$ **b** $\sqrt{30}$, $\sqrt[3]{150}$ **c** $\sqrt{20}$, $\sqrt[3]{60}$

     d $\sqrt{35}$, $\sqrt[3]{200}$ **e** $\sqrt{15}$, $\sqrt[3]{55}$ **f** $\sqrt{40}$, $\sqrt[3]{220}$

7 Write down two solutions to each of the following equations.

     a $x^2 = 9$ **b** $x^2 = 36$ **c** $x^2 = 49$ **d** $x^2 = 121$

Extension Work

Investigate each of the following statements to see which are:

i always true.   **ii** sometimes true.

For those which are sometimes true, state when they are true.

     a $\sqrt{A} + \sqrt{B} = \sqrt{(A + B)}$ **b** $\sqrt[3]{A} \times \sqrt[3]{B} = \sqrt[3]{(A + B)}$

     c $\sqrt{A} - \sqrt{B} = \sqrt{(A - B)}$ **d** $\sqrt{A} \div \sqrt{B} = \sqrt{(A \div B)}$

Constructing graphs involving time

Looking at real-life graphs involving time, three questions need to be asked.

- Is the measured quantity directly proportional to time?

  For example, when you walk at a constant speed, you travel the same distance every minute. So, if you draw a graph of the distance you covered against the time it took, you will get a straight line.

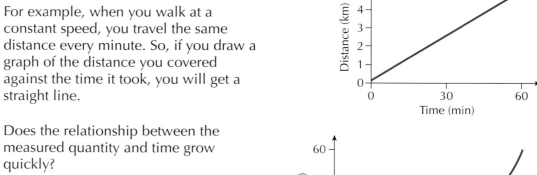

- Does the relationship between the measured quantity and time grow quickly?

  For example, when someone sets off in a car and accelerates, as each second passes that person covers increasing distances. So, if a graph is drawn of distance against time, a curved line is obtained which starts slowly then rapidly rises.

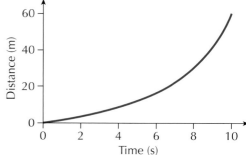

- Does the relationship between the measured quantity and time slow down?

  For example, when you pour a hot cup of tea, it will first cool quickly, but then after some minutes it will start to cool slowly to room temperature. So, if you draw the graph, it will show a sharp decrease initially, followed by a gentle curve down to room temperature.

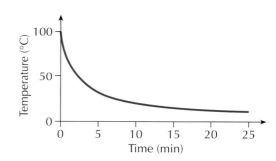

7

 1 Sketch a graph of the depth of water against time when water is poured steadily into these bottles.

a   **b**   **c**   **d**   **e**

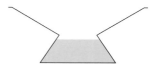

FM **2** Sketch the possible shape of the bottles which, when they are being filled, will give each graph of depth of water against time.

a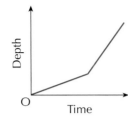

b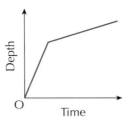

c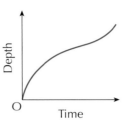

d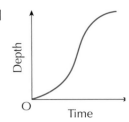

3 Sketch a graph of the number of hours of daylight throughout a year.

FM **4** Match each graph below to one of the situations described in **a** to **g**.

i 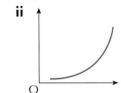   ii   iii 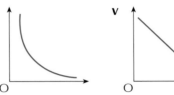   iv   v   vi

(a) The distance, y, travelled by a train moving at constant speed, plotted against time

(b) The number of litres of fuel, y, left in the tank of a lorry moving at constant speed, plotted against time

(c) The speed, y, of a braking car, plotted against time

(d) The temperature, y, of a room which gets hotter then colder

(e) The temperature, y, of a loaf of bread left to cool down after baking, plotted against time

(f) The distance, y, run by Giselle plotted against time. She starts quickly but then gradually slows down, coming to a standstill

(g) The number of computers, y, affected by a computer virus from its first being released up to a month later, plotted against time

5 In Question **4**, there is one situation which is not allocated a graph. Sketch a graph which will represent that situation.

Extension Work

1 A doctor prescribed for a patient one tablet four times daily. The drug took about 30 minutes to be absorbed into the bloodstream, from which it was slowly used up until the next dose was due.

Sketch a graph of the amount of drug in the bloodstream against time.

2 Sketch a graph of another patient who was prescribed the same drug, but who took the tablets five times daily.

3 Sketch a graph of a patient on the drug above who takes only one tablet twice daily.

5
I know the squares of the first 15 integers and the corresponding square roots.

I know the cubes of 1, 2, 3, 4, 5 and 10 and the corresponding cube roots.

I can calculate powers such as 5^3 and simplify algebraic expressions such as $3m \times 2m \times 4m$ using index form.

I can write down the highest common factor of a pair of numbers such as 6 and 8.

6
I can write down the highest common factor of a pair of algebraic expressions such as $4ab$ and $6a^2b$.

I can solve equations of the type $x^2 = 49$ and $(x - 2)^2 = 25$, giving two possible solutions.

I can draw and interpret graphs that show how variables change over time, such as the depth of water in a container.

7
I can use the index laws $x^m \times x^n = x^{m+n}$ and $x^m \div x^n = x^{m-n}$ to simplify expressions.

National Test questions

5

1 *2006 3–5 Paper 1*

   a I am thinking of a number. My number is a **multiple of 4**.

   Which of the statements below is true?
   - My number must be even
   - My number must be odd
   - My number could be odd or even

   Explain how you know.

   b I am thinking of a **different** number. My number is a **factor of 20**.

   Which of the statements below is true?
   - My number must be even
   - My number must be odd
   - My number could be odd or even

   Explain how you know.

2 *2007 5–7 Paper 1*

The graph shows the average heights of fir trees of different ages:

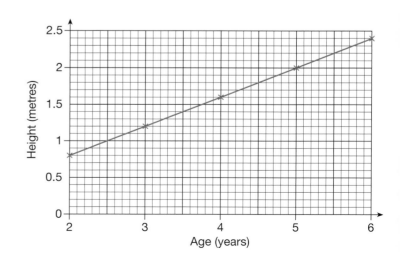

The table below shows the costs of fir trees of different heights:

	120 cm to 159 cm	160 cm to 199 cm	200 cm to 239 cm
Cost	£20.00	£25.00	£30.00

a One of these fir trees is $5\frac{1}{2}$ years old.

How much is it likely to cost?

b One of these fir trees costs **£25.00**.

How old is the tree likely to be?

Write your answer in the form 'Between …… and …… years old'.

3 *1998 Paper 1*

Here are five containers:

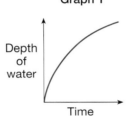

Water is poured at a constant rate into three of the containers.

The graphs show the depth of water as the containers fill up.

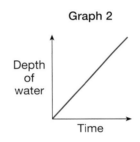

Copy and complete the sentences below to show which container matches each graph.

Graph 1 matches container ……

Graph 2 matches container ……

Graph 3 matches container ……

4 *2006 6–8 Paper 2*

Write the numbers missing from the following:

a $6x + 2 = 10$

so $6x + 1 = \ldots\ldots$

b $1 - 2y = 10$

so $(1 - 2y)^2 = \ldots\ldots$

Packages

Maximum package dimensions

The Post Office will only accept packages that follow the following rules.

Regular cuboidal packages

The length (greatest dimension) cannot be longer than 1.5 m.

The girth is the distance around the package (2 × width + 2 × height).

The girth and the length put together must not exceed 3 m in total.

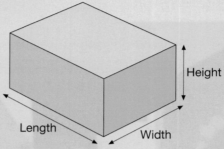

Irregular packages

Greatest dimension cannot exceed 1.5 m.

Girth is measured around the thickest part of package.

The girth plus the length must not exceed 3 m in total.

Girth measured around thickest part

Length measured as greatest dimension

Prices

Up to and including 10 kg:	£14.99
Every kg or part thereof:	Add 80p
Maximum weight:	30 kg

Use the information above to answer these questions.

1 For each of the following cuboidal packages:
  i write down the length.   **ii** work out the girth.   **iii** work out length plus girth.

a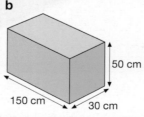

20 cm
100 cm   40 cm

b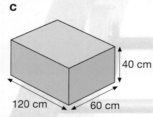

50 cm
150 cm   30 cm

c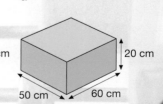

40 cm
120 cm   60 cm

d

20 cm
50 cm   60 cm

2 Which of the packages in Question 1 would not be acceptable to the Post Office?

3 For each of the cuboidal packages in the following table say whether it is acceptable to the Post Office. If it is not, give a reason why.

Package	Weight	Length	Width	Height
A	15 kg	1.2 m	70 cm	20 cm
B	22 kg	160 cm	30 cm	20 cm
C	10 kg	110 cm	80 cm	10 cm
D	40 kg	90 cm	50 cm	20 cm
E	16 kg	80 cm	60 cm	30 cm
F	20 kg	90 cm	70 cm	40 cm
G	32 kg	1 m	60 cm	60 cm
H	3000 g	1.8 m	20 cm	20 cm
I	4 kg	50 cm	50 cm	50 cm
J	18 kg	140 cm	50 cm	30 cm

4 For each of the acceptable packages in Question 1, work out the cost of postage.

5 Each of the following cuboidal packages is at the limit of acceptability. Work out the missing dimension.

a

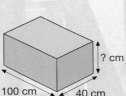

100 cm   40 cm   ? cm

b

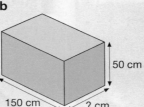

150 cm   ? cm   50 cm

c

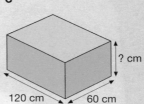

120 cm   60 cm   ? cm

d

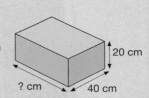

? cm   40 cm   20 cm

6 Cubes have the same length, width and height.
Work out the value of length plus girth for cubes with sides of:

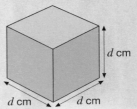

d cm

a 20 cm   **b** 25 cm   **c** 30 cm

d 40 cm   **e** 50 cm   **f** 60 cm

d cm d cm

g What is the largest possible acceptable dimension, in centimetres, of a cubical package?

7 Tubes are often used to send things through the post.

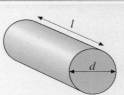

Are the following tubes acceptable to the Post Office? Show your calculations. Give answers to the nearest centimetre.

Remember: Circumference of a circle is given by $C = \pi d$

a $l = 150$ cm, $d = 10$ cm   **b** $l = 100$ cm, $d = 20$ cm

c $l = 80$ cm, $d = 25$ cm   **d** $l = 90$ cm, $d = 30$ cm

<table>
<tr><td colspan="2">

This chapter is going to show you
- How to interpret statements about probability
- How to identify mutually exclusive outcomes
- How to solve probability problems involving mutually exclusive outcomes
- How to use relative frequency to compare the outcomes of experiments

</td><td colspan="2">

What you should already know
- How to use a probability scale
- How to calculate probabilities for single events
- How to use a two-way table or sample space diagram to calculate probabilities
- How to compare fractions

</td></tr>
</table>

Probability statements

You have already studied many probability situations. Check, using the tables below, that you remember how each of the probabilities is worked out.

Also, make sure that you know and understand all the **probability** terms which are used in this chapter.

Single event	Outcome	Probability
Roll a dice	5	$\frac{1}{6}$
Toss a coin	Head	$\frac{1}{2}$
Two blue counters and three green counters in a bag	Blue	$\frac{2}{5}$

Two events	Outcome	Probability
Roll two dice	Double 6	$\frac{1}{36}$
Toss two coins	Two heads	$\frac{1}{4}$
Toss a coin and roll a dice	Head and 5	$\frac{1}{12}$

Most of the combined events you have dealt with so far have been **independent events**. Two events are said to be independent when the outcome of one of them does not affect the outcome of the other event. Example 9.1 illustrates this situation.

Example 9.1 ▷

A Glaswegian girl was late for school on Friday, the day before the world record for throwing the javelin was broken in Sydney by a Korean athlete. Were these events connected in any way?

The pupil's late arrival at school clearly could have no effect on the Korean's performance on the Saturday. So, the two events are independent.

Now look closely at the statements in Examples 9.2 and 9.3, and the comments on them. In Exercise 9A, you will have to decide which given statements are sensible.

Example 9.2 ▷ Daniel says: 'There is a 50–50 chance that the next person to walk through the door of a supermarket will be someone I know because I will either know them or I won't'.

The next person that walks through the door may be someone whom he knows, but there are far more people whom he does not know. So, there is more chance of she/he being someone whom he does not know. Hence, the statement is incorrect.

Example 9.3 ▷ Clare says: 'If I buy a lottery ticket every week, I am bound to win sometime'.

Each week, the chance of winning is very small (1 chance in 13 983 816), so it is highly unlikely that Clare would win in any week. Losing one week does not increase your chances of winning the following week.

Exercise 9A

1 Write a comment on each of the following statements, explaining why the statement is incorrect.

    a A game for two players is started by rolling a six on a dice. Ashad says: 'I never start first because I'm unlucky'.

    b It will rain tomorrow because it rained today.

    c There is a 50% chance of snow tomorrow because it will either snow or it won't.

    d There are mint, chocolate and plain sweets in the packet, so the probability of picking out a chocolate sweet is $\frac{1}{3}$.

2 Decide whether each of the following statements is correct or incorrect.

    a I fell down yesterday. I don't fall down very often, so it could not possibly happen again today.

    b I have just tossed a coin to get a Head three times in succession. The next time I throw the coin, the probability that I will get a Head is still $\frac{1}{2}$.

    c My bus is always on time. It will be on time tomorrow.

    d There is an equal number of red and blue counters in a bag. My friend picked a counter out and it was blue. She then put it back. It is more likely that I will get red when I pick one out.

3 Here are three coloured grids. The squares have either a winning symbol or a losing symbol hidden.

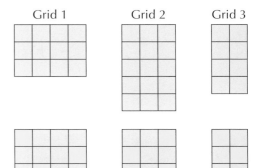

Grid 1   Grid 2   Grid 3

    a If you pick a square from each grid, is it possible to know on which you have the greatest chance of winning?

    b You are now told that on Grid 1 there are three winning squares, on Grid 2 there are five winning squares and on Grid 3 there are four winning squares. Which grid gives you the least chance of winning?

    c Helen says that there are more winning squares on Grid 2, which means that there is more chance of winning using Grid 2. Explain why she is wrong.

4 Here are three events, *A*, *B* and *C*.

    A Jonathan writes computer programs on Monday evenings.

    B Jonathan watches television on Monday evenings.

    C Jonathan wears a blue shirt on Mondays.

Which of these events are independent?

a   *A* and *B*   **b**   *A* and *C*   **c**   *B* and *C*

Extension Work

1   Draw each of the following different-sized grids.

     a   5 by 5 grid with seven winning squares

     b   6 by 6 grid with ten winning squares

     c   10 by 10 grid with 27 winning squares

2   Work out which grid in Question 1 gives you the best chance of finding a winning square. Explain your reasoning.

Mutually exclusive events and exhaustive events

In Year 8, you looked at **mutually exclusive events**. Remember that these are events which do *not* overlap.

Example 9.4 ▷   Which of these three types of number are mutually exclusive: odd, even and prime?

Odd and even numbers are mutually exclusive. Odd and prime numbers, and even are prime numbers are not: for example, 11 and 2.

Example 9.5 ▷   There are red, green and blue counters in a bag.
- Event A: Pick a red counter.
- Event B: Pick a blue counter.
- Event C: Pick a counter that is not green.

Which pairs of events are mutually exclusive?

Events A and B are mutually exclusive because there is no overlap. A red counter and a blue counter are different.

Events A and C are *not* mutually exclusive because they overlap. A red counter and a counter which is not green could be the same colour.

Events B and C are *not* mutually exclusive because they overlap. A blue counter and a counter which is not green could be the same colour.

Example 9.6 ▷

The eight counters shown are contained in a bag.
A counter is chosen at random.

a What is the probability of picking a red counter?
b What is the probability of not picking a red counter?
c What is the probability of picking a green counter?
d What is the probability of picking a blue counter?
e What is the sum of the three probabilities in **a**, **c** and **d**?

a There are three red counters out of a total of eight. This gives:
$$P(red) = \frac{3}{8}$$

b Since there are five outcomes which are not red counters, this means:
$$P(not\ red) = \frac{5}{8}$$

Notice that:
$$P(red) + P(not\ red) = \frac{3}{8} + \frac{5}{8} = 1$$

So, if you know P(Event happening), then:

P(Event not happening) = 1 − P(Event happening)

c There is one green counter, which means:
$$P(green) = \frac{1}{8}$$

d There are four blue counters, which means:
$$P(blue) = \frac{4}{8} = \frac{1}{2}$$

e The sum of the probabilities is:
$$P(red) + P(green) + P(blue)$$
$$= \frac{3}{8} + \frac{1}{8} + \frac{4}{8} = 1$$

All these events are mutually exclusive because only one counter is taken out at a time.

Also, because they cover all possibilities, they are called **exhaustive events**.

Note that the probabilities of exhaustive events which are also mutually exclusive **add up to 1**.

Exercise 9B

1 Discs lettered A, B, C, D and E, and the probability of choosing each, are shown.

A   B   C   D   E

P(A) = 0.3   P(B) = 0.1   P(C) = ?   P(D) = 0.25   P(E) = 0.05

a What is the probability of choosing a disc with either A or B on it?
b What is the probability of choosing a disc with C on it?
c What is the probability of choosing a disc which does not have E on it?

2 A set of 25 cards is shown.

a What is the probability of choosing a card with a fish on it?

b What is the probability of choosing a card with a fish or a cow on it?

c What is the probability of choosing a card with a sheep or a pig on it?

d What is the probability of choosing a card without a fish on it?

3 A spinner is shown with the probabilities of its landing on red, green or blue.

What is the probability of the spinner landing on one of the following?

a Red or green **b** Blue or green

c Blue, green or red **d** Yellow

4 The discs shown right are placed in a bag. One of them is chosen at random. Here are four events:

A A red disc is chosen.

B A blue disc is chosen.

C A green disc is chosen.

D A green or blue disc is chosen.

State which events are mutually exclusive, exhaustive, both or neither.

a *A* and *B* **b** *A* and *C* **c** *A* and *D* **d** *B* and *D*

Extension **Work**

You can work out how many times that you expect something to happen over a number of trials using this formula.

Expected number of successes = Probability of success in each trial × Number of trials

For example, the probability of the spinner in Question 2 landing on green is 0.25. If the spinner is spun 20 times, you have:

Expected number of times it lands on green = 0.25 × 20 = 5 times

Copy and complete the table of the expected number of successes in each case.

Probability of success	Number of trials	Expected number of successes
$\frac{1}{2}$	10	
$\frac{1}{4}$	80	
$\frac{2}{3}$	60	
0.24	100	
0.4	150	
0.75	120	

Estimates of probability

In an experiment to test whether a dice is biased, the dice was rolled 120 times. These are the results.

Number on dice	1	2	3	4	5	6
Frequency	18	25	20	22	14	21

Do you think that the dice is biased?

Number 2 was rolled 25 times out of 120. So, an **estimate of the probability** of rolling number 2 is given by:

$$\frac{25}{120} = 0.208$$

The fraction $\frac{25}{120}$ is called the **relative frequency**.

Relative frequency is an estimate of probability based on experimental data. The relative frequency may be the only way of estimating probability when events are not equally likely.

$$\text{Relative frequency} = \frac{\text{Number of successful trials}}{\text{Total number of trials}}$$

Number 2 was rolled 25 times out of 120. So, for example, you would expect it to be rolled 50 times out of 240. The expected number of successes can be calculated from the formula:

$$\text{Expected number of successes} = \text{Relative frequency} \times \text{Number of trials}$$

Hence, in this case, the expected number of times number 2 is rolled is given by:

$$\frac{25}{120} \times 240 = 50$$

Example 9.7 ▷

Look again at the example above.

A dice is rolled 120 times. Here are the results.

Number on dice	1	2	3	4	5	6
Frequency	18	25	20	22	14	21

a How could you obtain a more accurate estimate than the relative frequency?

b If the dice were rolled 1000 times, how many times would you expect to get a score of 2?

a A more accurate estimate could be obtained by carrying out many more trials.

b The expected number of times a score of 2 is rolled in 1000 trials is given by:
$$0.208 \times 1000 = 208 \text{ times}$$

Exercise 9C

1 A four-sided spinner was spun 100 times. Here are the results.

Number on spinner	1	2	3	4
Frequency	20	25	23	32

a What is the estimated probability of a score of 4?

b Do you think from these results that the spinner is biased? Give a reason for your answer.

c If the spinner were rolled 500 times, how many times would you expect to get a score of 4?

2 A drawing pin is thrown and the number of times that it lands point up is recorded at regular intervals and the results shown in the table.

a Copy and complete the table for the relative frequencies.

Number of throws	10	20	30	40	50
Number of times pin lands point up	6	13	20	24	32
Relative frequency of landing point up	0.6				

b What is the best estimate of the probability of the pin landing point up?

c How many times would you expect the pin to land point up in 200 throws?

3 A bag contains yellow and blue cubes. Cubes are picked from the bag, the colour recorded and the cubes replaced.

a Copy and complete the table for the relative frequencies for the number of times a blue cube was chosen.

Number of trials	10	25	50	100
Number of times blue cube chosen	3	8	15	28
Relative frequency	0.3			

b What is the best estimate of the probability of picking a blue cube from the bag?

c You are now told that there are 75 cubes in the bag altogether. What is the best estimate of the number of blue cubes in the bag?

Extension Work

Here is a graph showing the relative frequency of the number of times a darts player hits the target.

a How many times did the darts player hit the target in the first 10 throws?

b What is the best estimate of the probability of a hit?

c How many times would you expect the darts player to hit the target in 100 throws? State any assumptions that you make.

d Why is it not appropriate to use the graph to find out how many hits there were in the first 15 throws?

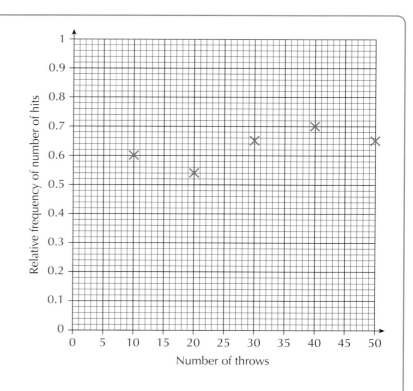

5
I understand and can use the probability scale from 0 to 1.
I know how to find and justify probabilities from equally likely events.
I can find probabilities based on experimental evidence.

6
I can identify outcomes from two events.
I can use tables and diagrams to show outcomes.
I can solve problems involving mutually exclusive events.
I can use the fact that the total probability of all mutually exclusive events of an experiment is 1.

7
I know how to take account of bias.
I can compare outcomes of experiments.
I understand relative frequency as an estimate of probability.

National Test questions

1 *2007 5–7 Paper 2*

The diagram below shows five fair spinners with grey and white sectors.

Each spinner is divided into equal sectors.

I am going to spin all the pointers.

a For one of the spinners, the probability of spinning **grey** is $\frac{3}{4}$.

Which spinner is this? Write its letter.

b For two of the spinners, the probability of spinning **grey** is **more than 60%** but **less than 70%**.

Which two spinners are these? Write their letters.

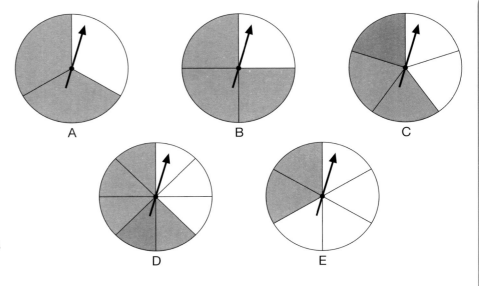

A   B   C

D   E

2 *2001 Paper 1*

Mark and Kate each buy a family pack of crisps.
Each family pack contains ten bags of crisps.

The table shows how many bags of each flavour
are in each family pack.

Flavour	Number of bags
Plain	5
Vinegar	2
Chicken	2
Cheese	1

a Mark is going to take a bag of crisps at random from
his family pack. Copy and complete these sentences.

The probability that the flavour will be ...... is $\frac{1}{2}$.

The probability that the flavour will be cheese is ......

b Kate ate two bags of plain crisps from her family pack of ten bags.
Now she is going to take a bag at random from the bags that are left.

What is the probability that the flavour will be cheese?

c A shop sells 12 bags of crisps in a large pack. I am
going to take a bag at random from the large pack.

The table on the right shows the probability of
getting each flavour.

Use the probabilities to work out how many bags of
each flavour are in this large pack.

Flavour	Probability	Number of bags
Plain	$\frac{7}{12}$	
Vinegar	$\frac{1}{4}$	
Chicken	$\frac{1}{6}$	
Cheese	0	

3 *2007 3–5 Paper 1*

Fred has a bag of sweets.

He is going to take a sweet from the bag at random.

a What is the **probability** that Fred will get a **black** sweet?

b Write down the missing **colour** from the sentence below:

The probability that Fred will get a ...... sweet is $\frac{1}{4}$.

Contents

3 yellow sweets
5 green sweets
7 red sweets
4 purple sweets
1 black sweet

4 *2005 5–7 Paper 2*

Here is some information about all the pupils in class 9A:
A teacher is going to choose a pupil from 9A at random.

a What is the probability that the pupil chosen will be a **girl**?

b What is the probability that the pupil chosen will be **left-handed**?

c The teacher chooses the pupil at random.
She tells the class that the pupil is **left-handed**.

What is the probability that this left-handed pupil is a **boy**?

	Number of boys	Number of girls
Right-handed	13	14
Left-handed	1	2

5 *2002 Paper 1*

I have a bag that contains blue, red, green and yellow counters.
I am going to take out one counter at random.

The table shows the probability of each colour being taken out.

	Blue	Red	Green	Yellow
Probability	0.05	0.3	0.45	0.2

a Explain why the number of yellow counters in the bag cannot be 10.

b What is the smallest possible number of each colour of counter in the bag? Copy and complete the table.

Blue	Red	Green	Yellow

6 *2006 5–7 Paper 2*

A pupil wants to investigate a report that Belgian one euro coins are biased in favour of heads.

Here is her plan for the investigation.

> I will spin **20** Belgian one euro coins to give one set of results.
>
> I will do this **10 times** to give a total of **200 results** to work out an estimated probability of spinning a head.
>
> If this probability is **greater than 56%** my conclusion will be that Belgian one euro coins are biased in favour of heads.

The table shows the 10 sets of results.

Number of each set of **20** coins that showed heads										
10	13	11	11	12	12	11	9	10	11

Using the pupil's plan, what should her conclusion be?

You **must** show your working.

7 *2005 5–7 Paper 1*

Meg and Ravi buy sweet pea seeds and grow them in identical conditions.

Meg's results:

Number of packets	Number of seeds in each packet	Number of seeds that germinate from each packet
5	20	18, 17, 17, 18, 19

Ravi's results:

Number of packets	Number of seeds in each packet	Total number of seeds that germinate
10	20	170

a Using Meg's results and Ravi's results, calculate two different estimates of the **probability** that a sweet pea seed will germinate.

b Whose results are likely to give the better estimate of the probability?

Explain why.

FM Class test

A Year 9 class sat some practice tests before their SATs. The following are their test results.

Name	Gender	English	Maths	Science
John Addy	M	17	45	32
Sean Allsop	M	43	37	41
Sally Emerson	F	65	54	48
Gerry Evans	M	28	65	55
Kay Gilbert	F	76	84	78
Zoe Ginn	F	49	46	57
Zahir Greer	M	87	24	43
Isabell Harding	F	93	75	68
Muhanad Hatamleh	M	72	56	51
Liah Huxter	F	69	74	78
Sahid Jallya	M	25	62	65
Molly Kenward	F	51	37	42
Brian Keys	M	48	53	49
Daniel Mann	M	55	85	73
John O'Dubhchair	M	62	39	35
Godwin Osakwe	M	38	41	27
Krishna Pallin	M	78	56	67
Joy Peacock	F	69	76	65
William Qui	M	87	92	89
Alan Runciman	M	92	34	45
Billie Speed	M	64	74	76
Robert Spooner	M	44	67	61
Joyce Tapman	F	53	43	39
Vi Thomas	F	37	57	64
Cliff Tompkins	M	48	43	51
Lesley Wallace	F	68	58	52
Madge Webb	F	74	42	44
John Wilkins	M	35	41	47
Jenny Wong	F	69	58	43
Jo Zunde	F	94	98	96

1
a Look at the results and write down your estimated guess of the mean test score for each subject for males and females separately.
b Calculate the mean test results for each subject.
c Comment on the accuracy of your guesses.

2 Draw a scatter diagram for the results in the following subjects.
a English and maths
b English and science
c Maths and science

3 Comment on the correlation shown in the three scatter diagrams you have drawn.

4 On your scatter diagrams, use colours to highlight the males and the females and comment on any gender differences now apparent from these results.

5 Draw a stem and leaf diagram for each set of results.

6 From your stem and leaf diagrams, state the median score of each and comment on your results.

7 Create a grouped frequency table for each set of results using the boundaries 1–20, 21–40, 41–60, 61–80 and 81–100.

8 Use the grouped frequency tables to draw a histogram for each set of results.

9 Use all the diagrams you have produced to comment on:
a which test appears to be the easiest and which the hardest.
b the differences between the male and female test results.

<table>
<tr><td>

This chapter is going to show you

- How to enlarge a shape by a fractional scale factor and a negative scale factor
- How to recognise planes of symmetry in 3-D shapes
- How to use map scales
- How to recognise congruent triangles

</td><td>

What you should already know

- How to enlarge a shape by a positive scale factor
- How to recognise reflective symmetry in 2-D shapes
- How to draw plans and scale drawings
- How to use ratio
- How to recognise congruent shapes

</td></tr>
</table>

Enlargements

Positive enlargement

In the diagram below, triangle ABC is **enlarged** by a **scale factor** of 3 to give triangle A'B'C'.

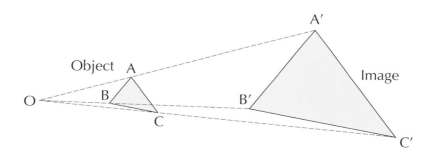

Lines called **rays** or **guidelines** are drawn from O through A, B, C to A', B', C'. Here, the scale factor is given as 3. So, OA' = 3 × OA, OB' = 3 × OB, OC' = 3 × OC. The length of each side of △A'B'C' is three times the length of the corresponding side of triangle ABC.

That is, the **object** triangle ABC is enlarged by a **scale factor** of 3 about the **centre of enlargement**, O, to give the **image** triangle A'B'C'.

The object and image are on the *same side* of O. The scale factor is positive. So, this is called **positive enlargement**.

Under any enlargement, corresponding angles on the object and image are the same.

In the diagram below, triangle ABC is enlarged by a scale factor of $\frac{1}{2}$ to give triangle A'B'C'.

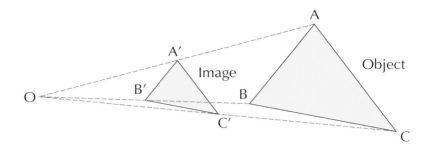

Each side of $\triangle$A'B'C' is half the length of the corresponding side of $\triangle$ABC. Notice also that OA' = $\frac{1}{2}$ of OA, OB' = $\frac{1}{2}$ of OB and OC' = $\frac{1}{2}$ of OC.

That is, the object $\triangle$ABC has been enlarged by a scale factor of $\frac{1}{2}$ about the centre of enlargement, O, to give the image $\triangle$A'B'C'.

The object and the image are on the *same side* of O, with the image *smaller* than the object. The scale factor is a fraction. This is called **fractional enlargement**.

The diagram below shows object flag A enlarged by a scale factor of –2 to give image flag B.

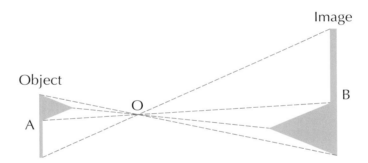

The size of the scale factor is 2 (ignoring the minus sign), so the length of each ray from O to flag B is double the length of the corresponding ray to flag A. The length of each line on flag B is double the length of the corresponding line on flag A.

However, this time the image is inverted (upside-down) and on the *other side* of O to the object. This is because the scale factor is negative (it has a minus sign). This is called **negative enlargement**.

When enlargement is on a grid, the principles are the same. The grid may or may not have coordinate axes, and the centre of enlargement may be anywhere on the grid.

The grid means that it is not always necessary to draw rays to find the image points.

Example 10.1 ▶ Enlarge the square WXYZ by a scale factor of –2 about the centre of enlargement, O.

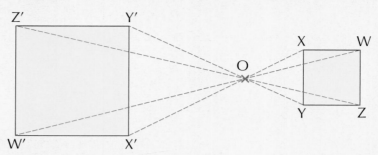

- Draw rays from points W, X, Y, Z to O.
- Measure their lengths and multiply each length by 2.
- Continue the rays beyond O by these new lengths to give points W′, X′, Y′ and Z′.
- Join these points to obtain W′X′Y′Z′.

The object WXYZ has been enlarged by a scale factor of –2 about the centre of enlargement O to give the image W′X′Y′Z′.

Example 10.2 ▶ Enlarge △ABC on the coordinate grid by a scale factor of –3 about the origin (0, 0).

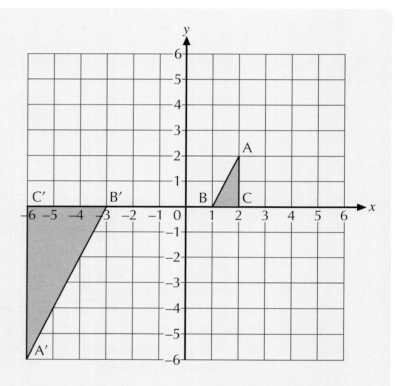

- Draw rays, or count grid units in the x- and y- directions, from points A, B, C to the origin.
- Multiply the ray lengths or the numbers of x, y units by 3.
- Continue beyond the origin by these new lengths or numbers of units to obtain points A′, B′, C′.
- Join these points to give △A′B′C′.

The object △ABC has been enlarged by a scale factor of –3 about the origin (0, 0) to give the image △A′B′C′.

If a negative enlargement is about the *origin* of a grid, as in this case, the coordinates of the image shape are the coordinates of the object shape multiplied by the negative scale factor. So here:

Object coordinates:	A(2, 2)	B(1, 0)	C(2, 0)
Image coordinates:	A′(–6, –6)	B′(–3, 0)	C′(–6, 0)

1 Draw copies of (or trace) the shapes below and enlarge each one by the given scale factor about the given centre of enlargement, O.

a   Scale factor $\frac{1}{2}$

O ×

b   Scale factor $\frac{1}{4}$

O ×

c   Scale factor $1\frac{1}{2}$

O ×

d   Scale factor –2

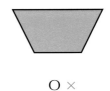

O ×

2 Draw copies of (or trace) the shapes below and enlarge each one by the given scale factor about the given centre of enlargement, O.

a   Scale factor –2

O ×

b   Scale factor –3

O ×

c   Scale factor –2

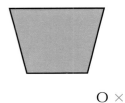

O ×

3 Copy the diagrams below onto a coordinate grid and enlarge each one by the given scale factor about the origin (0, 0).

a   Scale factor –2   **b**   Scale factor –2   **c**   Scale factor –3

a

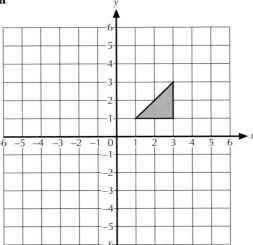

b

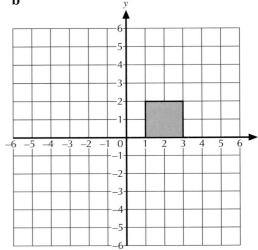

c

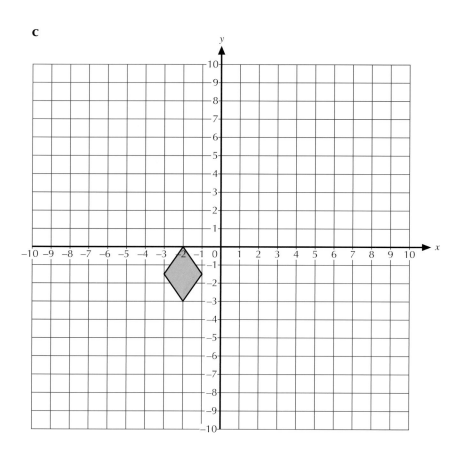

(4) Copy the diagram shown onto a coordinate grid.

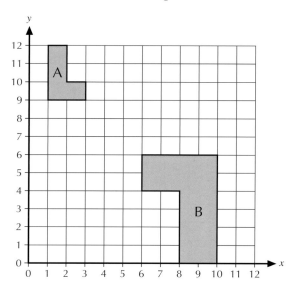

a Shape A is mapped onto shape B by an enlargement. What is the scale factor of the enlargement?

b By adding suitable rays to your diagram, find the coordinates of the centre of enlargement.

c Shape A can also be mapped onto shape B by a combination of a rotation followed by an enlargement. Carefully describe these two transformations.

5 Copy the diagram shown onto centimetre squared paper.

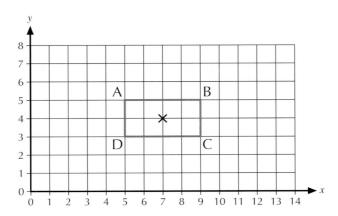

a Enlarge the rectangle ABCD by a scale factor of –2 about the point (7, 4). Label the new rectangle A′B′C′D′.

b Write down the coordinates of A′, B′, C′, D′.

c **i** Write down the lengths of AB and A′B′.
   ii Write down the ratio of the two sides in its simplest form.

d **i** Write down the perimeters of ABCD and A′B′C′D′.
   ii Write down the ratio of the two perimeters in its simplest form.

e **i** Write down the areas of ABCD and A′B′C′D′.
   ii Write down the ratio of the two areas in its simplest form.

Extension Work

1 Working in pairs or groups, design a poster to show how the letter 'A' shown on the right can be enlarged by different negative scale factors about any convenient centre of enlargement.

2 Use reference books or the Internet to explain how each of the following uses negative enlargements.
   a Camera   **b** Eye

3 Use ICT software, such as Logo, to enlarge shapes by different negative scale factors and with different centres of enlargement.

Planes of symmetry

A **plane** is a flat surface. That is, it is two dimensional.

All the two-dimensional (2-D) shapes you have met so far may have one or more lines of symmetry.

Three-dimensional (3-D) shapes, however, may have one or more planes of symmetry.

A plane of symmetry divides a 3-D shape into two identical parts or halves. That is, one half is a reflection of the other half in a plane of symmetry.

Example 10.3 A cuboid has three planes of symmetry. That is, it can be sliced into halves in three different ways.

Each plane of symmetry is a rectangle.

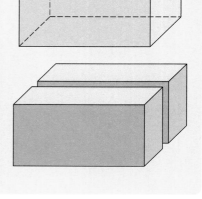

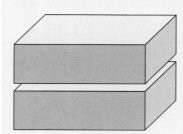 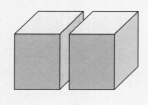

Exercise 10B

1 Write down the number of planes of symmetry for each of the following 3-D shapes.

   a Cuboid with two square faces   **b** Cube   **c** Regular tetrahedron   **d** Square-based pyramid   **e** Regular octahedron

2 Write down the number of planes of symmetry for each of the following regular prisms.

   a Triangular prism   **b** Hexagonal prism   **c** Octagonal prism

 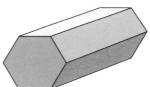 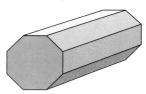

3 A prism has an n-sided regular polygon as its cross-section. How many planes of symmetry does it have?

4 Draw sketches to show the different planes of symmetry for each of the following solids.

  a   **b**   **c**

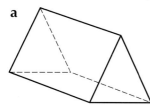 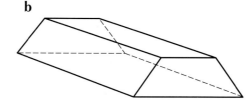 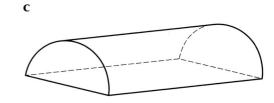

5 Draw sketches of some everyday objects which have one or more planes of symmetry. Below each sketch, write the number of planes of symmetry of the object.

6 Four cubes can be arranged to make the following different solids. Write down the number of planes of symmetry for each.

a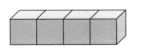

b

c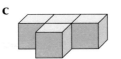

d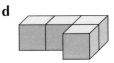

e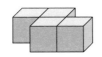

f

g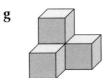

h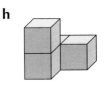

Extension Work

1 Draw separate diagrams to show all the planes of symmetry for a cube.

2 **Axes of symmetry**

The diagram shows an axis of symmetry for a cuboid. The cuboid has **rotational symmetry** of order 2 about this axis.

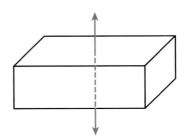

a Draw diagrams to show the other two axes of symmetry for the cuboid. What is the order of rotational symmetry about each of these axes?

b How many different axes of symmetry can you find for a cube?

3 Use reference books or the Internet to find the number of planes of symmetry for more complex 3-D shapes.

Map scales

Maps are two-dimensional **scale drawings** which can represent either local areas of land or geographical regions.

Distance on a map can be given in two different ways, as shown in Examples 10.4 and 10.5.

One way is to give a **map scale**. This relates a direct distance on the map to an actual direct distance on the ground. This is shown in Example 10.4.

The other way is to express the scale as the ratio of direct distance on the map to actual direct distance, measured in the same unit. Hence, a **map ratio** has no units. Example 10.5 explains how to use a map ratio.

Fine string can be used to estimate map distance along paths and roads.

Example 10.4 ▷

This is a map of Wales. Find the actual, direct distance between Aberystwyth and Milford Haven.

The direct distance between Aberystwyth and Milford Haven on the map is 3.5 cm. The scale is 1 cm to 30 km, so 3.5 cm represents 3.5 × 30 km = 105 km.

That is, the actual distance between Aberystwyth and Milford Haven is 105 km.

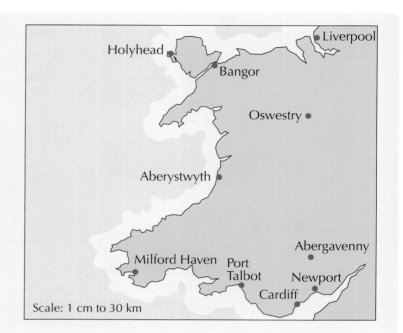

Scale: 1 cm to 30 km

Example 10.5 ▷

The scale of the map in Example 10.4 is 1 cm to 30 km.

There are 100 cm in a metre, and 1000 m in a kilometre.

So, 30 km = 30 × 100 × 1000 = 3 000 000 cm

Therefore, 1 cm to 30 km can also be written as 1 cm to 3 000 000 cm.

Hence, the map ratio will be given as 1 : 3 000 000.

When the ratio is used to find actual distances, each centimetre on a map will represent 3 000 000 cm or 30 km on the ground. Similarly, each inch on the map will represent 3 000 000 inches or 47.3 miles on the ground.

Exercise 10C

1 Write each of the following map scales as a map ratio.

   a 1 cm to 1 m   **b** 1 cm to 5 m   **c** 5 cm to 1 m

   d 1 cm to 1 km   **e** 4 cm to 1 km

2 Using the map in Example 10.4, find the actual direct distance between each of these places.

   a Cardiff and Bangor   **b** Holyhead and Newport

   c Milford Haven and Abergavenny

3 The map ratio on a map is 1 : 50 000. The direct distance between two towns on the map is 8 cm. What is the actual direct distance between the two towns?

4 The map ratio on Peter's map is 1 : 100 000. He has just been for a walk. Using a piece of string, he measures the map distance of his walk and finds it to be 8.5 cm. How far did Peter walk?

5 The map ratio on a map of Australia is 1 : 20 000 000. The actual direct distance between Sydney and Melbourne is 7400 km. What is the direct distance on the map?

6 The map shows York city centre. Find the actual direct distance between each of the following pairs of places.

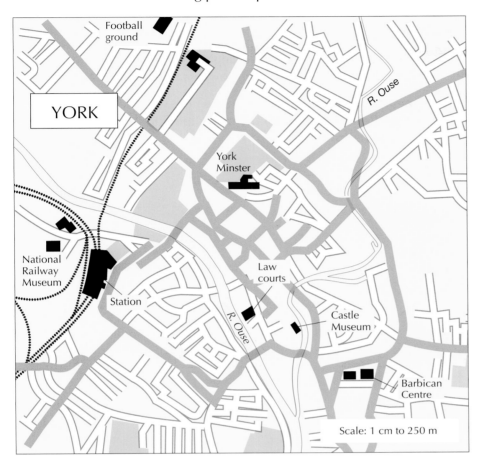

a The Law courts and the station

b The Castle Museum and the station

c The Castle Museum and the football ground

d The National Railway Museum and the Castle Museum

 7 The map shows Uluru (a large rock in the Australian desert). A group of tourists follow the base walk, making one complete circuit of the rock.

a Use a piece of string to find the distance walked by the tourists.

b Another group of tourists drive around the rock on a circuit drive. How much further does the second group travel in one complete circuit?

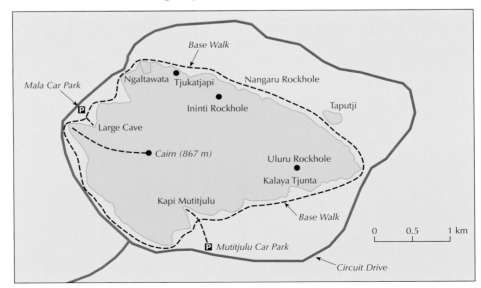

1 Write each of the following imperial map scales as a map ratio.

   a 1 inch to 1 mile   **b** 1 inch to 2 yards
   c 5 inches to $\frac{1}{2}$ mile   **d** 1 inch to 60 yards

2 Ask your teacher for a map of Europe. Using the scale given on the map, find the direct distances between various towns and cities.

3 Use the Internet to look for maps of the area where you live and find the scale that is used. Print out copies of the maps and find the distances between local landmarks.

Congruent triangles

You already know how to construct triangles from given dimensions, as summarised below.

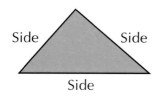

Three sides (SSS)

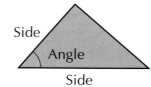

Two sides and the included angle (SAS)

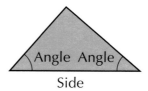

Two angles and the included side (ASA)

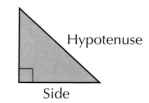

Right angle, hypotenuse and side (RHS)

You can use these conditions to show that two triangles are congruent, as Example 10.6 shows.

Example 10.6

Show that △ABC is congruent to △XYZ.

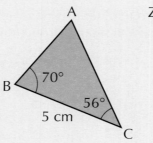

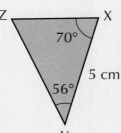

We have:
$\angle B = \angle X$
$\angle C = \angle Y$
$BC = XY$

So, △ABC is congruent to △XYZ (ASA).
This can be written as:
$\triangle ABC \equiv \triangle XYZ$

Exercise 10D

1 Show that each of the following pairs of triangles are congruent. Give reasons for each answer and state which condition of congruency you are using (that is, SSS, SAS, ASA or RHS).

a

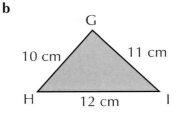

b

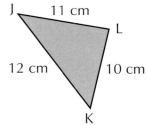

c

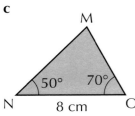
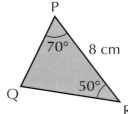

d

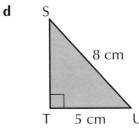
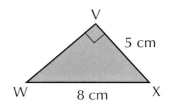

2 Explain why △ABC is congruent to △XYZ.

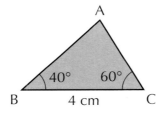
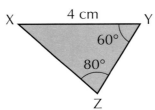

3 a Explain why △PQR is not necessarily congruent to △XYZ.

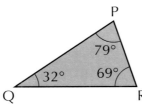
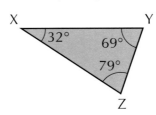

b Check your answer by trying to draw one of the triangles.

4 ABC is an isosceles triangle with AB = AC.
The perpendicular from A meets BC at D.
Show that △ABD is congruent to △ACD.

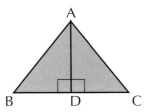

5 Draw a rectangle ABCD. Draw in the diagonals AC and BD to intersect at X. State the different sets of congruent triangles in your diagram.

Extension Work

1 Show that the opposite angles in a parallelogram are equal by using congruent triangles.

2 Draw a kite and label its vertices ABCD with AB = AD. Now draw the diagonals and label their intersection E.

    a Show that △ABC is congruent to △ADC.

    b State all other pairs of congruent triangles.

3 Construct as many different triangles as possible by choosing any three measurements from the following: 4 cm, 5 cm, 40° and 30°.

LEVEL BOOSTER

5 I can convert one metric unit to another.

6 I can I can use map scales.
I can enlarge a 2-D shape by a positive scale factor.

7 I know how to enlarge a 2-D shape by a fractional scale factor.
I can recognise planes of symmetry in 3-D shapes.
I can recognise congruent triangles.

National Test questions

5

1 *2002 Paper 2*

I have a paper circle. Then I cut a sector from the circle. It makes this net.

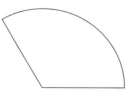

Which 3-D shape below could I make with my net?

A 　　B 　　C 　　D 　　E

2 *2005 4–6 Paper 2*

Draw an **enlargement** of this rectangle with **scale factor 2**.

Use **point A** as the **centre** of enlargement.

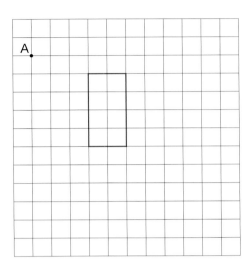

3 *2002 Paper 2* (adapted)

a The grid shows an arrow.

Copy the arrow onto squared paper. Draw an enlargement of scale factor −2 of the arrow.
Use point C as the centre of enlargement.

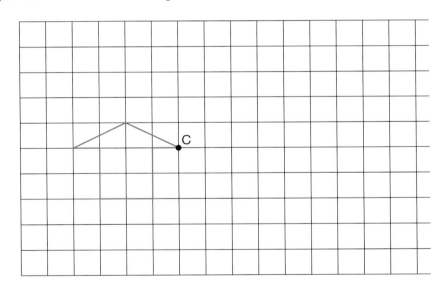

b The sketch below shows two arrows. The bigger arrow is an enlargement of scale factor 1.5 of the smaller arrow. Write down the three missing values.

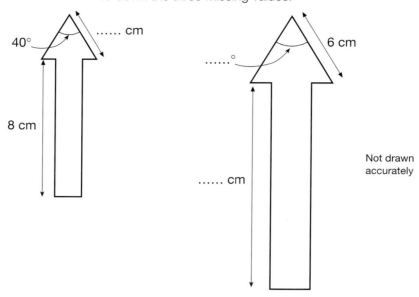

Not drawn accurately

4 *2003 5–7 Paper 2*

Here are four pictures, A, B, C and D. They are not to scale.

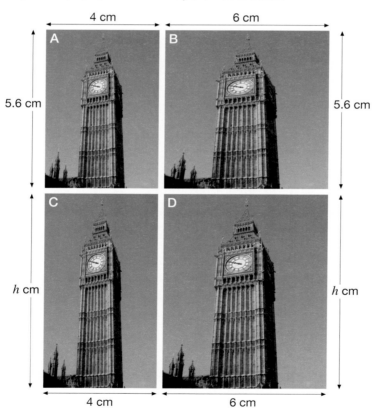

a Picture A can be stretched horizontally to make picture B.

Show that the horizontal factor of enlargement is **1.5**.

b Picture A can be stretched vertically to make picture C.

The vertical factor of enlargement is **1.25**.

What is the height, *h*, of picture C?

5 *2001 Paper 1*

The diagram shows five triangles. All lengths are in centimetres.

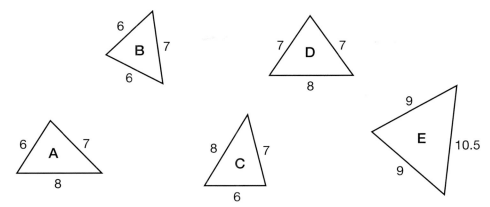

Write the letters of two triangles that are congruent to each other.

Explain how you know they are congruent.

Map reading

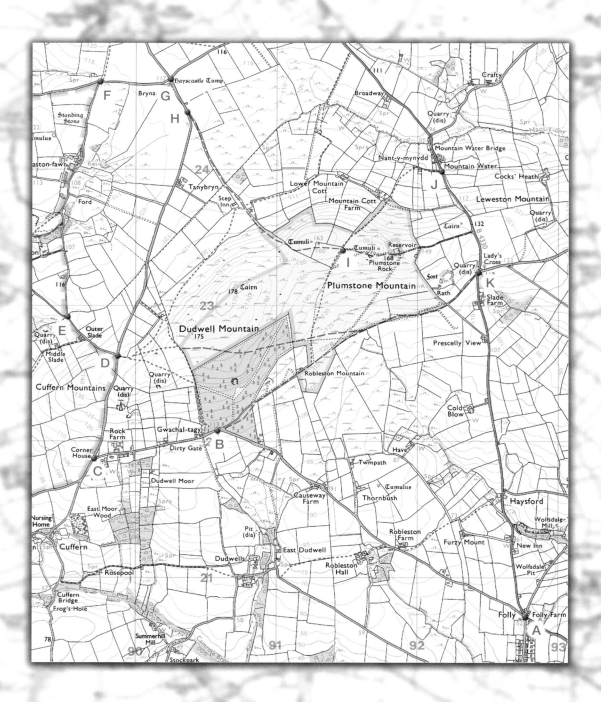

Katie and Richard go for a walk. The route they take is shown on the map. The map has a scale of 1 : 25000. They park their car at the point marked A. They walk from A to B, then B to C and so on until they arrive back at A.

Use the map to answer the questions below.

1 Copy and complete this table showing the distances that they walk.

From	To	Road or footpath	Distance on map	Distance on ground
A	B	Road	9.6 cm	2.4 km
B	C			
C	D			
D	E			
E	F			
F	G			
G	H			
H	I			
I	J			
J	K			
K	A			

2 What is the total distance that they walk on roads?

3 What is the total distance that they walk on footpaths?

4 How far do they walk altogether?

5 They walk at an average speed of 4 km/h. How long does the walk take them?

6 They leave their car at 10.00 am. They stop for a 1-hour lunch and a 30-minute rest. At what time do they get back to their car?

7 On a map, symbols are used to represent different things.

Represents a campsite   Represents a picnic site

a Draw an enlargement of the campsite symbol using a scale factor of 2.

b Draw an enlargement of the picnic site symbol using a scale factor of 3.

<table>
<tr><td>

This chapter is going to show you

- How to expand algebraic expressions
- How to factorise algebraic expressions
- How to substitute negative values and decimals into non-linear expressions
- How to use and create formulae
- How to change the subject of a formula
- How to generate points and plot graphs of linear equations

</td><td>

What you should already know

- How to multiply two expressions together
- How to apply the simple rules of powers
- How to read and plot coordinates and draw a graph

</td></tr>
</table>

Expansion

What is the area of this rectangle?

Split the rectangle into two smaller rectangles in order to find the area of each. Then the area of the original rectangle is the sum of the areas of the two smaller rectangles:

Area = $6x^2 + 8x$

This helps to illustrate the expansion of $2x(3x + 4)$, where the term outside the bracket multiplies every term of the expression inside the bracket. This is the principle of expanding brackets which you met first in Year 8.

Take, for example, the next two expressions:

$$3(2x + 5) = 3 \times 2x + 3 \times 5 = 6x + 15$$

$$t(8 - 3t) = t \times 8 - t \times 3t = 8t - 3t^2$$

Manipulation

Example 11.1 ▷ Find the two missing lengths, AB and CD, of this rectangle.

To find AB, consider

$$(2p + 7) - 3 = 2p + 7 - 3$$
$$= 2p + 4$$

Hence, the length of AB is $2p + 4$.

To find CD, consider

$$(5m + 6) - m = 5m + 6 - m$$
$$= 4m + 6$$

Hence, the length of CD is $4m + 6$.

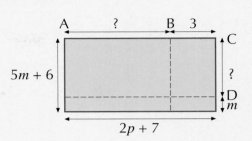

Exercise 11A

1 Expand each of the following.

     a $3(x + 2)$ **b** $5(t + 4)$ **c** $4(m + 3)$ **d** $2(y + 7)$

     e $4(3 + m)$ **f** $3(2 + k)$ **g** $5(1 + t)$ **h** $7(2 + x)$

2 Expand each of the following.

     a $2(x - 3)$ **b** $4(t - 3)$ **c** $3(m - 4)$ **d** $6(y - 5)$

     e $5(4 - m)$ **f** $2(3 - k)$ **g** $4(2 - t)$ **h** $3(5 - x)$

3 Expand each of the following.

     a $4(2x + 2)$ **b** $6(3t - 4)$ **c** $5(2m - 3)$ **d** $3(3y + 7)$

     e $3(3 - 3m)$ **f** $4(2 + 4k)$ **g** $6(1 - 2t)$ **h** $2(2 + 3x)$

4 Write down an expression for the area of each of the following rectangles. Simplify your expression as far as possible.

a 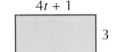   **b**   **c** 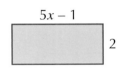   **d** 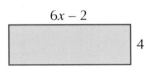   **e**

5 Expand each of the following.

     a $x(x + 3)$ **b** $t(t + 5)$ **c** $m(m + 4)$ **d** $y(y + 8)$

     e $m(2 + m)$ **f** $k(3 + k)$ **g** $t(2 + t)$ **h** $x(5 + x)$

6 Expand each of the following.

     a $x(x - 2)$ **b** $t(t - 4)$ **c** $m(m - 3)$ **d** $y(y - 6)$

     e $m(5 - m)$ **f** $k(2 - k)$ **g** $t(3 - t)$ **h** $x(6 - x)$

7 Expand each of the following.

     a $x(4x + 3)$ **b** $t(2t - 3)$ **c** $m(3m - 2)$ **d** $y(4y + 5)$

     e $m(4 - 5m)$ **f** $k(3 + 2k)$ **g** $t(4 - 3t)$ **h** $x(1 + 4x)$

8 Write down an expression for the area of each of the following rectangles. Simplify your expression as far as possible.

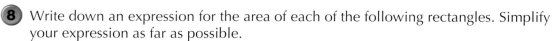

a 2x + 3, x   **b** 5 − 3t, t   **c** 4 + 5m, m   **d** k, 7k − 2

9 Expand and simplify each of the following.

a $3(x + 2) + 2(4 + 3x)$ **b** $4(t + 3) + 3(5 + 2t)$

c $4(m + 3) + 3(2 − 4m)$ **d** $5(2k + 4) + 2(3 − 4k)$

e $6(2x − 3) + 2(3 − 4x)$ **f** $5(3x − 2) + 3(1 − 2x)$

g $3(x + 4) − 2(3 + 2x)$ **h** $4(x + 5) − 3(4 + 2x)$

i $4(m + 2) − 3(2 − 3m)$ **j** $5(2m + 1) − 2(4 − 3m)$

k $5(2x − 1) − 2(1 + 3x)$ **l** $6(3x − 5) − 3(2 + 4x)$

m $3(x − 2) − 2(4 − 3x)$ **n** $4(2x − 1) − 3(5 − 2x)$

10 Write down the missing lengths in each of the following rectangles.

a
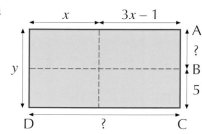

b
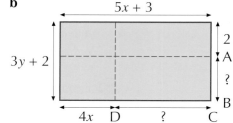

c
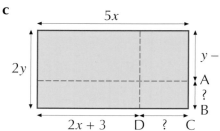

d
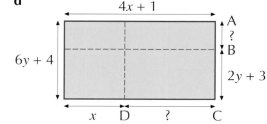

Extension Work

Think of a number. Multiply it by 3 and add 15. Then divide the result by 3 and take away 5.

a What is the number you end up with? What do you notice? Try this with a few more numbers.

b Show by algebra that this result will *always* be the answer.

c Find another similar routine which gives a constant answer.

Factorisation

Factorisation is the opposite (inverse) process to expanding a bracket. For example, expanding $3(2x + 5)$ gives:

$$3(2x + 5) = 3 \times 2x + 3 \times 5$$
$$= 6x + 15$$

Factorisation starts with an expression, such as $6x + 15$, and works back to find the factors which, when multiplied together and simplified, give that expression. (See page 126.)

Example 11.2 ▷

Factorise $6x + 15$.

Look for a factor which will divide into each term in the expression. Here that common factor is 3.

Now rewrite the expression using the common factor, which gives:

$$3 \times 2x + 3 \times 5$$

Insert brackets and move the common factor outside, to obtain:

$$3(2x + 5)$$

Example 11.3 ▷

Factorise $8t - 3t^2$.

Look for a factor which will divide into each term in the expression. Here, that is t.

Now rewrite the expression using the common factor, which gives:

$$t \times 8 - t \times 3t$$

Insert brackets and move the common factor outside, to obtain:

$$t(8 - 3t)$$

Always check your factorised expressions by expanding them. So, in the case of Example 11.2:

$$3(2x + 5) = 3 \times 2x + 3 \times 5$$
$$= 6x + 15$$

and in the case of Example 11.3:

$$t(8 - 3t) = t \times 8 - t \times 3t$$
$$= 8t - 3t^2$$

Exercise 11B

1 Factorise each of the following.

a	$3x + 6$	**b**	$4t + 6$	**c**	$4m + 8$	**d**	$5y + 10$
e	$8 + 2m$	**f**	$3 + 6k$	**g**	$5 + 15t$	**h**	$12 + 3x$

2 Factorise each of the following.

a	$2x - 4$	**b**	$4t - 12$	**c**	$3m - 9$	**d**	$6y - 9$
e	$14 - 7m$	**f**	$21 - 3k$	**g**	$12 - 8t$	**h**	$15 - 3x$

3 Factorise each of the following.

    a $12x + 3$ **b** $6t - 4$ **c** $9m - 3$ **d** $3y + 6$

    e $15 - 3m$ **f** $12 + 4k$ **g** $6 - 2t$ **h** $27 + 3x$

4 Write down an expression for the missing lengths of each of the following rectangles. Simplify your expression as far as possible.

a

?

Area = $3x^2 + 4x$ x

b

?

Area = $5t + 3t^2$ t

c

?

Area = $2m^2 - 3m$ m

d

?

Area = $4t - 2t^2$ t

5 Factorise each of the following.

    a $x^2 + 3x$ **b** $t^2 + 4t$ **c** $m^2 + 5m$ **d** $y^2 + 7y$

    e $3m + m^2$ **f** $4k + k^2$ **g** $3t + t^2$ **h** $x + x^2$

6 Factorise each of the following.

    a $x^2 - 3x$ **b** $3t^2 - 5t$ **c** $m^2 - 2m$ **d** $4y^2 - 5y$

    e $2m - m^2$ **f** $4k - 3k^2$ **g** $5t - t^2$ **h** $7x - 4x^2$

7 Factorise each of the following.

    a $3x^2 + 4x$ **b** $5t^2 - 3t$ **c** $3m^2 - 2m$ **d** $4y^2 + 5y$

    e $4m - 3m^2$ **f** $2k + 5k^2$ **g** $4t - 3t^2$ **h** $2x + 7x^2$

8 Write down an expression for the missing lengths of each of the following rectangles.

a

?

Area = $6x + 8$ 2

b

?

Area = $6 + 9m$ 3

c

?

Area = $12 - 8t$ 4

d

?

Area = $8x - 2$ 2

9 **a** Write down expressions for three consecutive integers where the smallest of these is n.

    b Write down an expression for the sum of these three consecutive integers. Simplify your expression as far as possible.

    c Factorise this expression.

    d Use your result to explain why the sum of *any* three consecutive integers is a multiple of 3.

Extension Work

1 The area of a rectangle is $2x^2 + 4x$. Write down *three* different pairs of expressions for the possible lengths of two adjacent sides of the rectangle.

2 Show by substitution of $x = 1$, $x = 2$ and $x = 3$ that each pair of values generate the *same* values of areas.

3 The area of another rectangle is $12x^2 + 18x$. Write down *seven* different pairs of expressions for the possible lengths of two adjacent sides of the rectangle.

Quadratic expansion

What is the area of this rectangle?

It is $(x + 3)(x + 2)$.

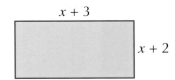

Its area can also be found by splitting each side into two sections, as shown below. The original rectangle is thus divided into four smaller rectangles.

The area of each smaller rectangle is then found, giving the area of the original rectangle as the sum of the areas of the four smaller rectangles.

	x	3	
	x^2	$3x$	x
	$2x$	6	2

The area of the four rectangles $= x^2 + 3x + 2x + 6 = x^2 + 5x + 6$

The area of the original rectangle $= (x + 3)(x + 2)$

Hence:

$$(x + 3)(x + 2) = x^2 + 5x + 6$$

This illustrates the expansion of $(x + 2)(x + 3)$, where every term in the first bracket is multiplied by every term in the second bracket, as shown below.

$$(x + 3)(x + 2) = x^2 + 3x + 2x + 6$$
$$= x^2 + 5x + 6$$

Using this method of curved arrows makes dealing with negative signs inside the brackets much easier, as Example 11.4 shows.

Example 11.4 ▷ Expand $(x - 3)(x - 4)$.

$$(x - 3)(x - 4) \quad \begin{aligned} &= x^2 - 4x - 3x + 12 \\ &= x^2 - 7x + 12 \end{aligned}$$

Example 11.5 ▷ Expand $(x + 3)^2$.

$$(x + 3)^2 = (x + 3)(x + 3) = x^2 + 3x + 3x + 9 = x^2 + 6x + 9$$

Exercise 11C

Expand each of the following expressions.

1 $(x + 3)(x + 4)$ **2** $(x + 5)(x + 1)$ **3** $(x + 2)(x + 7)$ **4** $(x + 2)(x - 4)$

5 $(x + 4)(x - 3)$ **6** $(x + 1)(x - 5)$ **7** $(x - 3)(x + 2)$ **8** $(x - 1)(x + 6)$

9 $(x - 4)(x + 3)$ **10** $(x - 1)(x - 2)$ **11** $(x - 3)(x - 6)$ **12** $(x - 4)(x - 5)$

13 $(4 + x)(1 - x)$ **14** $(5 + x)(2 - x)$ **15** $(3 + x)(6 - x)$ **16** $(x + 5)^2$

17 $(x - 3)^2$ **18** $(2 - x)^2$

7

19 **Investigation**

a Take a square piece of card or paper and label the two adjacent sides, x.

The area of the square is x^2.

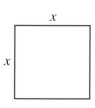

b In the unlabelled corner, draw a smaller square and label each side.

The area of the smaller square is y^2.

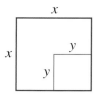

c Cut out this square of side y, and then label the remaining parts of the two sides $x - y$.

The area of this remaining shape must be $(x^2 - y^2)$.

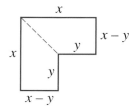

d Now cut this remaining shape diagonally, as indicated by the dashed line. Fit the two parts together, as shown.

The area remains, as before, $(x^2 - y^2)$.

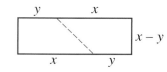

e This makes a rectangle of side $(x + y)$ and $(x - y)$.

Hence:
$$(x + y)(x - y) = x^2 - y^2$$

f It has been shown that the above identity is true geometrically. Now show it is also true algebraically.

20 The result $x^2 - y^2 = (x + y)(x - y)$ from Question **19** is called the **difference of two squares**, and can be used to solve certain arithmetic problems. For example, find the value of $32^2 - 28^2$ without squaring any numbers.

$$32^2 - 28^2 = (32 + 28)(32 - 28)$$
$$= 60 \times 4 = 240$$

Use this method to calculate each of the following.

a $54^2 - 46^2$ **b** $25^2 - 15^2$ **c** $17^2 - 3^2$

d $38^2 - 37^2$ **e** $29^2 - 21^2$ **f** $18^2 - 17^2$

g $8.1^2 - 1.9^2$ **h** $7.9^2 - 2.1^2$ **i** $999^2 - 998^2$

Extension **Work**

Expand each of the following quadratic expressions.

1 $(2x + 3)(4x + 1)$ **2** $(3x + 2)(4x + 5)$

3 $(4x + 3)(2x - 1)$ **4** $(5x - 2)(2x + 6)$

5 $(4x - 3)(2x - 4)$ **6** $(5x - 3)^2$

Change of subject

The cost, in pounds sterling, of advertising in a local paper is given by the formula:

$$C = 10 + 4A$$

where A is the area (in cm²) of the advertisement.

To find the cost of a 7cm² advertisement, substitute $A = 7$ into the formula to give:

$$C = 10 + 4 \times 7 = £38$$

To find the size of the advertisement you would get for, say, £60, you would take these two steps.

- Rearrange the formula to make it read $A = \dfrac{C - 10}{4}$.
- Substitute $C = 60$ into this formula.

When a formula is rearranged like this, it is called **changing the subject** of the formula. The subject of a formula is the variable (letter) in the formula which stands on its own, usually on the left-hand side of the equals sign. So, in this case, C is the subject in the original formula. In the rearranged formula, A becomes the subject.

To change the subject of a formula, use the same method as in solving equations. That is, do the same thing to both sides of the equals sign in order to isolate the variable which is to be the new subject. So, in this example:

$$C = 10 + 4A$$

- First, subtract 10 from both sides: $C - 10 = 4A$
- Then divide both sides by 4: $\dfrac{C - 10}{4} = A$

- Now switch the formula so that the subject is on the left-hand side:

$$A = \frac{C - 10}{4}$$

Hence, to find the size of advertisement which costs £60, substitute $C = 60$ to give:

$$A = \frac{60 - 10}{4} = 12.5 \text{ cm}^2$$

Exercise 11D

1 Change the subject of each of the following formulae as indicated.

  a i Make I the subject of $V = IR$. **ii** Make R the subject of $V = IR$.

  b i Make U the subject of $S = U + 2T$. **ii** Make T the subject of $S = U + 2T$.

  c Make b the subject of $P = 2b + 3$.

  d i Make b the subject of $A = \frac{b}{2}h$. **ii** Make h the subject of $A = \frac{b}{2}h$.

2 The formula $F = \dfrac{9C}{5} + 32$ is used to convert temperatures in degrees Celsius, C, to degrees Fahrenheit, F.

  a Make C the subject of the formula.

  b Use this formula to find the Celsius value of each of the following Fahrenheit temperatures.

   i Temperature on the planet Corus, −65 °F

   ii Body temperature of a reptile, 66.5 °F

   iii Recommended temperature for a tropical fish tank, 56.5 °F

3 The Greek mathematician Hero showed that the area A of a triangle with sides a, b and c is given by the formula:

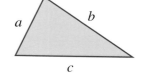

$$A = \sqrt{S(S-a)(S-b)(S-c)}$$

where $S = \dfrac{a+b+c}{2}$

Use Hero's formula to find the area of the following triangles.

a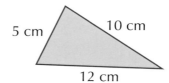

b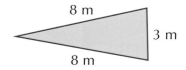

4 The estimated cost, £C, of making a pizza of radius r cm and depth d cm is given by:

$$C = \frac{r^2 d}{20}$$

a What is the estimated cost of making a pizza of radius 8 cm with a depth of 0.5 cm?

b i Rearrange the formula to make d the subject.

   ii What is the depth of a 10 cm radius pizza whose estimated cost to make is £3.75?

5 The area A cm^2 of an ellipse is given by $A = \pi ab$. Calculate to one decimal place each of these.

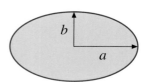

a The area of an ellipse with $a = 8$ cm and $b = 5$ cm.

b i Rearrange the formula to make a the subject.

   ii Calculate the length of a when $A = 150$ cm^2 and $b = 5$ cm.

c i Rearrange the formula to make b the subject.

   ii Calculate the length of b when $A = 45$ cm^2 and $a = 9.5$ cm.

6 Euler's theorem, which connects the number of nodes (N), the number of regions (R) and the number of arcs (A) of a figure, is stated as:

$$N + R - A = 2$$

Take, for example, the figure on the right. This shows 5 nodes, 3 regions (two inside and one outside the figure) and 6 arcs.

a Show that Euler's theorem is correct for the shape shown.

b Show that Euler's theorem is correct for a shape with 6 nodes and 5 regions.

c i Rearrange the formula to make A the subject.

   ii How many arcs will there be in a shape which has 10 nodes and 9 regions?

1 **a** Make r the subject of $A = \pi r^2$, which is the area of a circle.

   b Make r the subject of $V = \pi r^2 h$, which is the volume of a cylinder.

   c Make r the subject of $V = \dfrac{4\pi r^3}{3}$, which is the volume of a sphere.

2 What is the radius of a circle with an area of 100 cm²?

3 What is the radius of a cylinder with a volume of 200 cm³ and a height of 9 cm?

Graphs from equations in the form $Ay \pm Bx = C$

You have already met the linear equation $y = mx + c$, which generates a straight-line graph. It is this equation which is seen here as $Ay \pm Bx = C$. When its graph is plotted, it will, of course, still produce a straight line.

To construct the graph of $Ay \pm Bx = C$, follow these steps:

- Substitute $x = 0$ into the equation so that it becomes $Ay = C$.
- Solve for y, i.e. $y = \frac{C}{A}$, so that one point on the graph is $(0, \frac{C}{A})$.
- Substitute $y = 0$ into the equation so that it becomes $Bx = C$.
- Solve for x, i.e. $x = \frac{C}{B}$, so that one point on the graph is $(\frac{C}{B}, 0)$.
- Plot the two points on the axes and join them up.

Example 11.6

Draw the graph of $4y - 5x = 20$.

Substitute $x = 0 \Rightarrow 4y = 20$
$$y = 5$$

So the graph passes through $(0, 5)$.

Substitute $y = 0 \Rightarrow -5x = 20$
$$x = -4$$

So the graph passes through $(-4, 0)$.

Plot the points and join them up.

Note that this method is sometimes called the 'cover-up' method as all you have to do to solve for x or y is cover up the other term:

i.e. $4y$ 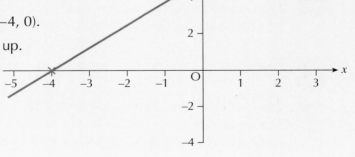 $= 20 \Rightarrow y = 5$

$- 5x = 20 \Rightarrow x = -4$

For both of these questions, use a grid that goes from –10 to +10 on both x and y axes.

1 Draw the graphs of the following.

a	$2y + 3x = 6$	**b**	$4y + 3x = 12$
d	$y + x = 6$	**e**	$5y + 2x = 10$

c $y + 2x = 8$

f $2y + 5x = 20$

2 Draw the graphs of the following.

a	$y - 5x = 10$	**b**	$2y - 3x = 12$	**c**	$x - 3y = 9$
d	$2y + 3x = -6$	**e**	$2y - 5x = 10$	**f**	$2x - 3y = 6$
g	$y + 3x = -9$	**h**	$3x - 4y = 12$	**i**	$y - 2x = 8$
j	$y + x = -8$	**k**	$5y - 2x = 10$	**l**	$x - 4y = 10$

Extension Work

1 Show clearly that when $4x + 5y = 20$ is rearranged to make y the subject, the answer is $y = -\frac{4}{5}x + 4$.

2 Describe how you would plot the graph $4x + 5y = 20$ using the 'cover up' method.

3 Describe how you would plot the graph $y = -\frac{4}{5}x + 4$ using the gradient-intercept method.

4 Compare the advantages of rearranging into the form $y = mx + c$ to draw the graph over using the cover up method.

LEVEL BOOSTER

5 I can substitute numbers into expressions to evaluate them, such as $a = 5$, $b = 6$ into $a^2 - 5b$ $(= -5)$.
I can substitute numbers into formulae to evaluate them, such as $P = 2w + 2b$.
I can expand brackets such as $3(2x - 3)$.

6 I can expand and simplify expressions such as $2(3x + 1) - 3(2x - 4)$.

7 I can factorise expressions such as $3x + 12$ and $4t^2 - 2t$.
I can rearrange formulae such as $P = 2T - 3$ to make T the subject.
I can draw graphs such as $2x - 5x = 10$ using the cover up method.

1 *2000 Paper 1*

    a Two of the expressions below are equivalent. Write them down.

        $5(2y + 4)$ $5(2y + 20)$ $7(y + 9)$ $10(y + 9)$ $2(5y + 10)$

    b One of the expressions below is not a correct factorisation of $12y + 24$. Which one is it? Write down your answer.

        $12(y + 2)$ $3(4y + 8)$ $2(6y + 12)$ $12(y + 24)$ $6(2y + 4)$

    c Factorise this expression: $7y + 14$.

    d Factorise this expression as fully as possible: $6y^3 - 2y^2$.

2 *12007 6–8 Paper 2*

    a Jenny wants to multiply out the brackets in the expression $3(2a + 1)$.

    She writes: $3(2a + 1) = 6a + 1$

    Show why Jenny is **wrong**.

    b Sandeep wants to multiply out the brackets in the expression $(k + 4)(k + 7)$.

    He writes: $(k + 4)(k + 7) = k^2 + 28$

    Show why Sandeep is **wrong**.

3 *2006 6–8 Paper 2*

    Multiply out these expressions. Write your answers as simply as possible.

    a $5(x + 2) + 3(7 + x)$

    b $(x + 2)(x + 5)$

4 *2005 6–8 Paper 2*

    Multiply out these expressions.

    Write your answers as simply as possible.

    a $y(y - 6) = \ldots\ldots$ **b** $(k + 2)(k + 3) = \ldots\ldots$

Trip to Rome

Tom and his wife Geri live in Silkstone. Their friends Stan and his wife Olive live in Barlborough. They both want to take a 7-day holiday in Rome. There are two airports in Rome, Ciampino (CIA) and Fiumicino (FCO).

The diagram shows the local airports, the costs of flights on the days they want to fly and the cost of parking a car for 7 days. Prices for flights are per person and include all taxes and fees.

The diagram also shows the main roads from their homes to the airports.

Motorways and dual carriageways are shown solid and minor roads are shown dotted.

Junctions are marked with arrows and the distances between arrows are shown in miles.

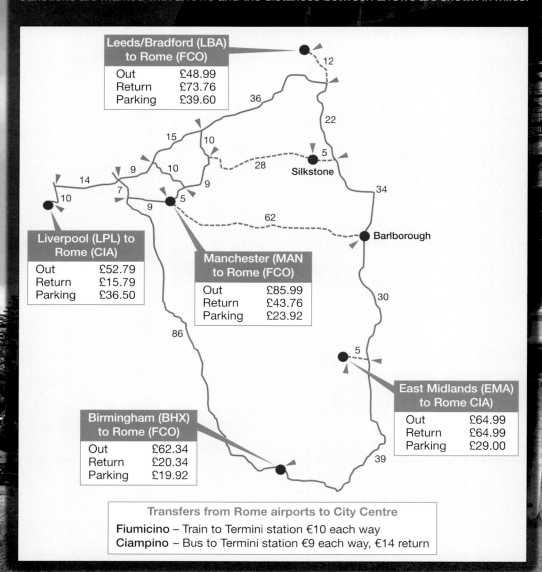

Leeds/Bradford (LBA) to Rome (FCO)

Out	£48.99
Return	£73.76
Parking	£39.60

Liverpool (LPL) to Rome (CIA)

Out	£52.79
Return	£15.79
Parking	£36.50

Manchester (MAN) to Rome (FCO)

Out	£85.99
Return	£43.76
Parking	£23.92

East Midlands (EMA) to Rome CIA)

Out	£64.99
Return	£64.99
Parking	£29.00

Birmingham (BHX) to Rome (FCO)

Out	£62.34
Return	£20.34
Parking	£19.92

Transfers from Rome airports to City Centre

Fiumicino – Train to Termini station €10 each way
Ciampino – Bus to Termini station €9 each way, €14 return

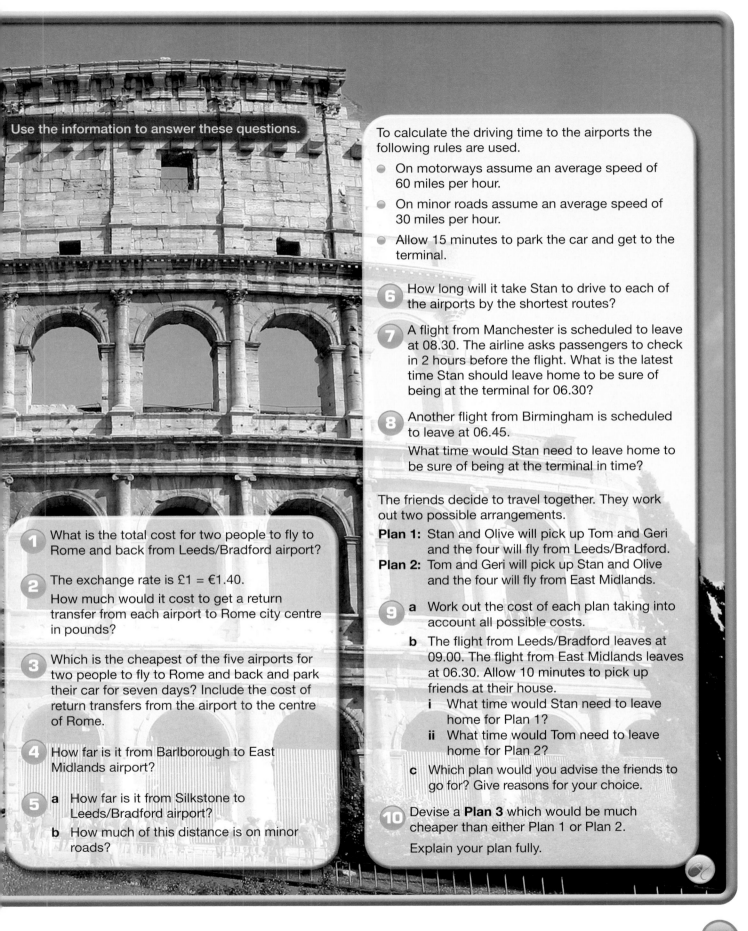

Use the information to answer these questions.

To calculate the driving time to the airports the following rules are used.

- On motorways assume an average speed of 60 miles per hour.
- On minor roads assume an average speed of 30 miles per hour.
- Allow 15 minutes to park the car and get to the terminal.

6 How long will it take Stan to drive to each of the airports by the shortest routes?

7 A flight from Manchester is scheduled to leave at 08.30. The airline asks passengers to check in 2 hours before the flight. What is the latest time Stan should leave home to be sure of being at the terminal for 06.30?

8 Another flight from Birmingham is scheduled to leave at 06.45.

What time would Stan need to leave home to be sure of being at the terminal in time?

The friends decide to travel together. They work out two possible arrangements.

Plan 1: Stan and Olive will pick up Tom and Geri and the four will fly from Leeds/Bradford.

Plan 2: Tom and Geri will pick up Stan and Olive and the four will fly from East Midlands.

9 **a** Work out the cost of each plan taking into account all possible costs.

b The flight from Leeds/Bradford leaves at 09.00. The flight from East Midlands leaves at 06.30. Allow 10 minutes to pick up friends at their house.

   i What time would Stan need to leave home for Plan 1?

   ii What time would Tom need to leave home for Plan 2?

c Which plan would you advise the friends to go for? Give reasons for your choice.

10 Devise a **Plan 3** which would be much cheaper than either Plan 1 or Plan 2.

Explain your plan fully.

1 What is the total cost for two people to fly to Rome and back from Leeds/Bradford airport?

2 The exchange rate is £1 = €1.40.

How much would it cost to get a return transfer from each airport to Rome city centre in pounds?

3 Which is the cheapest of the five airports for two people to fly to Rome and back and park their car for seven days? Include the cost of return transfers from the airport to the centre of Rome.

4 How far is it from Barlborough to East Midlands airport?

5 **a** How far is it from Silkstone to Leeds/Bradford airport?

b How much of this distance is on minor roads?

This chapter is going to give you practice in National Test questions about

- Number – fractions, percentages and decimals
- Number – the four rules, ratios and standard form
- Algebra – the basic rules and solving linear equations
- Algebra – graphs
- Geometry and measures
- Statistics

Number 1 – Fractions, percentages and decimals

Exercise 12A

Do not use a calculator for the first eight questions.

1 a About 33% of this rectangle is dotted.

About what **percentage** is: **i** striped? **ii** plain?

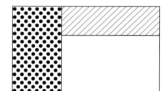

b About $\frac{1}{8}$ of this rectangle is red.

About what **percentage** is: **i** blue? **ii** white?

2 The following method can be used to work out 12% of 320:

$$10\% \text{ of } 320 = 32$$
$$1\% \text{ of } 320 = 3.2$$
$$\underline{1\% \text{ of } 320 = 3.2}$$
$$12\% \text{ of } 320 = 38.4$$

Use a similar method or a method of your own to work out 28% of 480.

3 If $\frac{5}{12}$ of the members of a youth club are girls, what fraction are boys?

FM **4** This is the sign at an airport's long-stay car park.

How much would it cost to park at the airport for 9 days?

FLYPARK

£6.50 per day or
£42.50 for a full week.

FM **5 a** A Scots pine tree is 4.35 m tall. A larch pine is 84 cm taller. How tall is the larch pine?

b From Barnsley to Sheffield via the motorway is 26.45 km. If you go via the ordinary roads it is 3.8 km shorter. How far is it from Barnsley to Sheffield via the ordinary roads?

FM **6** Some bathroom scales measure in stones and pounds, whilst others measure in kilograms. One way to change from stones and pounds to kilograms is shown below.

| number of stones | → | multiply by 14 | → | add number of pounds | → | divide by 2.2 | → | answer is weight in kilograms |

Convert 11 stone 10 pounds to kilograms.

FM **7** The train fare for an adult from Sheffield to London is £97. A child's fare is 35% less than this. How much is a child's fare?

FM **8** Jack's Jackets is having a sale.

Calculate the sale price of a jacket that is normally priced at £42.60.

You may use a calculator for the rest of the exercise.

9 Calculate the following, giving your answers as fractions.

a $\frac{3}{5} + \frac{1}{3}$ **b** $\frac{5}{9} - \frac{1}{6}$ **c** $2\frac{3}{4} + 1\frac{2}{5}$

FM **10** This table shows the populations (in **thousands**) of the eight largest towns in the UK in 1991 and in 2001. It also shows the percentage change in the populations of the towns over that 10-year period.

Town	London	Birmingham	Leeds	Glasgow	Sheffield	Liverpool	Manchester	Bristol
1991	6 800	1 007	717	660	529	481	439	407
2001	7 200	1 017	731	692	531	456		423
% change	5.9%	1%	2.0%	4.8%	0.3%	−5.2%	−3.2%	

a How many more people lived in Leeds than Sheffield in 2001?

b Calculate the population of Manchester in 2001.

c Calculate the percentage change in the population of Bristol over the 10 years.

11 Identify which four of the following numbers are equivalent.

0.06   60%   0.60 $\frac{6}{100}$ $\frac{3}{5}$ 6% $\frac{6}{10}$

12 A garage records the sales of fuel in one morning.

Fuel	Number of litres sold	Takings
Unleaded	345	£262.89
Premium	180	£142.56
Diesel	422	£289.07
LP Gas	25	£12.15
Lead replacement	125	£96.25
Total	1097	£802.92

a What percentage of the total litres sold was Unleaded?

b What percentage of the total money taken was for Diesel?

c Which is cheaper per litre, Unleaded or Lead replacement?

13 **a** Calculate: **i** 0.2×0.4 **ii** $600 \div 0.3$

  b Estimate the answer to $\dfrac{479 \times 0.48}{0.59}$.

Number 2 – The four rules, ratios and directed numbers

Exercise 12B

Do not use a calculator for the first eight questions.

1 **a** Copy each number sequence below and put in the correct sign, '<', '=' or '>', to make each one true.

  i $-6 \dots -2$ **ii** $8 - 6 \dots -2$ **iii** $7 - 7 \dots 5 - 8$

  b Here is a list of numbers.

$$-8 \quad -6 \quad -4 \quad -2 \quad 0 \quad 1 \quad 3 \quad 5$$

  i Choose two numbers from the list that have a total of -1.

  ii What is the total of all the numbers in the list?

  iii Choose two different numbers from the list to make the lowest possible value when put in these boxes:

$$\boxed{} - \boxed{} = \dots\dots$$

2 Write a number at the end of each equation to make it correct.

  a $27 + 53 = 17 + \dots$ **b** $76 - 28 = 66 - \dots$

  c $50 \times 17 = 5 \times \dots$ **d** $400 \div 10 = 4000 \div \dots$

3 Use $+$, $-$, $\times$ or $\div$ to make each calculation correct.

  For example, for $3 \dots 7 = 2 \dots 5$, you could insert '+' and '×' to give $3 + 7 = 2 \times 5$.

  a $9 \dots 6 = 20 \dots 5$ **b** $15 \dots 3 = 4 \dots 3$

  c $5 \dots 2 = 15 \dots 5$ **d** $8 \dots 4 = 4 \dots 2$

4 A teacher has 32 pupils in her class. She decides to buy each pupil a pen for Christmas, costing 98p. How much will it cost her altogether?

5 Give the missing number for each of these number chains.

a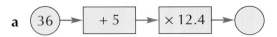

b

c (36) → [×] → (450)

d (364) → [÷] → (35)

 6 Litter bins cost £29 each. A school has a budget of £500 to spend on bins. How many bins can the school afford?

 7 Alf and Bert are paid £48 for doing a job. They decide to share the money in the ratio 3 : 5. How much does Alf get?

8 Work out: **a** 24×0.6 **b** $54 \div 0.6$ **c** 0.2×0.3

You may use a calculator for the rest of the exercise.

 9 A car company wants to move 700 cars by rail. Each train can carry 48 cars.

    a   How many trains will be needed to move the 700 cars?

    b   Each train costs £3745. What is the total cost of the trains?

    c   What is the **cost per car** of transporting them by train?

 10 **a**   A bus travels 234 miles in 4 hours and 30 minutes. What is the average speed of the bus?

    b   A car travels 280 miles at an average speed of 60 miles per hour. How long was the car travelling for? Give your answer in hours and minutes.

11 Concrete is made by mixing cement and sand in the ratio 1 : 4.

    a   What weight of sand is needed to mix with four bags of cement, each weighing 25 kg?

    b   Frank needs one tonne of concrete. How many 25 kg bags of cement will he need?

 12 Parking tickets cost £1.25 each. In one day a ticket machine takes the following coins.

How many tickets were sold that day?

Coin	Number of coins
£1	126
50p	468
20p	231
10p	185
5p	181

13 Look at the six cards with numbers on below.

 $(-1)^2$ 4^4 $(-2)^6$ 8^2 5^9 $(-3)^4$

  a Which card has the largest value?
  b Which two cards have the same value?
  c Which card is equal to 2^8?
  d Which cards have values that are cube numbers?

Algebra 1 – Rules of algebra and solving equations

Exercise 12C   **Do not use a calculator for this exercise.**

1 **a** What is the next coordinate in the list below?

   (2, 1),   (4, 3),   (6, 5),   (8, 7),   …

  b Explain why the coordinate (29, 28) could not be part of this sequence.

2 a, b and c represent the weights in kilograms of three children, Ali, Billie and Charlie.

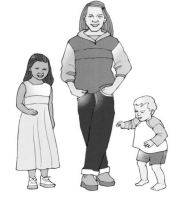

  a Match each of the following algebraic expressions with one of the statements below.

   $a = 30$ $b = 2a$

   $b + c = 75$ $\dfrac{a + b + c}{3} = 35$

   Statement 1: Billie weighs twice as much as Ali.
   Statement 2: The mean weight of all three children is 35 kg.
   Statement 3: Ali weighs 30 kg.
   Statement 4: Billie and Charlie weigh 75 kg together.

  b Use the information to work out Billie's weight and Charlie's weight.

3 The diagram shows a square with sides of length $(n + 4)$ cm.

The square has been split into four smaller rectangles. The area of one rectangle is shown.

  a Fill in the three missing areas with a number or an algebraic expression.

  b Write down an expression for the total area of the square.

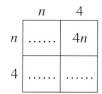

4 Expand the brackets and simplify the following expressions if possible.

  a $4(x - 5)$ **b** $3(2x + 1) + 5x$ **c** $3(x - 2) + 2(x + 4)$
  d $5(3x + 4) + 2(x - 2)$ **e** $4(2x + 1) - 3(x - 6)$

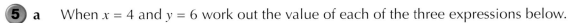

5 a When $x = 4$ and $y = 6$ work out the value of each of the three expressions below.

    i $3x + 9$ **ii** $4x - y$ **iii** $2(3x + 2y + 1)$

b Solve the equations below to find the value of z in each case.

    i $5z + 9 = 24$ **ii** $\dfrac{z - 8}{2} = 7$ **iii** $5z + 9 = 3z + 7$

6 Two friends, Selma and Khalid are revising algebra.

Selma says 'I am thinking of a number. If you multiply it by 6 and add 3 you get an answer of 12'.

Khalid says 'I am thinking of a number. If you multiply it by 3 and subtract 6 you get the same answer as adding the number to 7'.

a Call Selma's number x and form an equation. Then solve the equation.

b Call Khalid's number y and form an equation. Then solve the equation.

7 Solve each of the following equations.

    a $3x + 7 = x + 10$ **b** $5x - 6 = 10 - 3x$ **c** $3(x + 3) = x + 8$

8 Look at the algebraic expressions on the cards below.

$2 \times n$	$n^3 \div n$	$n + n$	$0.5n$	$n \div 2$

$n \times n$	$3n - n$	$n \times 2$	$6n \div 3$

a Which two expressions will always give the same answer as $\dfrac{n}{2}$?

b Which two expressions will always give the same answer as n^2?

c Five of the expressions are the same as $2n$. Write an expression of your own that is the same as $2n$.

9 a You are told that $2a + 4b = 15$ and that $2b - c = 13$.

    Write down the values of the following.

    i $6a + 12b = \ldots$ **ii** $4b - 2c = \ldots$ **iii** $2a + 2c = \ldots$

b Factorise each of the following.

    i $3x + 6y$ **ii** $x^2 + x$ **iii** $4ab + 6a$

10 For each equation below, fill in the missing card to make the equation true.

a $\boxed{3n - 1}$ + $\boxed{\ldots\ldots\ldots}$ = $\boxed{5n + 3}$ **b** $\boxed{6n + 9}$ − $\boxed{\ldots\ldots\ldots}$ = $\boxed{5n + 3}$

c $\boxed{6n + 1}$ + $\boxed{\ldots\ldots\ldots}$ = $\boxed{5n + 3}$ **d** $\boxed{8n + 2}$ − $\boxed{\ldots\ldots\ldots}$ = $\boxed{5n + 3}$

11 a Two of the expressions below are equivalent. Which ones are they?

    $3(4x - 6)$ $2(6x - 4)$ $12(x - 3)$ $6(2x - 3)$ $8(4x - 1)$

b Factorise the expression below.

    $6y - 12$

c Factorise the following expression as fully as possible.

    $9y^2 - 6y$

Algebra 2 – Graphs

Do not use a calculator for this exercise.

You will need graph paper or centimetre-squared paper.

For any graphs you are asked to draw, axes the size of the ones in the first question will be big enough.

1 Each of the lines labelled l_1, l_2, l_3 and l_4 has one of the equations in the list below. Match each line to its equation.

    a $x = 2$ **b** $y = x$

    c $x = -3$ **d** $y = -x$

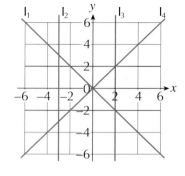

2 Draw and label each of the following graphs.

    a $y = 2x + 1$ **b** $y = \frac{1}{2}x - 1$ **c** $x + y = 3$

3 Does the point (20, 30) lie on the line $y = 2x - 10$? Explain your answer.

FM **4** The distance–time graph shows the journey of a jogger on a 5-mile run. At one point she stopped to admire the view and at another point she ran up a steep hill.

    a   For how long did she stop to admire the view?

    b   What distance into her run was the start of the hill?

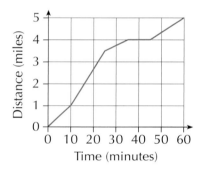

FM **5** In a house, the hot water tank automatically refills with cold water whenever hot water is taken out. The heating system then heats the water to a pre-set temperature.

Dad always has a shower in the morning. Mum always has a bath and the two children get up so late that all they do is wash their hands and faces.

The graph shows the temperature of the water in the hot water tank between 7 am and 9 am one morning.

    a   At what time did Dad have his shower?

    b   At what time did Mum have her bath?

    c   At what time did the first child wash?

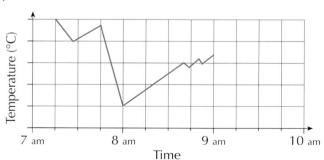

    d   Gran likes to have as hot a bath as possible, once everyone else has left the house at 9 am. Estimate at what time the water will be back to its maximum temperature.

6 For every point on the graph of $x + y = 6$, the x- and y-coordinates add up to 6. Which of the following points lie on the line?

a **i** (3, –3)   **ii** (6, 0)   **iii** (–7, –1)   **iv** (–1, 7)

b On a grid draw the graph of $x + y = 6$.

FM **7** The prison population of Britain is increasing rapidly as is the use of illegal drugs. These graphs show the change in prison population and drug use between 1998 and 2001.

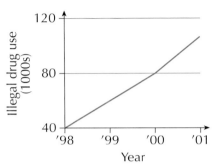 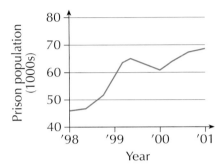

Use the graphs to decide for each of the statements below, **a**, **b** and **c**, if:
- the statement is **true**.
- the statement is **false**.
- you cannot be sure if it is true or false from the information given.

Use only the information given in the graphs. Do not use any facts that you might know about the subject already. Explain your answers.

a There is a positive correlation between prison population and illegal drug use.

b The prison population will reach 70 000 before 2008.

c Reducing illegal drug use will decrease the prison population.

8 The graph shows the line $y = 2x + 2$.

a Copy the graph and draw and label the line $y = 2x - 1$ on the same axes.

b Draw and label the line $y = x + 2$ on the same axes.

c Write down the coordinates of the point where the graphs $y = 2x - 1$ and $y = x + 2$ intersect.

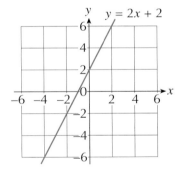

9 The diagram shows a rectangle ABCD.

a The equation of the line AB is $x = 1$. What is the equation of the line CB?

b The equation of the diagonal AC is $y = 2x + 2$. What is the equation of the diagonal BD?

c Write down the equations of the two lines of symmetry of the rectangle.

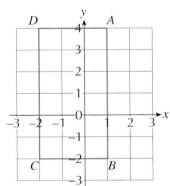

10 a On the same axes, draw and label the graphs of $y = -3$, $x = 2$ and $y = 3x$.

b The three lines you have drawn enclose a triangle. Work out the area of this triangle in square units.

11 Here are the equations of six graphs.

A $y = 2x - 1$ B $y = x$ C $y = 2$

D $x = 2$ E $y = 2x + 3$ F $y = \frac{1}{2}x - 1$

a Which two graphs are parallel?

b Which two graphs are perpendicular?

c Which pair of graphs cross the y-axis at the same point?

d Which pair of graphs cross the x-axis at the same point?

Geometry and measures

Exercise 12E

Do not use a calculator for Questions 1 to 5.

You will find squared paper useful for Questions 3 and 11.

1 a What is the area of this rectangle?

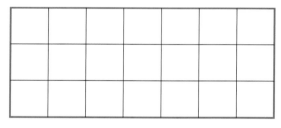

b The rectangle is cut into four triangles as shown. What is the area of one of the larger triangles?

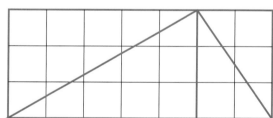

c The four triangles are put together to form a kite. What is the area of the kite?

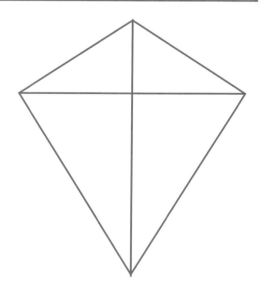

2 a Describe angles A–E in the diagram using the correct words chosen from below.

Acute   Obtuse
Reflex   Right-angled

b Is angle A bigger, smaller or the same size as angle C? Explain your answer.

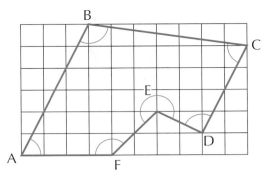

3 Copy each of the following diagrams and shade in more circles so that the dotted lines are lines of symmetry. You may find squared paper helpful.

a

○ ○ ○ ┊ ○ ○ ○
● ○ ○ ┊ ○ ○ ○
○ ● ○ ┊ ● ○ ○
○ ○ ● ┊ ● ● ●
○ ○ ● ┊ ○ ○ ○
○ ○ ○ ┊ ○ ○ ○

b

◌ ○ ○ ○ ○ ○
○ ◌ ○ ○ ○ ○
○ ○ ● ○ ○ ○
○ ● ● ◌ ○ ○
○ ● ● ○ ◌ ○
○ ● ○ ○ ○ ◌

c

○ ○ ○ ● ○ ○
○ ○ ○ ● ● ○
○ ○ ○ ● ○ ●
‑ ‑ ‑ ┊ ‑ ‑ ‑
○ ○ ○ ┊ ○ ○ ○
○ ○ ○ ┊ ○ ○ ○
○ ○ ○ ┊ ○ ○ ○

4 a Copy and complete the two-way table to show the symmetries of each of the shapes shown. Shape A has been done for you.

A   B   C   D   E   F   G

		Number of lines of symmetry				
		0	**1**	**2**	**3**	**4**
	1		A			
Order of rotational symmetry	**2**					
	3					
	4					

b Name a quadrilateral that has two lines of symmetry and rotational symmetry of order 2.

5 a Make an accurate construction of this triangle.
b Measure the angle at A.

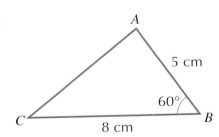

You may use a calculator for the rest of this exercise.

6 **a** A rectangle measures 24 cm by 12 cm.
What is its area?

b The rectangle is folded in half several times until it
measures 6 cm by 3 cm.
How many times was it folded?

c What is the ratio of the **areas** of the original rectangle
and the smaller rectangle?
Give your answer in its simplest form.

12 cm

24 cm

3 cm

6 cm

FM **7** This car speedometer shows speed in both miles per
hour (mph) and kilometres per hour (kph). Use the
speedometer to answer the following questions.

a How many kilometres are equivalent to 50 miles?

b Is someone travelling at 100 kph breaking the
speed limit of 70 mph? Justify your answer.

c About how many miles is 150 km? Explain your
answer.

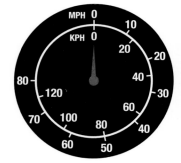

8 Find the values of angles *a*, *b* and *c* in this
diagram. The lines marked with arrows
are parallel.

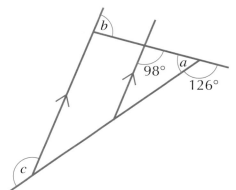

9 *ABCD* is an isosceles trapezium.

a Work out the size of angles
a, *b* and *c* in the diagram.

b Explain how you know that BE is
parallel to AD.

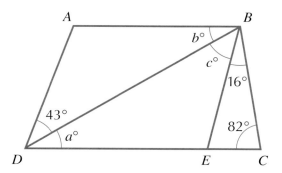

10 Copy the diagram onto squared paper
and enlarge the shape by a scale factor
of 3, using the point O as the centre of
enlargement.

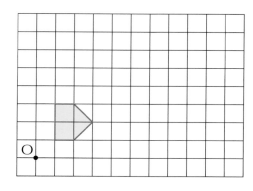

11 The diagram shows a cuboid and a triangular prism. Both solids have the same volume. Use this information to calculate the length of the prism.

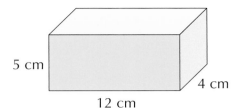

5 cm

12 cm

4 cm

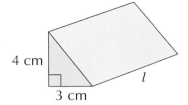

4 cm

3 cm

l

12 a Calculate the length of the side marked x in this right-angled triangle.

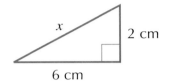

x

2 cm

6 cm

b Calculate the length of the side marked y in this right-angled triangle.

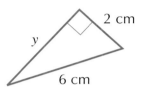

2 cm

y

6 cm

Statistics

Exercise 12F

You do not need to use a calculator for questions 1 to 9.

1 Hakim has 5 cards.

a What is the mode of the numbers on the cards?
b What is the median of the numbers on the cards?
c What is the mean of the numbers on the cards?

2 Look at the three different spinners, P, Q and R, below.

P   Q 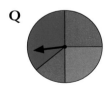   R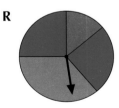

a Which spinner has the greatest chance of landing on red?
b Which spinner has an evens chance of landing on blue?
c Which two spinners have an equal chance of landing on green?

3 a Zeenat rolls an ordinary six-sided dice. What is the probability that the dice shows an even number?

b Zeenat now rolls the dice and tosses a coin. One way that the dice and the coin could land is to show a head and a score of 1. This can be written as (H, 1).

Copy and complete the list below to show all the possible outcomes.

(H, 1), (H, 2), …

c Zeenat rolls the dice and it shows a score of 6. She rolls the dice again. What is the probability that the dice shows a score of 6 this time?

4 Two four-sided dice, each numbered 1, 2, 3, 4 are thrown. The table shows all the possible total scores.

	Score on first dice			
	1	**2**	**3**	**4**
1	2	3	4	5
2	3	4	5	6
3	4	5	6	7
4	5	6	7	8

Score on second dice (label on left of table)

a When the two dice are thrown what is the probability that the total score is a square number?

b When the two dice are thrown what is the probability that the score is greater than 5?

c i Draw a table to show all the possible products if the numbers on each of the dice are multiplied together.

ii What is the probability that the product is a number less than 17?

5 A bag contains only red and blue marbles. A marble is to be taken from the bag at random.

It is twice as likely that the marble will be red as blue. Give a possible number of red and blue marbles in the bag.

6 Paul's marks for his last nine maths homeworks are:

9,　3,　5,　4,　4,　7,　5,　8,　6

a What is the range of his marks?

b What is the median mark?

c After checking the final homework, Paul realised that his teacher did not mark one of the questions. Once this had been marked, Paul's mark increased from 6 to 8.

Say whether each of the statements, **i**, **ii** and **iii** are true, false or if it is not possible to say.

Explain your answers.
i The mode of the marks has increased.
ii The median mark has increased.
iii The mean mark has increased.

7 The probability that a ball taken at random from a bag is black is 0.7. What is the probability that a ball taken at random from the same bag is **not** black?

8 Lee and Alex are planning a survey of what pupils at their school prefer to do at the local entertainment complex, where there is a cinema, a bowling alley, a games arcade and a disco.

    a Alex decides to give out a questionnaire to all the pupils in a Year 7 tutor group. Explain why this may not give reliable results for the survey.

    b Lee decides to include this question in his questionnaire:

How many times in a week do you go to the entertainment complex?

Never ☐   1–2 times ☐   2–5 times ☐   every day ☐

Explain why this is not a good question.

9 x is a whole number bigger than 1. For each of the five values on the cards below:

    a what is the median value?

    b what is the mean value?

$3x$	$2x + 1$	$x + 1$	$3x + 2$	$6x + 1$

You may use a calculator for questions 10 and 11.

10 The scatter diagram shows the value and the mileage for a number of cars. (The mileage is the total distance the car has travelled since new.) The value of each car is given as a percentage of its value when it was new.

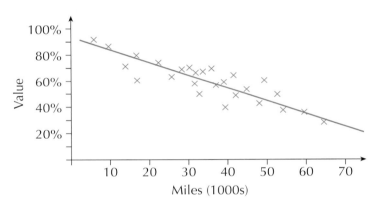

A line of best fit has been drawn on the scatter diagram.

    a What does the scatter diagram show about the relationship between the value of a car and its mileage?

    b A car has a mileage of 45 000. Estimate its value, as a percentage of its value when new.

    c A car cost £12 000 when it was new. It is now worth £7800. Use this information to estimate how many miles it has travelled.

11 The table shows the SATs Levels awarded to a class in Mathematics.

Level	3	4	5	6
Number of pupils	2	7	13	8

    a How many pupils were there altogether in the class?

    b Work out the mean SATs score for the class.

 More National Test practice provided in the Interactive Book.

CHAPTER 13

Statistics 3 and Revision

<table>
<tr><td>This chapter is going to show you</td><td>What you should already know</td></tr>
<tr><td>

- Some of the statistical techniques you have met before
- How to make a hypothesis
- How to carry out a handling data investigation

</td><td>

- How to carry out a survey
- How to write a questionnaire
- How to collect data
- How to construct and interpret two-way tables
- How to construct and interpret frequency diagrams
- How to construct and interpret scatter graphs
- How to calculate averages

</td></tr>
</table>

Statistical techniques

This lesson will remind you of the statistical techniques that you have met before. You will be using these to carry out a handling data project.

The following tables show the vocabulary you should know before you start an investigation.

Handling Data vocabulary

Collecting data

	Definition	**Example**
Questionnaire	A set of questions used to collect information from people	Here is an example of a poor question: How old are you? ☐ 0–10 ☐ 10–20 ☐ 20–30 ☐ over 30 It is poor because the categories overlap, so that both 10 and 20 are in two response sections.
Population	The set of people or objects being investigated	A school with 1000 pupils
Sample	Part of the whole population being used for analysis	50 pupils picked from the 1000 in a school
Survey	The collection of data from a sample of the population	Investigating the favourite colour of pupils in a school by asking 50 pupils
Census	The collection of data from an entire population	Investigating the favourite colour of pupils in a school by asking *every* pupil in the school

	Definition	Example
Data collection sheet or Observation sheet	A form for recording results	Favourite colours of 50 pupils: Blue ⊥⊥⊥⊥ ⊥⊥⊥⊥ Red ⊥⊥⊥⊥ ⊥⊥⊥⊥ ⊥⊥⊥⊥ ∥ Green ⊥⊥⊥⊥ ⊥⊥⊥⊥ ⊥⊥⊥⊥ Other ⊥⊥⊥⊥ ∥∥∥
Tally	A means of recording data quickly	
Raw data	Data which has not been sorted or analysed	Ages of 10 pupils: 12, 14, 13, 11, 12, 12, 15, 13, 11, 12
Primary data	Data that *you* have collected, usually by observation, surveys or experiments	Colours of cars on your street
Secondary data	Data collected by someone else and then used by you	Acceleration times of different cars
Two-way table	A table for combining two sets of data	<table><tr><td></td><td>**Ford**</td><td>**Vauxhall**</td><td>**Peugeot**</td></tr><tr><td>**Red**</td><td>3</td><td>5</td><td>2</td></tr><tr><td>**Blue**</td><td>1</td><td>0</td><td>4</td></tr><tr><td>**Green**</td><td>2</td><td>0</td><td>1</td></tr></table>
Frequency table	A table showing the quantities of different items or values	<table><tr><td>**Weight of parcels W (kg)**</td><td>**Number of parcels (frequency)**</td></tr><tr><td>$0 < W \le 1$</td><td>5</td></tr><tr><td>$1 < W \le 2$</td><td>7</td></tr><tr><td>$W > 2$</td><td>3</td></tr></table>
Frequency diagram	A diagram showing the quantities of different items or values	 **BAR CHART** **PIE CHART** **LINE GRAPH**

	Definition	Example
Stem-and-leaf diagram	A way of grouping data, in order	**Recorded speeds of 17 cars** 2 | 3 7 7 8 9 9 3 | 1 2 3 5 5 5 7 9 4 | 2 2 5 Key: 2 | 3 means 23 miles per hour
Population pyramid	A statistical diagram often used for comparing large sets of data	 **Age distribution in France (2000)**
Scatter graph or scatter diagram	A graph to compare two sets of data	

Processing data

	Definition	Example
Mode	The value that occurs *most* often	Find the mode, median, mean and range of this set of data: 23, 17, 25, 19, 17, 23, 21, 23
Median	The *middle* value when the data is written in order (or the average of the middle two values)	Sorting the data into order, smallest first, gives: 17, 17, 19, 21, 23, 23, 23, 25 Mode = 23
Mean	The sum of all the values divided by the number of items of data	Median = $\dfrac{21+23}{2} = 22$ Mean = $\dfrac{17+17+19+21+23+23+23+25}{8} = 21$
Range	The difference between the largest and smallest values	Range = 25 − 17 = 8

1 Calculate the mode, the median and the mean for each set of data below.

    a   1, 1, 1, 4, 8, 17, 50

    b   2, 5, 11, 5, 8, 7, 6, 1, 4

    c   £2.50, £4.50, £2, £3, £4.50, £2.50, £3, £4.50, £3.50, £4, £3.50

    d   18, 18, 19, 21, 24, 25

2 Criticise each of the following questions that were used in a questionnaire about travelling to school.

    a   How do you travel to school?

          ☐ Walk   ☐ Bus   ☐ Car

    b   How long does your journey take?

          ☐ 0 – 5 minutes   ☐ 5 – 10 minutes

          ☐ 10 – 15 minutes   ☐ 15 – 20 minutes

    c   What time do you usually set off to school?

          ☐ Before 8.00 am   ☐ 8.00 am – 8.15 am

          ☐ 8.15 – 8.30 am   ☐ Other

3 19 pupils take a test. The total marks available were 20. Here are the results.

    17, 16, 12, 14, 19, 15, 9, 16, 18, 10, 6, 11, 11, 14, 20, 8, 12, 19, 5

    a   Use the data to copy and complete the stem and leaf diagram below.

```
0 |
1 |
2 |
Key: ☐ | ☐ means  [          ]
```

    b   Work out the median mark.

    c   State the range of the marks.

    d   How many pupils scored 75% or more in the test?

4 A school quiz team is made up of pupils from four different classes. The table shows the number of pupils in the team from each class.

Class	Number of pupils
A	4
B	3
C	8
D	5

    a   Represent this information in a pie chart.

    b   Holly says 'The percentage of pupils chosen from class C is double the percentage chosen from class A.' Explain why this might not be true.

5 Below are the times taken (*T* seconds) by 20 pupils to run 100 m.

Boys	13.1	14.0	17.9	15.2	15.9	17.5	13.9	21.3	15.5	17.6
Girls	15.3	17.8	16.3	18.0	19.2	21.4	13.5	18.2	18.4	13.6

a Copy and complete the two-way table to show the frequencies.

	Boys	Girls
$12 \le T < 14$		
$14 \le T < 16$		
$16 \le T < 18$		
$18 \le T < 20$		
$20 \le T < 22$		

b What percentage completed the 100 m in less than 16 seconds?

c Which is the modal class for the girls?

d In which class is the median time for the boys?

6 Look at the population pyramid for France in the year 2000 on page 198.

a Compare the number of females and males alive in the year 2000 who were born during or before World War II, which lasted from 1939 to 1945.

b Suggest some possible reasons for the difference in the number of males and females in this age range.

Extension **Work**

It was estimated that there were 58 836 700 people living in the UK in mid 2001. This was an increase of 1.4 million people (2.4 per cent) since 1991.

The graph shows the population (in thousands) of the UK between 1991 and 2001. Explain why it may be misleading.

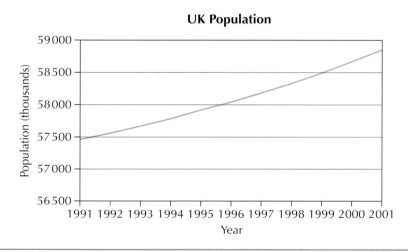

UK Population

A handling data project

In this section you are going to plan and write a handling data investigation. Look at the handling data cycle below. This shows the basic steps in an investigation.

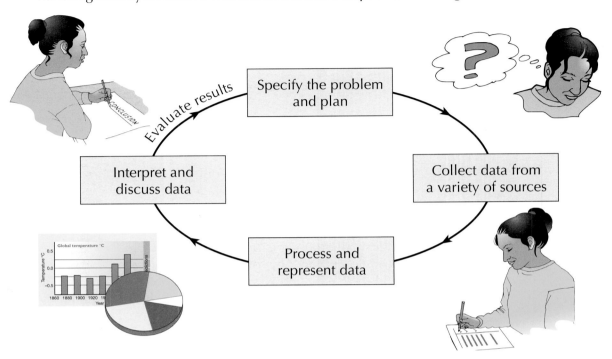

More detail is given about each step below. Follow this checklist when doing your investigation and writing your report.

- **Specify the problem and plan**
  - Statement of problem or topic to investigate
  - Hypothesis stating what you think the investigation will show
  - How you will choose your sample and sample size
  - Any practical problems you foresee
  - How you will obtain your data, possibly including how to avoid bias

- **Collect data from a variety of sources**
  - Follow initial plan and use a suitable data-collection sheet

- **Process and represent data**
  - Analysis of your results using appropriate statistical calculations and diagrams

- **Interpret and discuss data**
  - Comparison of results with your original hypothesis
  - List of any factors which might have affected your results and how you could overcome these in future
  - A final conclusion

Exercise 13B In small groups investigate one of the following topics.

 1 Compare people's hand-span with their shoe size.

2 Compare the reaction times of two different groups of people, for example girls and boys.

 3 Investigate the ability of people to estimate the lengths of lines (straight or curved) and to estimate the size of angles.

 4 Compare the word lengths in a newspaper with those in a magazine, or compare the word lengths in two different newspapers.

 5 Choose your own investigation.

Extension Work

Choose one of the following tasks.

1 Working individually, write a report of your investigation using the checklist. Look again at the limitations of your investigation and think how you could overcome these, for example by increasing your sample size or choosing your sample using a different method.

2 In your small group, create a display which can be used as part of a presentation to show the other groups in your class how you carried out your investigation and what results you obtained. Look again at the limitations of your investigation and think how you could overcome these, for example by increasing your sample size or choosing your sample using a different method.

3 If you have completed your report, then consider a different problem from the list in Exercise 13B. Write a plan of how you would investigate it, including how to overcome any problems encountered in your first project.

 More National Test practice provided in the Interactive Book.

<table>
This chapter is going to show you	**What you should already know**
• Some of the methods already met to determine shapes and their properties • How to carry out a shape and space investigation • How to carry out a symmetry investigation	• How to find the surface area of 2-D shapes • How to find the volume of 3-D shapes • How to use reflective and rotational symmetry
</table>

Geometry and measures revision

Before starting an investigation into geometry and measures, you must be familiar with all the formulae and terms which you have met so far.

This section provides a checklist before you start your investigation.

Perimeter and area

Square	Rectangle	Parallelogram	Triangle	Trapezium	Circle
	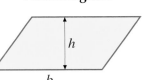	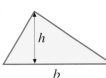		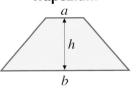	
$P = 4l$ $A = l^2$	$P = 2l + 2w$ $A = lw$	$A = bh$	$A = \frac{1}{2}bh$	$A = \frac{1}{2}(a + b)h$	$C = \pi d = 2\pi r$ $A = \pi r^2$

Volume and surface area

Cube	Cuboid	Prism
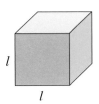	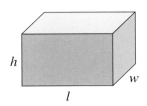	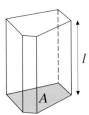
$V = l^3$ $A = 6l^2$	$V = lwh$ $A = 2lw + 2lh + 2hw$	$V = Al$

Exercise 14A

1   For each of the following shapes, find: **i** the perimeter.   **ii** the area.

a
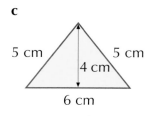

b
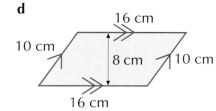

c   **d**   **e**
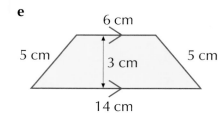

2   For each of the following circles, calculate:
i   the circumference.
ii   the area.

Take π = 3.14 or use the [π] key on your calculator. Give your answers to one decimal place.

a   **b**   **c**   **d**
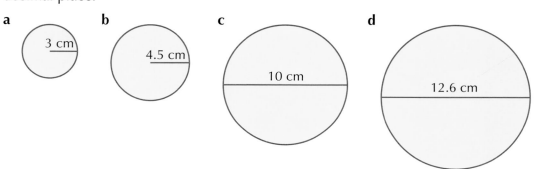

3   For each of the following 3-D shapes, calculate:
i   the surface area.
ii   the volume.

a   **b**
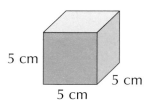
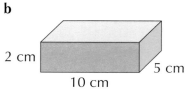

c   **d**
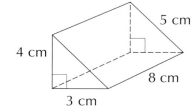
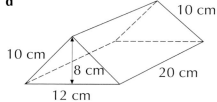

4 Calculate the area of the square drawn on the centimetre grid.

5 A circle has a circumference of 20 cm.

  a   Calculate the diameter of the circle.

  b   Calculate the area of the circle.

Take π = 3.14 or use the $\boxed{\pi}$ key on your calculator. Give each answer to one decimal place.

Extension   Work

Calculate the perimeter and the area of the shape below.

Take π = 3.14 or use the $\boxed{\pi}$ key on your calculator. Give your answers to three significant figures.

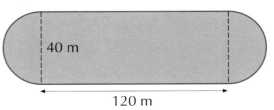

40 m

120 m

Geometry and measures investigations

When undertaking an investigation, you should carry out the following.

●   Draw some easy examples first, making all diagrams clear with all measurements shown.

●   Put your results in a table with suitable headings.

●   Look for any patterns among the entries in the table.

●   Describe and explain any patterns you spot.

●   Try to find a rule or formula to explain each pattern.

●   Try another example to see whether your rule or formula does work.

●   Summarise your results with a conclusion.

●   If possible, extend the investigation by introducing different questions.

Working in pairs or small groups, investigate one of the following.

1 Investigate whether the perimeter and the area of a square can have the same value. Extend the problem by looking at rectangles.

2 For the growing squares on the grid below, investigate the ratio of the length of a side to the perimeter and the ratio of the length of a side to the area.

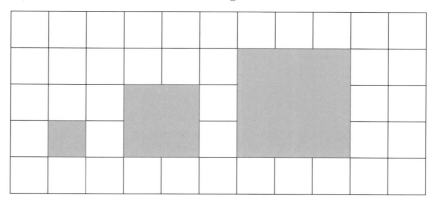

3 A coin is stamped from a square sheet of metal. Investigate the percentage waste for coins of different sizes.

4 The diagram below represents a 6 × 2 snooker table with a pocket at each corner, A, B, C and D.

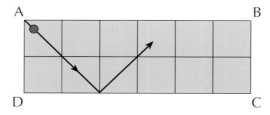

A snooker ball is hit from the corner at A at an angle of 45° and carries on bouncing off the sides of the table until it goes down one of the pockets.

a How many times does the ball bounce off the sides before it goes down a pocket?

b Down which pocket does the ball go?

c Investigate for different sizes of snooker tables.

Symmetry revision

Before starting an investigation into symmetry, you must be familiar with terms which you have met so far.

This section provides a checklist before you start your investigation.

There are two types of symmetry: **reflection symmetry** and **rotational symmetry**.

Some 2-D shapes have both types of symmetry, while some have only one type.

All 2-D shapes have rotational symmetry of order 1 or more.

Reflection symmetry

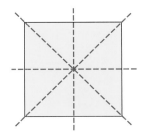 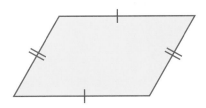

A square has 4 lines of symmetry   A parallelogram has no lines of symmetry

Remember that tracing paper or a mirror can be used to find the lines of symmetry of a shape.

Rotational symmetry

A 2-D shape has rotational symmetry when it can be rotated about a point to look exactly the same in its new position.

The **order of rotational symmetry** is the number of different positions in which the shape looks the same when rotated about the point.

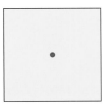 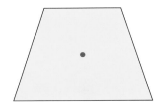

A square has rotational symmetry   This trapezium has rotational symmetry
of order 4   of order 1

Remember that tracing paper can be used to find the order of rotational symmetry of a shape.

Planes of symmetry

A **plane of symmetry** divides a 3-D shape into two identical parts. Each part is a reflection of the other in the plane of symmetry.

A cuboid has three planes of symmetry, as shown below.

  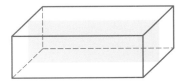

Each plane of symmetry is a rectangle.

Exercise 14C

1 Copy each of these shapes and draw its lines of symmetry. Write below each shape the number of lines of symmetry it has.

a 　　b 　　c 　　d 　　e

2 Write down the number of lines of symmetry for each of the following shapes.

a 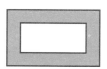　　b 　　c 　　d

3 Copy each of the following diagrams and write the order of rotational symmetry below each one.

a 　　b 　　c 　　d 　　e

4 Write down the order of rotational symmetry for each of the following shapes.

a 　　b 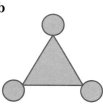　　c 　　d

5 Write down the number of planes of symmetry for each of the following 3-D letters.

a 　　b 　　c 　　d

6 Draw a 3-D shape that has five planes of symmetry.

Extension Work

Find pictures in magazines which have reflection or rotational symmetry.

Make a poster of your pictures to display in your classroom.

Symmetry investigations

When undertaking a symmetry investigation, you should carry out the following.

- Draw some easy examples first, showing any lines of symmetry and/or stating the order of rotational symmetry on the diagrams.
- Explain anything you notice from the diagrams.
- Describe and explain any patterns which you spot.
- Summarise your results with a conclusion.
- If possible, extend the investigation by introducing different questions.

Exercise 14D

Working in pairs or small groups, investigate one of the following.

1 Three squares are shaded on the 3 × 3 tile shown so that the tile has one line of symmetry.

    a Investigate the line symmetry of the tile when three squares are shaded.

    b Investigate the line symmetry when different numbers of squares are shaded.

Extend the problem by looking at different sizes of tiles.

2 Pentominoes are shapes made from five squares which touch edge to edge. Here are some examples.

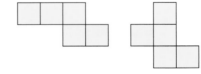

    a Investigate line symmetry and rotational symmetry for different pentominoes.

    b Extend the problem by looking at hexominoes. These are shapes made from six squares which touch edge to edge.

3 **a** In how many ways will the T-shape fit inside the 3 × 3 grid?

    b Investigate the number of ways the T-shape will fit inside a 1 cm square grid of any size.

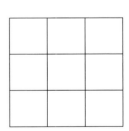

4 The **symmetry number** for a 3-D solid is the number of ways the solid can be placed through a 2-D outline of the solid.

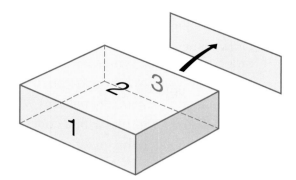

For example, the outline of a cuboid is a rectangle and the cuboid can be 'posted' (so that it fits exactly) through the rectangle in four different ways. These are:

- Side 3 first, with side 2 facing up (shown above)
- Side 3 first, with 2 facing down
- Side 1 first, with 2 facing up
- Side 1 first, with 2 facing down

So, the symmetry number for a cuboid is 4.

Investigate the symmetry number for other 3-D solids.

 More National Test practice provided in the Interactive Book.

This chapter is going to show you

- Different topics within probability
- How to use probability to make a hypothesis
- How to carry out a handling data investigation using experimental and theoretical probabilities

What you should already know

- Probabilities are numbers between 0 and 1
- How to work out simple probabilities
- How to calculate probabilities for two or more outcomes using sample spaces
- The difference between experimental and theoretical probability
- The vocabulary of probability

Revision of probability

Make sure that you are familiar with the vocabulary to do with probability which is listed in the table below.

Probability vocabulary

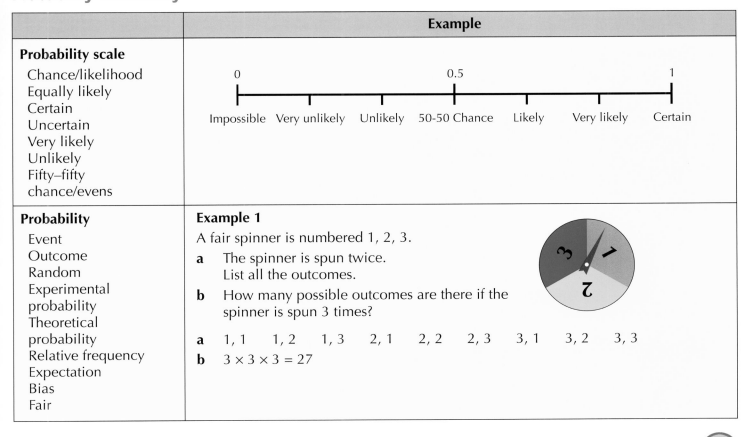

	Example
Probability scale Chance/likelihood Equally likely Certain Uncertain Very likely Unlikely Fifty–fifty chance/evens	0 0.5 1 Impossible Very unlikely Unlikely 50-50 Chance Likely Very likely Certain
Probability Event Outcome Random Experimental probability Theoretical probability Relative frequency Expectation Bias Fair	**Example 1** A fair spinner is numbered 1, 2, 3. a The spinner is spun twice. List all the outcomes. b How many possible outcomes are there if the spinner is spun 3 times? a 1, 1 1, 2 1, 3 2, 1 2, 2 2, 3 3, 1 3, 2 3, 3 b $3 \times 3 \times 3 = 27$

	Example

Probability (continued)	**Example 2**
	A six-sided dice is rolled 60 times.
	It lands on a 6 fifteen times.
	  a What is the experimental probability of landing on a 6?
	  b If the dice were rolled 300 times, how many times would you expect it to land on a 6?
	  c If the dice were fair, what would be the theoretical probability of landing on a 6?
	
	  a $\dfrac{15}{60} = \dfrac{1}{4}$
	
	  b $\dfrac{1}{4} \times 300 = 75$ times
	
	  c $\dfrac{1}{6}$

Probability diagrams
Sample
Sample space
	Example 3
	A coin is thrown and a dice is rolled.
	  a Draw a sample space diagram.
	  b Write down the probability of getting a head and a 6.
	
	  a
	<table><tr><td colspan="2"></td><td colspan="6">Dice</td></tr><tr><td colspan="2"></td><td>1</td><td>2</td><td>3</td><td>4</td><td>5</td><td>6</td></tr><tr><td rowspan="2">Coin</td><td>Head</td><td>H,1</td><td>H,2</td><td>H,3</td><td>H,4</td><td>H,5</td><td>H,6</td></tr><tr><td>Tail</td><td>T,1</td><td>T,2</td><td>T,3</td><td>T,4</td><td>T,5</td><td>T,6</td></tr></table>
	  b $\dfrac{1}{12}$

Events
Exhaustive
Independent
Mutually exclusive
	Example 4
	In a raffle there are blue, green and yellow tickets. The table shows the probability of each colour being chosen.
	
	| Ticket colour
		Probability |
		|---|---|
		| Blue | $\dfrac{1}{2}$ |
		| Green | ? |
		| Yellow | $\dfrac{1}{8}$ |
		
		  a What is the probability of picking a blue or a yellow ticket?
		  b What is the probability of picking a green ticket?
		
		  a $\dfrac{1}{2} + \dfrac{1}{8} = \dfrac{5}{8}$
		
		  b $1 - \dfrac{5}{8} = \dfrac{3}{8}$

Probability notation P(Event)	$P(\text{Green}) = \dfrac{3}{8}$

1 Three coins are thrown.

    a How many different outcomes are there? Make a list to show all the possibilities.

    b Work out the probability of getting no heads.

    c Work out the probability of getting exactly one head.

    d Work out the probability of getting at least one head.

2 Matthew is either late, on time or early for school. The probability that he is late is 0.1 and the probability that he is on time is 0.3.

    a What is the probability that he is late or on time?

    b What is the probability that he is early?

3 A group of 50 pupils are told to draw two straight lines on a piece of paper. Seven pupils draw parallel lines, twelve draw perpendicular lines and the rest draw lines which are neither parallel nor perpendicular.

Use these results to estimate the probability that a pupils chosen at random has

    a drawn parallel lines.

    b drawn perpendicular lines.

    c drawn lines that are neither parallel nor perpendicular.

4 A five-sided spinner is spun 50 times. Here are the results.

Number on spinner	1	2	3	4	5
Frequency	8	11	10	6	15

    a Write down the experimental probability of the spinner landing on the number 4.

    b Write down the theoretical probability of a fair, five-sided spinner landing on the number 4.

    c Compare the experimental and theoretical probabilities and say whether you think the spinner is fair.

    d How many fours would you expect if the spinner were spun 250 times?

Extension Work

1 State whether each of the following pairs of events are independent or not independent. Explain your answers.

    a Rolling a dice and getting a 6.
       Rolling the dice a second time and getting a 6.

    b Picking out a winning raffle ticket.
       Picking out a second winning raffle ticket.

    c It raining in London on Monday.
       It raining in London on Tuesday.

2 State whether each of the following pairs of outcomes are mutually exclusive or not mutually exclusive. Explain your answers.

    a An ordinary, six-sided dice landing on an even number.
       The dice landing on a prime number.

    b Two coins being thrown and getting at least one head.
       The two coins being thrown and getting two tails.

    c Two coins being thrown and getting at least one tail.
       The two coins being thrown and getting two tails.

3 State whether each of the following outcomes are exhaustive or not exhaustive. Explain your answers.

    a A dice landing on an odd number.
       The dice landing on a multiple of 2.

    b A spinner numbered 1, 2, 3, 4, 5 landing on a number greater than 3.
       The spinner landing on a number less than 3.

    c A spinner numbered 1, 2, 3, 4, 5 landing on a number greater than 2.
       The spinner landing on a number less than 4.

A probability investigation

Look again at the handling data cycle.

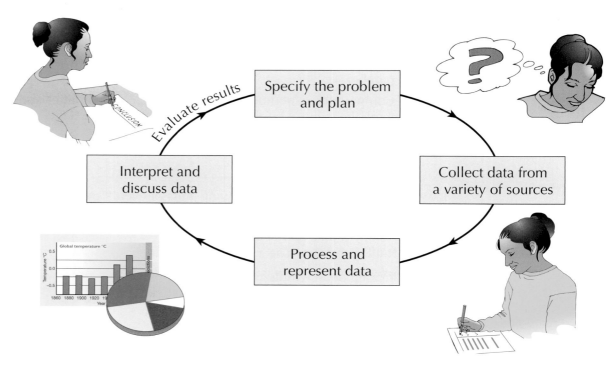

Use the handling data cycle to help you when completing your probability investigation. More detail is given about each step below.

- **Specify the problem and plan**
  - Statement of problem or topic to investigate
  - Hypothesis stating what you think the investigation will show
  - How you will choose your sample and sample size
  - Any practical problems you foresee
  - How you will obtain your data, possibly including how to avoid bias

- **Collect data from a variety of sources**
  - Follow initial plan and use a suitable data-collection sheet

- **Process and represent data**
  - Analysis of your results using appropriate statistical calculations and diagrams

- **Interpret and discuss data**
  - Comparison of results with your original hypothesis
  - List of any factors which might have affected your results and how you could overcome these in future
  - A final conclusion

Exercise 15B

In small groups carry out an experiment to investigate one of the following.

1 Organise a class lottery. Get each person to choose 10 numbers, from 1 to 20. Have 10 separate draws and record who has a winning number each time (there may be more than one winner for each draw). Compare the theoretical and experimental probabilities of each player winning.

2 Investigate whether a drawing pin will land point up more often than point down. Use different-sized drawing pins to test whether the results are always the same.

3 Ask a member of your group to put ten coloured cubes in a bag, so that the rest of the group do not know what the colours are. Investigate how many times you need to pick a cube out and replace it in order to be able to predict accurately the contents of the bag.

4 Some people are luckier than others when rolling a dice.

5 A playing card usually lands face-up when dropped.

Choose one of the following tasks.

1 Working individually, write a report of your experiment using the checklist. Look again at the limitations of your experiment and think how you could overcome these, for example by increasing your sample size or choosing your sample using a different method.

2 In your small group, create a display which can be used as part of a presentation to show the other groups in your class how you carried out your experiment and what results you obtained. Look again at the limitations of your experiment and think how you could overcome these, for example by increasing your sample size or choosing your sample using a different method.

3 If you have completed your report, then consider a different problem from the list in Exercise 15B. Write a plan of how you would investigate it, including how to overcome any problems encountered in your first project.

 More National Test practice provided in the Interactive Book.

CHAPTER 16

GCSE Preparation

This chapter is going to

- Get you started on your GCSE course

Long multiplication

You have already met several ways of doing long multiplication. Two of these are shown in the examples below. You may use any method you are happy with for Exercise 16A.

Example 16.1

Work out 164×56.

This multiplication could be done using the box method, as shown below.

×	100	60	4
50	5000	3000	200
6	600	360	24

```
 5000
 3000
  200
  600
  360
   24
 ────
 9184
```

Example 16.2

Work out 238×76.

This multiplication could be done using the standard column method, as shown right.

```
    238
 ×   76
 ──────
   1428
    2 4
  16660
    2 5
 ──────
  18088
      1
```

Exercise 16A

Use any method you are happy with for the following questions and show all your working. Check your answers with a calculator afterwards.

1. Work out each of the following. Remember to show your working.

   a 157×24 b 324×33 c 513×32 d 189×23

2. Work out each of the following.

   a 258×34 b 276×47 c 139×62 d 126×39

3. Work out each of the following.

   a 637×28 b 377×44 c 265×75 d 753×63

4. Work out each of the following.

   a 207×14 b 620×26 c 805×63 d 199×99

Long division

You should remember meeting two different ways of doing long division. These are shown below. You may use any method you are happy with to answer the questions in Exercise 16B.

Example 16.3 ▷

Work out 858 ÷ 22.

This division could be done using the standard column method, as below.

Step 1: Start by asking how many 22s there are in 8. There are none of course. So, include the next digit, which is 5, and ask how many 22s there are in 85. Working up the 22 times table (22, 44, 66, 88), we can see that there are 3. Write the 3 above the 5.

Step 2: Work out the value of 3 × 22 (= 66) and write it underneath 85. Then subtract 66 from 85 to find the remainder of 19.

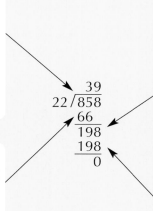

$$\begin{array}{r} 39 \\ 22\overline{)858} \\ 66 \\ \hline 198 \\ 198 \\ \hline 0 \end{array}$$

Step 3: Bring down the 8, next to the 19, to give 198.

Step 4: Now ask how many 22s there are in 198. Once again work up the 22 times table: 22, 44, 66, 88, 110, 132, 154, 176, 198. So there are exactly nine 22s in 198. Write the 9 above the 8.

As there is no remainder we can stop. The answer is 39.

Example 16.4 ▷

Work out 938 ÷ 36.

This division has been done below, using repeated subtraction or 'chunking'.

$$\begin{array}{r} 938 \\ -720 \quad (20 \times 36) \\ \hline 218 \\ -180 \quad (5 \times 36) \\ \hline 38 \\ -36 \quad (1 \times 36) \\ \hline 2 \end{array}$$

As the remainder is less than 36 we can stop.

We have subtracted 36 a total of 20 + 5 + 1 = 26 times, so the answer is 26 rem 2.

Exercise 16B

Use any method you are happy with for the following questions and show your working. Check your answers with a calculator afterwards.

1. Work out each of the following. These divisions have exact answers with no remainders. Remember to show your working.

   a 644 ÷ 23   **b** 1224 ÷ 34   **c** 522 ÷ 18   **d** 868 ÷ 28

(2) Work out each of the following. These divisions have exact answers with no remainders.

    a $840 \div 24$ **b** $2021 \div 47$ **c** $532 \div 38$ **d** $741 \div 39$

(3) Work out each of the following. These divisions will give remainders.

    a $637 \div 28$ **b** $877 \div 41$ **c** $865 \div 25$ **d** $658 \div 33$

(4) Work out each of the following. These divisions will give remainders.

    a $407 \div 14$ **b** $820 \div 16$ **c** $915 \div 39$ **d** $799 \div 29$

Long multiplication and division in real-life problems

Example 16.5

Mr Winston buys a car for £36 480. He agrees to pay for it in 24 equal, monthly instalments. How much does he pay each month?

First you need to identify that this is a division problem, then choose which method to use.

The calculation is done below using the repeated subtraction method. We can ignore the zero on the end of £36 480, as long as we multiply the final answer by 10.

The 24 times table has been written out on the right to help.

$$
\begin{array}{ll}
3648 & \\
-\ 2400 & (100 \times 24) \\
\hline
1248 & \\
-\ 1200 & (50 \times 24) \\
\hline
\ \ 48 & \\
-\ \ \ \ 48 & (2 \times 24) \quad + \\
\hline
\ \ \ \ 0 & (152 \times 24)
\end{array}
\qquad
\begin{array}{l}
1 \times 24 = 24 \\
2 \times 24 = 48 \\
5 \times 24 = 120 \\
10 \times 24 = 240 \\
20 \times 24 = 480 \\
100 \times 24 = 2400 \\
50 \times 24 = 1200
\end{array}
$$

Don't forget that we divided the starting number by 10, so the answer is £1520 per month.

Example 16.6

On checking his running diary, Paul finds that he has run an average of 65 miles a week during the last year. How many miles did he run in the year altogether?

You need to identify that this is a multiplication problem, recall that there are 52 weeks in a year, and then decide which method you are going to use.

The multiplication has been done below using the box method.

×	60	5
50	3000	250
2	120	10

So Paul has run a total of $3000 + 250 + 120 + 10 = 3380$ miles

Work out each of the following, showing your working.
Check your answers with a calculator afterwards.

1 A typist can type 54 words per minute on average. How many words can he type in 15 minutes?

 2 Small chocolate eggs cost 43p each. Mrs Owen wants to buy an egg for each of her class of 28 pupils. How much will this cost her?

3 There are 972 pupils in a school. Each tutor group has 27 pupils in it. How many tutor groups are there?

 4 In a road-race, there were 2200 entrants.

   a To get them to the start, the organisers used a fleet of 52-seater buses. How many buses were needed?

   b The race was 15 miles long and all the entrants completed the course. How many miles in total did all the runners cover?

 5 At a school fair, cups of tea were 32p each. The school sold 182 cups.

   a How much money did they take?

   b The school used plastic cups which came in packs of 25. They bought 24 packs. How many cups were left over?

 6 a A cinema has 37 rows of seats. Each row contains 22 seats. How many people can sit in the cinema altogether?

   b Tuesday is 'all seats one price' night. There were 220 customers who paid a total of £572. What was the cost of one seat?

7 A library gets 700 books to distribute equally among 12 local schools.

   a How many books will each school get?

   b The library keeps any books left over. How many books is this?

 8 The label on the side of a 1.5 kg cereal box says that there are 66 g of carbohydrate in a 100 g portion. How many grams of carbohydrate will Dan consume if he eats the whole box at once?

 9 A first-class stamp costs 28p and a second-class stamp costs 19p. How much does it cost to send 63 letters first class and 78 letters second class?

 10 12 members of a running club hire a minivan to do the Three Peaks race (climbing the highest mountains in England, Scotland and Wales). The van costs £25 per day plus 12p per mile. The van uses a litre of petrol for every 6 miles travelled. Petrol costs 78p per litre. The van is hired for 3 days and the total mileage covered is 1500.

   a How much does it cost to hire the van?

   b How many litres of petrol are used?

   c If the total cost is shared equally how much does each member pay?

Equivalent fractions

Example 16.7

Cancel the following fractions to lowest terms.

a $\dfrac{9}{30}$ b $\dfrac{8}{18}$ c $\dfrac{15}{55}$

To cancel a fraction we need to find the highest common factor (HCF) of the numerator and the denominator, then divide both by it.

a   The HCF of 9 and 30 is 3. $\dfrac{9}{30} = \dfrac{9 \div 3}{30 \div 3} = \dfrac{3}{10}$

b   The HCF of 8 and 18 is 2. $\dfrac{8}{18} = \dfrac{\cancel{8}^{4}}{\cancel{18}_{9}} = \dfrac{4}{9}$

c   The HCF of 15 and 55 is 5. $\dfrac{15}{55} = \dfrac{\cancel{15}^{3}}{\cancel{55}_{11}} = \dfrac{3}{11}$

Example 16.8

Find $\dfrac{4}{9}$ of 450 marbles.

First work out $\dfrac{1}{9}$ of $450 = 450 \div 9 = 50$

Then work out $\dfrac{4}{9}$ of 450, which is $4 \times 50 = 200$ marbles

Examples 16.9 and 16.10 could also be done using a calculator.

Example 16.9

Which is larger: $\dfrac{3}{5}$ of 13 million or $\dfrac{5}{6}$ of 9 million?

$\dfrac{3}{5}$ of 13 million is $3 \times \dfrac{1}{5}$ of 13 million $= 3 \times 0.2 \times 13$ million $= 7.8$ million

$\dfrac{5}{6}$ of 9 million is $5 \times \dfrac{1}{6}$ of 9 million $= 5 \times 1.5$ million $= 7.5$ million

Hence $\dfrac{3}{5}$ of 13 million is larger.

Example 16.10

Which of the fractions below is closest to $\dfrac{1}{2}$?

$\dfrac{3}{5}$ $\dfrac{4}{9}$ $\dfrac{6}{11}$ $\dfrac{5}{12}$

It would be very difficult to find a common denominator, so convert all the fractions to decimals.

$\dfrac{3}{5} = 0.6$ $\dfrac{4}{9} = 0.444$ $\dfrac{6}{11} = 0.545$ $\dfrac{5}{12} = 0.417$

Of these $\dfrac{6}{11}$ is closest to $\dfrac{1}{2}$ (0.5).

Exercise 16D

1 Cancel down the following fractions.

a $\frac{9}{12}$ b $\frac{15}{25}$ c $\frac{7}{21}$ d $\frac{9}{15}$

e $\frac{14}{35}$ f $\frac{16}{40}$ g $\frac{12}{30}$ h $\frac{18}{24}$

i $\frac{10}{45}$ j $\frac{16}{36}$

2 Fill in the missing numbers in these equivalent fractions.

a $\frac{5}{15} = \frac{\square}{45}$ b $\frac{6}{21} = \frac{\square}{7}$ c $\frac{12}{21} = \frac{4}{\square}$ d $\frac{8}{28} = \frac{\square}{35}$

e $\frac{12}{15} = \frac{\square}{25}$ f $\frac{9}{24} = \frac{\square}{16}$ g $\frac{18}{30} = \frac{12}{\square}$ h $\frac{10}{35} = \frac{\square}{21}$

3 Calculate these amounts.

a $\frac{6}{7}$ of £420   b $\frac{3}{8}$ of 320 counters   c $\frac{2}{5}$ of 365 days

d $\frac{5}{12}$ of 60 minutes   e $\frac{2}{9}$ of £63   f $\frac{6}{11}$ of 44 litres

4 32 000 runners took part in the London Marathon, of which $\frac{3}{16}$ were female. How many women ran the race?

5 A house is valued at £130 000. A couple take out a mortgage for $\frac{3}{5}$ of this amount. How much is the mortgage?

6 A lottery syndicate has 25 shares. Jane has 3 of these. How much will Jane receive out of a win of £15 700?

7 By writing each pair of fractions with a common denominator, put the sign > or < between them.

a $\frac{4}{5}, \frac{7}{9}$ b $\frac{2}{7}, \frac{3}{8}$ c $\frac{1}{4}, \frac{2}{9}$ d $\frac{5}{8}, \frac{3}{5}$

8 Which of the following is larger?

a $\frac{6}{7}$ of 84 or $\frac{5}{6}$ of 90   b $\frac{3}{8}$ of 44 or $\frac{2}{9}$ of 72

c $\frac{3}{10}$ of 85 or $\frac{3}{11}$ of 88   d $\frac{5}{12}$ of 96 or $\frac{5}{7}$ of 63

9 Which of the fractions below is closest to $\frac{1}{4}$?

$\frac{3}{11}$ $\frac{3}{8}$ $\frac{5}{18}$ $\frac{3}{10}$

10 210 000 candidates entered a GCSE examination. Of these, $\frac{3}{8}$ took the Foundation paper, $\frac{4}{7}$ took the Intermediate paper and the rest took the Higher paper.

    a   How many candidates took the Foundation paper?

    b   How many candidates took the Intermediate paper?

    c   How many candidates took the Higher paper?

Adding and subtracting fractions

Example 16.11 ▷

Work out the following.

a $\frac{3}{7} + \frac{2}{9}$ **b** $\frac{5}{8} + \frac{9}{10}$ **c** $2\frac{5}{6} + 1\frac{7}{15}$

To add fractions with different denominators we need to find the lowest common denominator. This is the same as the lowest common multiple (LCM) of the denominators. Answers should be cancelled to lowest terms and converted to mixed numbers if necessary.

a   The LCM of 7 and 9 is 63.

$$\frac{3}{7} + \frac{2}{9} = \frac{27}{63} + \frac{14}{63} = \frac{41}{63}$$

b   The LCM of 8 and 10 is 40.

$$\frac{5}{8} + \frac{9}{10} = \frac{25}{40} + \frac{36}{40} = \frac{61}{40} = 1\frac{21}{40}$$

c   The LCM of 6 and 15 is 30. Work out the whole-numbers separately: 2 + 1 = 3

$$\frac{5}{6} + \frac{7}{15} = \frac{25}{30} + \frac{14}{30} = \frac{39}{30} = 1\frac{9}{30}$$

Add the whole-number part, to give:

$$3 + 1\frac{9}{30} = 4\frac{9}{30} = 4\frac{3}{10}$$

Example 16.12 ▷

Work out the following.

a $\frac{7}{10} - \frac{3}{8}$ **b** $3\frac{3}{4} - 1\frac{5}{6}$

a   The LCM of 10 and 8 is 40.

$$\frac{7}{10} - \frac{3}{8} = \frac{28}{40} - \frac{15}{40} = \frac{13}{40}$$

b   The LCM of 4 and 6 is 12. Work out the whole numbers separately: 3 − 1 = 2

$$\frac{3}{4} - \frac{5}{6} = \frac{9}{12} - \frac{10}{12} = \frac{-1}{12}$$

Now add on the whole-number part, to give:

$$2 + \frac{-1}{12} = 1\frac{11}{12}$$

Example 16.13 ▷ Of all the candidates taking mathematics in Year 11, $\frac{3}{8}$ were taking the Foundation paper and $\frac{4}{7}$ were taking the Intermediate paper. What fraction were taking the Higher paper?

$$\frac{3}{8} + \frac{4}{7} = \frac{21}{56} + \frac{32}{56} = \frac{53}{56}$$

$$1 - \frac{53}{56} = \frac{56}{56} - \frac{53}{56} = \frac{3}{56}$$

So $\frac{3}{56}$ of the year were taking the Higher paper.

Exercise 16E

1 There are 1500 children in a school. $\frac{2}{5}$ of them come by bus, $\frac{1}{3}$ walk and the rest come by car.
  a What fraction come by car?
  b How many pupils come by bus?

2 In a small village there are 620 children, of which $\frac{9}{20}$ are boys. $\frac{5}{9}$ of the boys go to secondary school.
  a How many boys go to secondary school?
  b How many girls are there in the village?

3 On checking his e-mails Mr Smith finds that $\frac{1}{5}$ of them are junk mail, $\frac{3}{8}$ are about business and the rest are personal. What fraction of his e-mails are personal?

4 Mr Berry collects beer-mats. He has 630. Of these $\frac{4}{9}$ are square and $\frac{1}{18}$ are rectangular.
  a What fraction of the collection are not square or rectangular?
  b How many square mats are in the collection?

5 On a large farm, $\frac{3}{8}$ of the fields are used for crops, $\frac{1}{6}$ are used to graze cattle and the rest is lying fallow. Of the fields used for crops $\frac{2}{3}$ are planted with wheat.
  a What fraction of the farm is lying fallow?
  b There are 240 acres on the farm. How many acres are planted with wheat?

6 Two packets of nails weigh $3\frac{3}{5}$ kg and $2\frac{1}{6}$ kg. How much do they weigh altogether?

7 a Work out the following.
  i $\frac{1}{2} + \frac{1}{4}$ **ii** $\frac{1}{2} + \frac{1}{4} + \frac{1}{8}$ **iii** $\frac{1}{2} + \frac{1}{4} + \frac{1}{8} + \frac{1}{16}$

  b What is the answer to the infinite sum below?

$$\frac{1}{2} + \frac{1}{4} + \frac{1}{8} + \frac{1}{16} + \frac{1}{32} + \frac{1}{64} + \frac{1}{128} + \frac{1}{256} + \frac{1}{512} + \ldots\ldots$$

8 Work out the following. Cancel answers to lowest terms and make any top-heavy fractions into mixed numbers.
  a $\frac{1}{12} + \frac{2}{3}$ **b** $\frac{3}{4} + \frac{5}{8}$ **c** $\frac{2}{7} - \frac{1}{8}$ **d** $\frac{11}{15} - \frac{1}{6}$
  e $\frac{7}{9} - \frac{3}{8}$ **f** $\frac{17}{20} + \frac{7}{15}$ **g** $\frac{9}{10} - \frac{2}{3}$ **h** $\frac{3}{7} + \frac{5}{6}$

9 Work out the following. Cancel answers to lowest terms and make any top-heavy fractions into mixed numbers.

a $2\frac{7}{15} + 1\frac{2}{3}$ b $2\frac{5}{12} - 1\frac{5}{8}$ c $3\frac{11}{20} + 1\frac{5}{6}$ d $3\frac{9}{10} - 1\frac{1}{6}$

e $4\frac{4}{7} - 1\frac{7}{8}$ f $3\frac{6}{7} + 1\frac{1}{2}$ g $4\frac{1}{3} - 2\frac{1}{6}$ h $7\frac{8}{15} + 3\frac{5}{12}$

 10 A tin contains $3\frac{3}{8}$ litres of syrup. If $1\frac{3}{4}$ litres of syrup is poured out, how many litres are left?

11 Find the perimeter of each of these shapes.

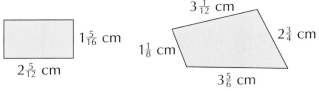

Multiplying and dividing fractions

Example 16.14 ▶

Multiply the following fractions.

a $\frac{3}{10} \times \frac{2}{9}$ b $2\frac{2}{9} \times 1\frac{1}{5}$

To multiply fractions together you simply multiply together the numerators to get the new numerator and multiply together the denominators to get the new denominator.

Before multiplying you should convert mixed numbers into top-heavy fractions and then cancel any numerators and denominators that have common factors.

After multiplying you should cancel, if possible, and convert back to a mixed number, if necessary.

a $\frac{3}{10} \times \frac{2}{9} = \frac{\cancel{3}^1}{\cancel{10}_5} \times \frac{\cancel{2}^1}{\cancel{9}_3} = \frac{1}{5} \times \frac{1}{3} = \frac{1}{15}$

b $2\frac{2}{9} \times 1\frac{1}{5} = \frac{20}{9} \times \frac{6}{5} = \frac{\cancel{20}^4}{\cancel{9}_3} \times \frac{\cancel{6}^2}{\cancel{5}_1} = \frac{4}{3} \times \frac{2}{1} = \frac{8}{3} = 2\frac{2}{3}$

Example 16.15 ▶

Divide the following fractions.

a $\frac{9}{10} \div \frac{3}{8}$ b $3\frac{3}{4} \div 4\frac{1}{6}$

The only rule to remember when dividing fractions is to turn the dividing fraction upside down and multiply by it. After that the same rules apply as for multiplying.

a $\frac{9}{10} \div \frac{3}{8} = \frac{9}{10} \times \frac{8}{3} = \frac{\cancel{9}^3}{\cancel{10}_5} \times \frac{\cancel{8}^4}{\cancel{3}_1} = \frac{3}{5} \times \frac{4}{1} = \frac{12}{5} = 2\frac{2}{5}$

b $3\frac{3}{4} \div 4\frac{1}{6} = \frac{15}{4} \div \frac{25}{6} = \frac{15}{4} \times \frac{6}{25} = \frac{3}{2} \times \frac{3}{5} = \frac{9}{10}$

Example 16.16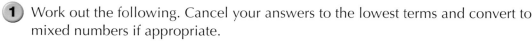

A bottle of pop holds $1\frac{1}{8}$ litres. Jenny has 6 full bottles of pop and one which is $\frac{2}{3}$ full. How many $\frac{1}{4}$ litre glasses of pop can Jenny make?

First we multiply the number of bottles by the capacity, to get the total volume of pop and then divide by the amount needed for one glass.

$$6\frac{2}{3} \times 1\frac{1}{8} = \frac{20}{3} \times \frac{9}{8} = \frac{5}{1} \times \frac{3}{2} = \frac{15}{2}$$

$$\frac{15}{2} \div \frac{1}{4} = \frac{15}{2} \times \frac{4}{1} = \frac{15}{1} \times \frac{2}{1} = 30 \text{ glasses}$$

Exercise 16F

1 Work out the following. Cancel your answers to the lowest terms and convert to mixed numbers if appropriate.

   a $\frac{1}{2} \times \frac{2}{3}$ **b** $\frac{1}{10} \times \frac{5}{9}$ **c** $\frac{2}{3} \times \frac{9}{10}$ **d** $\frac{9}{14} \times \frac{7}{15}$

2 Work out the following. Cancel your answers to the lowest terms and convert to mixed numbers if appropriate.

   a $1\frac{7}{15} \times 1\frac{2}{3}$ **b** $\frac{13}{15} \times 1\frac{7}{8}$ **c** $2\frac{1}{10} \times 1\frac{1}{3}$ **d** $2\frac{1}{4} \times 1\frac{1}{6}$

3 Work out the following. Cancel your answers to the lowest terms and convert to mixed numbers if appropriate.

   a $\frac{2}{9} \div \frac{2}{3}$ **b** $\frac{7}{20} \div \frac{7}{15}$ **c** $\frac{9}{10} \div \frac{3}{25}$ **d** $\frac{2}{9} \div \frac{4}{27}$

4 One sack of flour weighs $1\frac{7}{8}$ kg. How much do $2\frac{1}{2}$ sacks of flour weigh?

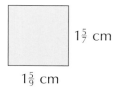 **5** Of all the pupils in a school, $\frac{2}{5}$ come by bus, $\frac{1}{3}$ walk and the rest come by car. $\frac{3}{8}$ of the pupils that come by bus are girls. $\frac{1}{2}$ of the pupils that come by car are girls.

   a What fraction of the pupils in the school are girls that come by bus?

   b If $\frac{11}{20}$ of the pupils in the school are girls, then what fraction of the pupils that walk are girls?

   [*Hint:* Assume that there are 1200 pupils in the school]

6 Work out the following. Cancel your answers to the lowest terms and convert to mixed numbers if appropriate.

   a $2\frac{2}{7} \div \frac{8}{21}$ **b** $2\frac{2}{3} \div 1\frac{3}{5}$ **c** $2\frac{1}{8} \div \frac{1}{16}$ **d** $1\frac{7}{15} \div 2\frac{1}{5}$

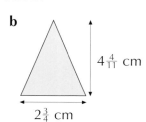 **7** A recipe for a smoothie requires a pint of milk. A small tub of milk contains $\frac{5}{8}$ of a centilitre. How many small tubs would be needed to make a pint of milk, which is $5\frac{5}{8}$ centilitres?

8 Find the areas of the shapes below.

   a
$1\frac{5}{7}$ cm

$1\frac{5}{9}$ cm

   b
$4\frac{4}{11}$ cm

$2\frac{3}{4}$ cm

9 In a small village $\frac{9}{20}$ of the children are boys. $\frac{5}{9}$ of the boys go to secondary school and $\frac{5}{11}$ of the girls go to secondary school.

  a What fraction of all the children in the village are boys who go to secondary school?

  b What fraction of the children in the village go to secondary school?

 10 On checking his e-mails Mr Smith finds that $\frac{1}{5}$ of them are junk mail. Of the remainder, $\frac{3}{4}$ are about business. What fraction of Mr Smith's e-mails are about business?

 11 Mr Berry collects stamps. $\frac{4}{9}$ of his collection are British and $\frac{2}{5}$ of the rest of the collection are French. What fraction of the whole collection are French?

Directed Numbers

This section will remind you how to work with directed numbers.

Example 16.17 ▷ Work out the following.

  a $2 + {-3}$ **b** $-2 - {-5} - {+6}$ **c** -2×-6 **d** $-3 \times -8 \div +4$

When two alike signs occur together, they combine to make a single plus sign
$(+ + = +$ and $- - = +)$.
Two unlike signs combine to make a single minus sign $(+ - = -$ and $- + = -)$.

Once the signs are combined, we work out addition and subtraction on the number line, starting at zero and counting left for negative numbers and right for positive numbers.

  a $2 + {-3} = 2 - 3 = -1$

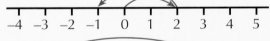

  b $-2 - {-5} - {+6} = -2 + 5 - 6 = -3$

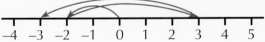

When multiplying or dividing, two alike signs again combine to make a positive number $(+ \times + = +$ and $- \times - = +)$, whilst two unlike signs combine to make a negative number $(+ \times - = -$ and $- \times + = -)$.

  c $-2 \times -6 = +12$

  d $-3 \times -8 \div +4 = +24 \div +4 = +6$

Example 16.18 ▷ When $a = -2$, $b = +4$ and $c = -6$, evaluate the following algebraic expressions.

  a $a^2 + bc$ **b** $(a + b) \times (c - a)$

  a First substitute the numbers into the expression. Using brackets will help.
$a^2 + bc = (-2)^2 + (4) \times (-6) = +4 - 24 = -20$

  b $(a + b) \times (c - a) = [(-2) + (+4)] \times [(-6) - (-2)] = [-2 + 4] \times [-6 + 2] = +2 \times -4 = -8$

1 Work out the following.

a	+3 − 7	**b**	−3 − 9	**c**	7 − −4	**d**	+5 − +6 − −8
e	−2 × +6	**f**	−5 × −4	**g**	−32 ÷ −8	**h**	+24 ÷ −6
i	+4 × −6 ÷ −3	**j**	$(−3)^2 + −6$	**k**	$(−2 + 3) × −4$	**l**	$(−2 − 1)^2 + 7$
m	$+4 − (2 − −1)^2$	**n**	$(−3 + −7) ÷ (−5 + 3)$	**o**	$(+4 + −2)^2 + (−5 − 4)$		

2 Find the missing number in each of the expressions below.

a   ($\boxed{}$ − +3) × −7 = +14

b   −6 × $\boxed{}$ ÷ −8 = −1.5

c   (−6 − $\boxed{}$)² = 4 (two answers possible)

3 What number do I have to **add** to −10 to get an answer of: **a** −6?   **b** −12?

4 What number do I have to **subtract** from −5 to get an answer of: **a** −7?   **b** +7?

5 What number do I have to **multiply** −6 by to get an answer of: **a** −9?   **b** +24?

6 What number do I have to **divide** −32 by to get an answer of: **a** −4?   **b** +64?

7 What number do I have to **divide** −3 into to get an answer of: **a** −7?   **b** +1.5?

8 You are told that $a = −4$, $b = −3$ and $c = +6$. Work out the value of the expressions below.

a	$a^2 + b^2$	**b**	$(a + b)(a − b)$	**c**	$3a − 4b + 6c$
d	abc	**e**	$(a + c)^2 − (a − c)^2$	**f**	$3(a − 2b) + 4(b − 2c)$

9 $\boxed{-5}$ $\boxed{-3}$ $\boxed{-2}$ $\boxed{+2}$ $\boxed{+4}$ $\boxed{+7}$

Pick out cards from the set above that give the following answers.

a $\boxed{}$ + $\boxed{}$ = +2   b $\boxed{}$ − $\boxed{}$ = +2

c $\boxed{}$ − $\boxed{}$ = −2   d $\boxed{}$ + $\boxed{}$ = −5

10 $\boxed{-6}$ $\boxed{-3}$ $\boxed{-2}$ $\boxed{+2}$ $\boxed{+4}$ $\boxed{+8}$

Pick out cards from the set above that give the following answers.

a $\boxed{}$ × $\boxed{}$ = +12   b $\boxed{}$ ÷ $\boxed{}$ = −2

c $\boxed{}$ × $\boxed{}$ ÷ $\boxed{}$ = +12   d $\boxed{}$ ÷ $\boxed{}$ × $\boxed{}$ = −6

Basic percentages

Example 16.19 A television that normally costs £320 is reduced in a sale by 12%. How much does the television cost after the reduction?

According to the 'road-sign' the formula to work this out is:
Final value = Original value × Multiplier

For a reduction of 12%, the multiplier is 0.88.

So the final value = £320 × 0.88 = £281.60

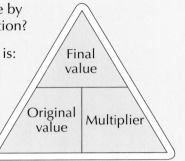

Example 16.20 What percentage of 75 is 45?

According to the road sign:
Multiplier = Final value ÷ Original value = 45 ÷ 75 = 0.6

A multiplier of 0.6 is the same as 60%.

Example 16.21 Fran measures her sunflower at Midday on Monday and at Midday on Tuesday. She finds its height has increased by 5% in this time. The height of the sunflower on Tuesday is 73.5 cm.

What was the sunflower's height on Monday?

A 5% increase is a multiplier of 1.05.

According to the road sign:
Original value = Final value ÷ Multiplier = 73.5 ÷ 1.05 = 70 cm

Exercise 16H

1 Increase each of the following by the given percentage.

a £78 by 10%	**b** £107 by 20%	**c** 650 g by 5%
d 54 m by 15%	**e** £89 by 25%	**f** 120 km by 30%

2 Decrease each of the following by the given percentage.

a £54 by 10%	**b** 92 kg by 5%	**c** £450 by 20%
d 68 m by 15%	**e** £150 by 25%	**f** 240 cm by 2%

 3 A car that normally costs £12 500 is reduced by 15%. What does it cost now?

4 Work out the percentage that the first number is of the second.

a 12 out of 20	**b** 34 out of 50	**c** 56 out of 200
d 23 out of 25	**e** 7 out of 10	**f** 153 out of 300

D

5 Increase each of the following by the given percentage. Round your answers if necessary.

    a £98 by 12%   **b** 645g by 17%   **c** £650 by 8%

    d 44 m by 16%   **e** £85 by $17\frac{1}{2}$%   **f** 243 cm by 32%

6 Decrease each of the following by the given percentage. Round your answers if necessary.

    a £108 by 8%   **b** 970 g by 18%   **c** £624 by 36%

    d £64 by 12%   **e** £195 by 33%   **f** 256 cm by 42%

 7 A cooker that normally costs £248 is reduced by 12%. What does it cost now?

8 Work out the percentage that the first number is of the second.

    a 18 out of 60   **b** 45 out of 75   **c** 63 out of 90

    d 28 out of 40   **e** 24 out of 30   **f** 162 out of 270

 9 Donald puts £1000 in a savings account which pays 5% compound interest per year. How much is in the account after 2 years?

 10 Enid puts £1000 in a savings account which pays 3.2% compound interest per year. How much is in the account after 6 years?

 11 After a 10% wage increase, Beryl now earns £6.60 per hour. What did she earn before?

 12 After losing 16% of her weight on a diet, Francis now weighs 63 kg. What did she weigh before the diet?

Basic algebra

Example 16.22 ▷   Expand and then simplify the following expressions.

    a $2(x - 2) + 3(x + 1)$ **b** $2(3x - 1) - 3(x - 2)$

    a Expand each bracket and then collect like terms together:

        $2(x - 2) + 3(x + 1) = 2x - 4 + 3x + 3 = 2x + 3x - 4 + 3 = 5x - 1$

    b $2(3x - 1) - 3(x - 2) = 6x - 2 - 3x + 6 = 6x - 3x - 2 + 6 = 3x + 4$

Example 16.23 ▷   Expand and then simplify the following expressions.

    a $x(x - y) + 2x(y + 3x)$ **b** $x(x + 2y) - y(2x - y)$

    a Expand each bracket and then collect like terms together:

        $x(x - y) + 2x(y + 3x) = x^2 - xy + 2xy + 6x^2 = x^2 + 6x^2 - xy + 2xy = 7x^2 + xy$

    b $x(x + 2y) - y(2x - y) = x^2 + 2xy - 2yx + y^2 = x^2 + y^2$

    Note that $2xy$ and $2yx$ are the same expression.

Example 16.24 ▷ Solve the following equations.

    a $3(x - 1) + 2(2x - 1) = 23$ **b** $3(x + 1) = 2(x - 2) + 12$

    a $3(x - 1) + 2(2x - 1) = 23$

                $3x - 3 + 4x - 2 = 23$ (expand brackets)

                       $7x - 5 = 23$ (collect terms together)

                           $7x = 28$ (add 5 to both sides)

                              $x = 4$ (divide by 7)

    b $3(x + 1) = 2(x - 2) + 12$

           $3x + 3 = 2x - 4 + 12$ (expand brackets)

       $3x - 2x = -4 + 12 - 3$ (collect letter terms on left and numbers on right of equals sign)

                    $x = 5$ (add or subtract the like terms)

Exercise 16I

(1) Expand and simplify the following expressions.

    a $2(x - 4) + 3(x + 2)$ **b** $3(x - 1) - 2(x + 3)$

    c $4(2x + 5) - 3(3x - 2)$ **d** $4(x + 5) - 2(x - 10)$

    e $3(3x + 1) + 2(2x - 7)$ **f** $3(x - 5) - 3(2x - 1)$

    g $x(x + 2y) - x(3y - x)$ **h** $x(2x - y) - 2x(x + 2y)$

    i $3x(2x - 3y) - x(3x + 2y)$ **j** $3x(2x - 3y) + x(y + 5x)$

(2) Solve the following equations.

    a $2(x - 4) + 3(x + 2) = 18$ **b** $3(x - 1) - 2(x + 3) = 19$

    c $4(x + 1) - 2(x - 3) = 20$ **d** $2(x + 3) + 4(x - 3) = 15$

    e $3(x + 2) - 4(x - 3) = 19$ **f** $5(x + 2) - 6(x + 1) = 6$

    g $2(3x - 1) + 2(x + 3) = 4$ **h** $5(2x + 1) + 4(x - 3) = 21$

    i $4(2 - 3x) + 2(2x - 1) = 14$ **j** $2(4x + 2) + 3(2x + 7) = 4$

(3) Solve the following equations.

    a $5(x - 1) = x + 3$ **b** $9(x - 3) = 3(x + 1)$

    c $4(x + 2) + 5 = 2(x - 1) + 18$ **d** $6(x - 2) + 9 = 6(2x - 2)$

    e $3(x - 1) = 4(x + 2) - 9$ **f** $3(2x - 1) = 2(4x - 3) - 2$

(4) The angles of a triangle, in degrees, are $3x$, $2x + 15$ and $4x - 60$.

    Calculate the value of x.

(5) The perimeter of this rectangle is 22 cm.

    Calculate the value of x.

                                 $2x + 3$ cm

                                                       $4x - 7$ cm

C

GCSE past-paper questions

EDEXCEL non calc, 2005

1 a Work out: **i** $3 - 11$ **ii** -3×-5

b Work out $\frac{7}{8} - \frac{1}{4}$.

EDEXCEL non calc, 2005

2 Linda's mark in a maths test was 36 out of 50.

Find 36 out of 50 as a percentage.

AQA Spec B calc, 2006

3 a Work out $25 - (11 + 6)$.

b Insert brackets to make this calculation correct.

$15 - 6 \times 2 = 18$

AQA Spec A non calc, 2006

4 Write in order, starting with the smallest.

$0.22 \qquad \frac{3}{20} \qquad 19\%$

AQA Spec A non calc, 2006

5 Romana picks a number.

a One number that she could pick is 36.

Write down the other **two** numbers that Romana could pick.

My number has 2 digits and is a factor of 36.

b Romana gives some more clues about the number.

What number does Romana pick?

You must show your working.

If I add the digits in my number, I get a square number.

If I multiply the digits in my number, I get a cube number.

AQA Spec A calc, 2006

6 Jack buys 1.5 kilograms of oranges at 98 pence per kilogram.

He also buys some bananas at 85 pence per kilogram.

His total bill is £2.49.

What is the weight of the bananas that he buys?

AQA Spec B calc, 2006

7 a Work out 38% of £146.

b What percentage is £108 of £150?

232

OCR non calc, 2004

8 Mrs Brown has double glazing, costing £8000, installed in her house.

  To pay for the double glazing, she must first pay a deposit of 15% of the cost.

  The rest of the cost is paid in 20 equal instalments

  How much is one of these equal payments?

AQA Spec B non calc, 2006

9 You are given that $56 \times 245 = 13\,720$.

  Use this to work out:

  a 560×2450

  b 5.6×0.245

EDEXCEL non calc, 2005

10 Work out the value of $\frac{2}{3} \times \frac{3}{4}$.

  Give your answer as a fraction in its simplest form.

EDEXCEL calc, 2005

11 Andy sells CDs.

  He sells each CD for £8.80 plus VAT at $17\frac{1}{2}\%$.

  He sells 650 CDs.

  Work out how much money Andy receives.

OCR non calc, 2004

12 **a** Expand $x(x + 2)$.

  b Expand and simplify $3(4x + 1) + 2(2x - 1)$.

AQA Spec A non calc, 2006

13 Expand and simplify:

  $3(2x - 1) + 2(3x + 5)$

OCR calc, 2004

14 **a** Maria invested £2000 for 3 years at 2.7% per annum compound interest.

  How much was her investment worth at the end of 3 years?

  b Maria used some of the money to buy a dress in a sale. The price of the dress had been reduced by 35% to the sale price of £37.70.

  What was the price of the dress before the sale?

FM The Eden Project

1 The Eden Project business plan expected 700 000 visitors in the first year, followed by a 9% increase in visitor numbers each year for each of the next 8 years.

How many visitors did they expect to get in the fifth year?

Round your answer to a sensible number.

2 Two families visited the Eden Project.

It cost the Brown family of one adult and two children £24.

It cost the Kahnaan family of two adults and two children £38.

How much does it cost Mrs McDonald and her three children to enter the Eden Project?

3 The Schools Visit Manager at the Eden Project estimates that the ratio of men : women : children visiting the project is 1 : 2 : 4.

On the first Wednesday in March, there were 7700 visitors to the project.

   a How many of the 7700 visitors were children?

   b Every person visiting that day was given a ticket with a number on, and one was chosen at random for a prize.

      What is the probability that the prize went to a child?

4 The biomes cover a total of 22130 m² and contain about 135 000 plants.

   a Find the planting density (the number of plants per square metre) of the biomes.

   b Is it reasonable to think that every square metre has this planting density? Explain your answer.

5 In the information centre, Joel saw this table showing the number of visitors to the Eden Project from 2000 to 2006.

Year	2000	2001	2002	2003	2004	2005	2006
Visitor numbers (millions)	2.0	1.9	1.6	1.7	1.8	1.8	1.8

Find the mean number of visitors per year.

6 The extract below is part of a UK website.

The largest greenhouse in the world is the 'Humid Tropics Biome' (HTB) at the Eden Project, Cornwall, England.

The HTB is 55 m high, 100 m wide and 200 m long.

This information needs to be placed in an American web page.

The standard unit used in the USA for this type of measurement is feet (not metres).

Rewrite the website information for the American web page using the information below.

     1 meter = 39.37 inches
     1 foot   = 12 inches

7 Using a ruler and a protractor, make an accurate copy of this diagram of a regular hexagon – the shape used in making the biomes at the Eden Project.

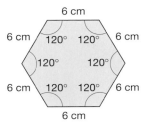

6 cm
6 cm 120° 120° 6 cm
120°   120°
6 cm 120° 120° 6 cm
6 cm

8 The total site of the Eden Project covers 502 022 m² , of which 97 843 m² is landscaped and 1231 m² is a man-made lake.

  a What percentage of the total site has been landscaped? Give your answer correct to two significant figures.

  b What percentage of the total site is the man made lake? Give your answer correct to two decimal places.

9 The graph below shows the change in temperature for part of one day last June in the Humid Tropics Biome (HTB).

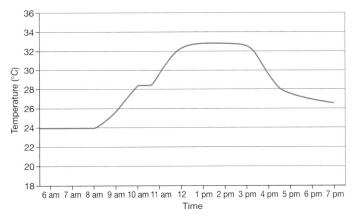

  a What time did the Sun rise?

  b The Sun went behind a cloud in the morning. For how long?

  c The automatic vents start working when the temperature rises too high. At what time did they start working?

  d What was the minimum temperature in the HTB?

  e What was the maximum temperature in the HTB?

  f What do you think happens to the temperature in the HTB after 7 pm?

10 The largest hexagon in making the biomes is 11 m across! The length of each side is 5.5 m.

A hexagon can be made from two identical trapeziums.

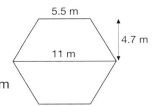

5.5 m
4.7 m
11 m

The formula for the area of a trapezium is:
$$\frac{1}{2}(a + b)h$$

Find the area of the hexagon above.

11 The total weight of steel that the biomes are made from is 700 tonnes.

The total length of all of these steel beams is 36 000 m.

What is the mean weight of the steel beams in kilograms per metre?

12 The percentage humidity is the amount of water vapour in the air.

The 'apparent' temperature is people's average guess of the temperature.

A biology student compared the percentage humidity in different parts of the different biomes with the 'apparent' temperature, and also with the number of plants per square metre (m²).

Her results are shown on the two scatter diagrams below.

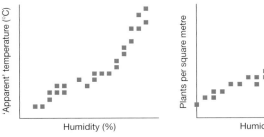
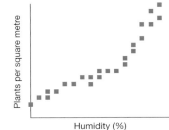

Humidity (%)   Humidity (%)

  a Describe the type of correlation between humidity and apparent temperature.

  b Describe the type of correlation between mhumidity and the number of plants per square metre (m²).

  c Describe the relationship between the apparent temperature and the number of plants per square metre (m²).

  d Draw a scatter diagram to show the correlation between the apparent temperature and the number of plants per square metre (m²). Plot about 10 points on your graph.

13 Bambusa Gigantica, a type of bamboo, can grow up to 45 cm a day.

A display shows one week's growth from one of the large bamboo plants. This piece has a diameter of 11 cm.

Diameter of bamboo = 11 cm

Calculate the volume, in cm³, of bamboo that grew in one week from this bamboo plant.

1 Here are some road signs.

For each part, copy the sign and draw in all the lines of symmetry.

a   b   c

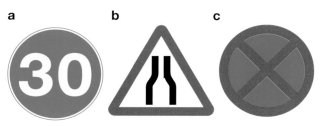

a   Minimum 30 mph sign

b   Road narrows sign

c   Clear way sign (with the cross on it)

2 Here are some road signs.

For each part, state the order of rational symmetry.

a   b   c

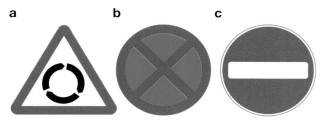

a   Roundabout

b   Clear way sign (as above)

c   No entry sign

3 Here are three advertisements for driving schools.

Fast Pass

First four lessons £8 each

Then £20 per lesson

All lessons 1 hour

Easy Drive

Standard hourly rate £20

First five hours £60

Block bookings
10 hours £150
15 hours £225

Safe Motoring

First lesson free

Normal price £20 per hour

£2 off per hour for block booking of 10 or more lessons

a   Work out the cost of 40 hours of lessons using Fast Pass.

b   Work out the cost of 40 hours of lessons using Easy Drive. Remember to save money by using the block booking prices.

c   Work out the cost of 40 hours of lessons using Safe Motoring. Remember to save money by using the block booking prices.

d   Which driving school is the cheapest for 40 hours of lessons?

4 The table shows the percentage of casualties in road accidents for different age groups.

Age	Percentage
17–25 years	33%
26–39 years	28%
40–59 years	24%
60 years and over	15%

a Draw a pie chart to show this information.

b Give a reason why there are more casualties in the 17–25 years age group.

5 Research shows that it is safer for pedestrians to walk facing traffic than walking with their back to traffic on rural roads.

10% of those involved in an accident when walking with their back to traffic are killed or seriously injured.

6% of those involved in an accident when facing traffic are killed or seriously injured.

a If 2000 pedestrians are involved in accidents when walking with their back to traffic, how many of these are likely to be killed or seriously injured?

b If 2000 pedestrians are involved in accidents when facing traffic, how many of these are likely to be killed or seriously injured?

6 The driving test is made up of two parts: the theory test and the practical test.

A learner has to pass the theory test before taking a practical test.

In April 2008, the theory test cost £30 and the practical test cost £56.50 for weekdays and £67.00 for weekday evenings or weekends.

a The probability that a driver passes the theory test is 0.9. What is the probability that the driver fails the theory test?

b A driver passes her theory test first time and the practical test on the third attempt. How much more does it cost if the practical tests are taken at the weekend than if they are taken on a weekday?

7 A practical test lasts for 40 minutes and covers 12 miles. Work out the average speed in miles per hour.

8 The table shows the number of attempts that some drivers take to pass their driving test.

Number of attempts to pass	Number of drivers
1	16
2	9
3	7
4	4
5	3
6	1
	Total = 40

a What fraction of the drivers pass at the first attempt?

b Work out the median number of attempts to pass.

c Work out the mean number of attempts to pass for these drivers.

9 The scatter diagram shows the relationship between the age and the number of driving lessons taken by students at a driving school.

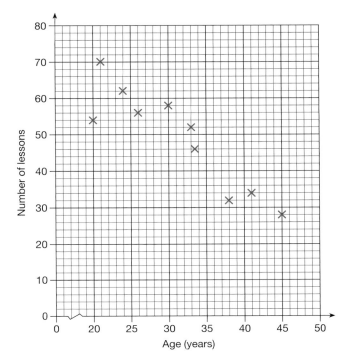

a Describe the correlation.

b Estimate the number of lessons taken by a 36-year-old person at this driving school.

c Explain why it would not be sensible to use the scatter diagram to estimate the number of lessons needed by a 50-year-old person.

10 Here is a formula for working out stopping distance, d (feet), when travelling at speed, v (mph).

$$d = v + \frac{v^2}{20}$$

a Work out the stopping distance in feet when $v = 20$ mph.

b By working out the stopping distance in feet when $v = 30$ mph, show that a car would travel almost twice as far when stopping from 30 mph than 20 mph.

FM Squirrels

Red squirrels are native to Britain. In 1870 some North American grey squirrels were released in the North of England. The grey squirrel thrived in the conditions in Britain and slowly took over the habitats of the red squirrel, reducing their numbers dramatically.

1 Today it is estimated that there are 180 000 red squirrels and 2.7 million grey squirrels in Britain.

a Write 2.7 million in figures.

b Write the ratio number of red squirrels : number of grey squirrels in its simplest form.

2 The population of red squirrels in England, Wales and Scotland is estimated as:

Country	Number of red squirrels
England	35 000
Scotland	120 000
Wales	25 000

Draw a fully-labelled pie chart to show this information.

3 A study on the body weights of squirrels gave the following data for red squirrels over a 12-month period.

Month	Jan	Feb	Mar	Apr	May	Jun	Jul	Aug	Sep	Oct	Nov	Dec
Average weight (g)	273	265	274	280	285	290	310	325	345	376	330	290

This graph shows the same data for grey squirrels.

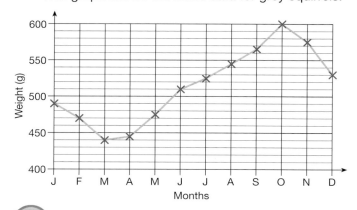

a On a copy of the graph, draw a line graph to show the average body weight of the red squirrels.

b Why do you think the weights of the squirrels increase in the autumn?

c Comment on the differences in the weights of the red and grey squirrels over the year.

4 One reason that grey squirrels do better than red squirrels is that they are more aggressive feeders. This table shows how many of each type can be supported in different types of habitats.

Grizedale forest in Cumbria has an area of 2445 hectares. The table also shows the percentage of Grizedale forest given over to different habitats.

Type of habitat	Number of grey squirrels per hectare	Number of red squirrels per hectare	Land use (%) of forest
Broad-leaved woodland	8	1	65
Coniferous woodland	2	0.1	12
Agricultural	0	0	10
Wildlife management	10	2	2
Open areas	0	0	11

a How many hectares of Grizedale forest are broad-leaved woodland?

Give your answer to an appropriate degree of accuracy.

b Assuming no red squirrels live in the forest, estimate how many grey squirrels the forest could support.

c In fact the ratio of grey to red squirrels in the forest in n : 1.

Show that the value of n is approximately 8.

10 adult male red and 10 adult male grey squirrels are trapped and studied.

This is the data obtained

Red squirrels

	A	B	C	D	E	F	G	H	I	J
Body length (mm)	202	185	215	192	205	186	186	199	235	222
Tail length (mm)	185	164	198	175	182	173	162	184	210	203
Weight (g)	320	292	340	305	335	341	295	325	360	357

Grey squirrels

	A	B	C	D	E	F	G	H	I	J
Body length (mm)	272	243	278	266	269	280	251	272	278	281
Tail length (mm)	223	196	220	218	218	222	198	220	226	225
Weight (g)	530	512	561	512	542	551	520	530	558	564

5 **a** Work out the mean and range of the weights of the red squirrels.

b Work out the mean and range of the weights of the grey squirrels.

c Comment on the differences in the weights of each species.

6 For red squirrel A the tail length is 92% (to the nearest percentage) of the body length and for grey squirrel A the tail length is 82% of the body length.

a Work out the same data for red and grey squirrels D, G and J.

b The data for another squirrel is:

Body length: 240 mm   Tail length: 215 mm

Unfortunately the species was not recorded.

Is the squirrel a red or grey squirrel? Give a reason for your answer.

7 The scatter diagram below shows the relationship between the body length and tail length of red squirrels.

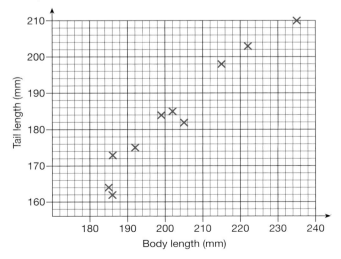

a Estimate the tail length of a red squirrel with a body length of 210 mm.

b Describe the correlation between the body length and tail length of red squirrels.

c **i** Using the data for grey squirrels, draw a scatter diagram to show the relationship between body length and tail length.

Use a horizontal axis for body length from 240 mm to 290 mm and a vertical axis for tail length from 190 mm to 230 mm.

ii Draw a line of best fit on the diagram.

iii Use your line of best fit to estimate the body length of a grey squirrel with a tail length of 205 mm.

iv Explain why the diagram could not be used to estimate the tail length of a young grey squirrel with a body length of 180 mm.

8 The normal diet of red squirrels is mainly seeds and pine cones with some fungi and plant shoots.

This table shows the percentage of each type of food in the diet of some red squirrels.

Food	Seeds	Pine cones	Fungi	Shoots
Percentage	42%	34%	14%	10%

Copy and complete a percentage bar chart to show the information.

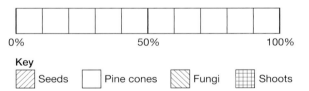

9 This table shows the number of baby red squirrels born 100 nests.

Number of baby squirrels	Frequency
1	24
2	42
3	19
4	10
5	5

a Work out the mean number of baby squirrels per nest.

b The probability of a baby squirrel surviving to adulthood is 0.4.

How many of the squirrels in the table above would you expect to survive to adulthood?

10 A male red squirrel can roam over an area of up to 42 acres. This is about the size of 34 football pitches. Assuming that a football pitch is 100 m by 50 m, calculate (to 2 decimal places) how many acres are in one hectare (10 000 m²).

Mobile shops were very common in the 1960s but as supermarkets started to open and people had access to cars, they fell out of favour. Nowadays, with people wanting fresher produce and concerned about driving long distances to shop, they are returning to some remote rural areas.

Jeff and Donna decide to start a Mobile shop in a rural area of North Devon.

1 This is a map of the villages they decide they will serve with the distances between villages shown.

The distances are in kilometres.

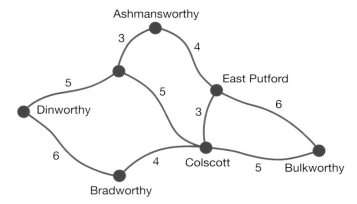

They plan this route: Ashmansworthy – Dinworthy – Bradworthy – Colscott – Bulkworthy – East Putford – Ashmansworthy.

a How many kilometres is this route?

b They plan a timetable.

They intend to be open for 30 minutes in each village.

It takes 5 minutes to pack all the groceries safely after they close before they can drive off.

It takes 5 minutes to unpack the groceries after they arrive and before they can open.

They know they need to allow 2 minutes per kilometre on the rural roads.

They intend to open the shop at 9 am in Ashmansworthy.

This is the timetable for the first two villages.

Copy and complete the timetable for the opening times at each village.

Event	Time
Open Ashmansworthy	9.00
Close Ashmansworthy	9.30
Leave Ashmansworthy	9.35
Arrive Dinworthy	9.51
Open Dinworthy	9.56
Close Dinworthy	10.26
Leave Dinworthy	10.31

c What time do they arrive back in Ashmansworthy?

2 Most mobile shops are often converted single-decker buses.

Jeff and Donna see this advert and decide to buy this bus.

> **1983 Leyland Tiger** – Mid engine, Plaxton Paramount 3200, Semi-automatic, 53 seats with belts, Air Door, Very clean inside and out. Drives well, MOT Jan 2008. Length: 12 metres, height 3.2 metres, width 2.5 metres. For more photos please visit our website www.usedcoachsales.co.uk

They know that fitting out the bus will cost £5000.

Insuring and taxing the bus will cost £1500.

Buying the initial stock for the bus will be £2000.

They have savings of £7500.

a What is the minimum amount they need to borrow from the bank to get started?

b The bank agrees to lend them up to £10 000 at an interest rate of 7.5% per annum.

i How much will the interest be on £10 000 for one year?

ii If they only borrow the minimum amount they need and decide to pay the loan back over one year, what will be the approximate monthly payment?

3 Health and Safety rules state that they must have adequate lighting, hot water for washing hands, a fridge for storing chilled foods and heating for the winter. They consult an electrician who estimates the power for each item to be:

Lighting	500 W
Water heater	2 kW
Fridge	1 kW
Heating	kW

a W stands for Watts. What does k stand for?

b What is the total maximum power needed? Answer in Watts.

4 Before they go ahead with the plan, Jeff and Donna decide to do a survey of the villages to see if there will be enough business to make the venture worthwhile.

a Jeff says, 'We need to find out the population of each village and survey about 20% of the residents in each of them'.

Donna says, 'We need to find out how many households there are in each village and survey about 20% of them'.

Who is correct and why?

b The number of households in each village is given in the table.

How many households in each village should be surveyed?

Village	Households
Ashmansworthy	322
Dinworthy	178
Bradworthy	476
Colscott	150
Bulkworthy	483
East Putford	189

c This is one of the questions that Jeff prepares for the survey.

> How much do you spend each week?
> Up to £20 ☐   £20 – £30 ☐   More than £30 ☐

Give two criticisms of this question.

d This is a question that Donna prepares for the survey.

Please tick the appropriate box.
How much do you spend each week on:

Item	£0 to £9.99	£10 to £19.99	£20 to £29.99	£30 or more
Meat				
Fruit				
Vegetables				
Cleaning products				
Other household items				

Give two reasons why this is a good question.

e This is one of the tables they compile after doing the survey of how much households spend each week on meat.

Amount, m, £	Frequency, f	Midpoint, m	$m \times f$
£0 ≤ m < £10	48	5	
£10 ≤ m < £20	97	15	
£20 ≤ m < £30	38	25	
£30 ≤ m < £40	17	35	
Total		Total	

Copy the table and work out the mean amount each household spends on meat each week.

5 The bus is 12 m long and 2.5 m wide.

This is a scale drawing of the bus with 1 cm representing 1 m.

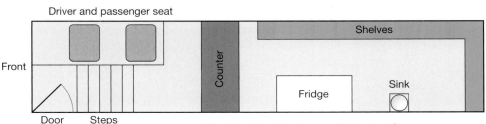

a What is the total area of the bus?

b What is the actual width of the counter?

c The area behind the counter is the 'shop area'. What percentage of the total area is the 'shop area'?

Give your answer to the nearest percentage.

d The fridge is $1\frac{1}{2}$ m high. What is the volume of the fridge?

6 Donna uses the following formula to work out the profit the shop will make each week.

P is the profit. T is the total amount taken over the counter in pounds in a week.

$$P = \frac{T}{5} - 150$$

a What does 150 represent?

b What is the profit if the weekly takings are £1600?

c Jeff says that they need to make a weekly profit of £400.

How much do they need to take each week to do this?

d They apply for a grant to the European Union community fund who agree to subsidise them by 10% of their takings each week.

i How much profit do they make when their weekly takings are £1000 and they receive a subsidy?

ii Show that they need to take between £1800 and £1850 each week to make a profit of £400 taking the subsidy into account.

Index

A

algebra 1–11, 40–53, 126–33
  revision 186–7
angles
  bisectors 66–7
  exterior 55–7
  interior 55–7
  polygons 55–60
APR (Annual Percentage Rate)
  26
arc 61
areas
  circles 99–101, 177
  ellipse 176
  formulae and revision 203–5
  metric units 101–2
  ratio 28
axes of symmetry 157

B

BIDMAS 31
bisectors
  angles 66–7
  perpendicular 66–7
BODMAS 20, 31
box method 114, 217, 219

C

calculator
  fraction key 117–18
  π key 97–8
  power key 21, 117–18
  reciprocal key 118
  x^2 key 100
capacity, metric units 101–2
centre of enlargement 150
changing the subject of
  formulae 175–7
chord 61
circles 61–3, 96–9
  area 99–101
  circumscribed 66
circumference 61, 96–9
column method 114, 217,
  218, 219

common denominators 16–17
comparing data 85–7
compound interest 21–3
concentric circles 62
congruent triangles 160–2
constructing, right-angled
  triangles 64–6
conventions 69–70
coordinate grids 152–5
correlations 76–9
counter-example 30
cover-up method 177–8
cube roots 130–1
cylinders, volumes 105, 177

D

data
  comparing 85–7
  handling investigation 201–2
  handling vocabulary 196–8
decimals
  dividing 115–17
  multiplying 114–15
definitions 69–70
derived properties 69–70
diagonals 5
diameter 61, 96–7
difference of two squares 174
direct proportion graphs 50–3
directed numbers 184–6,
  227–8
distance–time graphs 8–10
dividing decimals 115–17
drawing, parallel lines 58

E

efficient calculator use
  117–18
ellipse, area 176
enlargements 150–5
equations 40–2
  cover-up method 177–8
  with fractions 44–5
  gradient–intercept method
    178

solving problems 43–4
trial and improvement
  48–50
with x^2 46–7
estimation 33–4, 112–13
Euler's theorem 176
events
  independent 138–40, 212
  mutually exclusive 140–2,
    212
expansion 168–70
  quadratic 173–4
  revision 230–1
exterior angles 55–7

F

factorisation 126–8, 171–2
factors, algebraic 126–8
Fibonacci sequences 119
finite sequences 11
flow diagrams 7
formulae 40–2
  changing the subject 175–7
fractional enlargements 151
fractions
  adding and subtracting
    16–18, 223–5
  in equations 44–5
  equivalent 221–2
  multiplying and dividing
    18–20, 225–7
  revision 182–4
frequency diagrams 197–8
Functional Maths
  APR 26
  best value problems 119,
    121, 122
  comparing data 86–7, 200
  compound interest 23
  data investigations 201–2
  distance–time graphs 10, 11
  fractions revision 224, 225,
    226, 227
  graphs revision 188–9
  loci problems 68–9, 72–3

map scales   159
metric to imperial conversions   192
numbers revision   185
percentages revision   229, 230
real-life graphs   9–10, 132–3, 135
solving problems revision   182–3, 220
statistical investigations   90, 93
time series graphs   81–2
two-way tables   83–5
VAT   25
Mobile phone tariffs   14–15
The London Olympics 2012   38–9
Garden design   74–5
Rainforest deforestation   94–5
Athletics stadium   108–9
Paper   124–5
Packages   136–7
Class test   148–9
Map reading   166–7
Trip to Rome   180–1
Road safety   238–9
Squirrels   240–1
Mobile shop   242–3
The Eden Project   236–7
functions   6–8

G

GCSE
    past papers   232–3
    preparation   217–31
geometry and measures   55–70, 96–105
    investigations   205–6
    revision   190–3, 203–6
gradients   50
gradient–intercept method   178
graphs
    direct proportion   50–3
    of functions   8
    linear equations   177–8
    real-life   9–10, 132–3
    revision   188–90
    time series   79–82

H

HCF (highest common factor)   26, 126–8, 221

Hero's formula   176
hypotenuse   160

I

identities   41–2
identity functions   6
imperial units
    length   103
    map scales   160
independent events   138–40
index notation   128–9
infinite sequences   11
inputs   6–7
interior angles   55–7
inverse functions   6
investigations
    data handling   201–2
    geometry and measures   205–6
    probability   214–16
    statistical   88–90
    symmetry   209–10

L

LCM (lowest common multiple)   17, 223
limits of sequences   11
lines of symmetry   207–8
loci   66–9
Logo   155
long division   218–20
long multiplication   217, 219–20

M

magic squares, fractions   18
manipulation   169–70
map
    ratios   157, 158
    scales   157–60
mapping   6
mean   198
median   198
metric units
    areas   101–2
    capacity   101–2
    prefixes   111
    volumes   101–2
mnemonics   99
mode   198
multipliers, percentage   21–3, 24–5
multiplying decimals   114–15

mutually exclusive events   140–2

N

negative enlargements   151
*n*th terms   1–5
number   16–34, 110–20
numbers
    between 0 and 1   29–30
    directed revision   184–6, 227–8

O

order of operations   31–2
outputs   6–7

P

π (pi)   97–9
parallel lines   57–8
pentominoes   209
percentages   21–6
    reverse   24–6
    revision   182–4, 229–30
perimeters   203–5
perpendicular bisectors   63, 66–7
planes of symmetry   155–7, 207–8
polygons
    angles of   55–60
    diagonals   5
positive enlargements   150–1
powers
    of ten   110–11
    of variables   128–30
prefixes, metric units   111
prisms, volume and surface area   103–5
probability   138–42
    estimates   143–4
    investigations   214–16
    revision   194, 211–14

Q

quadratic
    expansion   173–4
    sequences   4–5

R

radius   61, 96–7
range   198
ratios   26–8
    revision   185

real-life graphs   9–10, 132–3
reflection symmetry   206–8
regular polygons   59–60, 63–4,
      156
relative frequency   143–4
rotational symmetry   157, 206–8
rounding   33–4, 112–13

 S

SAMDOB   32
scale factors   150–1
scatter graphs   76–9, 195, 198
sector   61
segment   61
self-inverse functions   7
semicircle   61
sequences   1–5
   finite   11
   infinite   11
   repeating   120
significant figures   33–4, 112–13
solutions   40

solving problems
   best value problems   118–19
   by equations   43–4
spheres, volume   177
square number sequences   3–5
square roots   130–1
squares, difference of two   174
statistical investigations   88–90
statistics   76–90, 138–44
   revision   193–5, 198–200,
      211–14
surface area, prisms   103–4
symmetry   155–7
   investigations   209–10
   number   210
   revision   191, 206–10

 T

tables, two-way   83–5
tangent   61
term-to-term rule   1
tessellations   63–4

time series graphs   79–82
trial and improvement   48–50
triangles
   congruent   160–2
   right-angled   64–6
two-way tables   83–5, 197

 U

unitary method   24–5

 V

variables   40
volumes
   cylinders   105, 177
   formulae and revision   203–4
   metric units   101–2
   prisms   103–4
   ratio   28
   spheres   177

 X

x^2 in equations   46–7

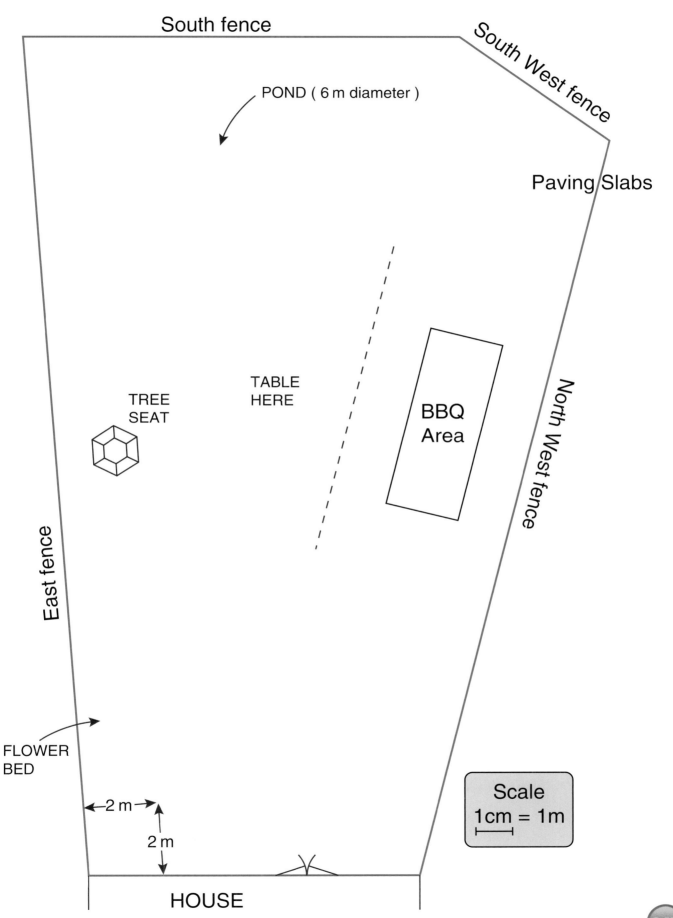

South fence

South West fence

POND (6 m diameter)

Paving Slabs

TABLE
HERE

TREE
SEAT

BBQ
Area

North West fence

East fence

FLOWER
BED

←2 m→

2 m

Scale
1cm = 1m

HOUSE

William Collins' dream of knowledge for all began with the publication of his first book in 1819. A self-educated mill worker, he not only enriched millions of lives, but also founded a flourishing publishing house. Today, staying true to this spirit, Collins books are packed with inspiration, innovation and practical expertise. They place you at the centre of a world of possibility and give you exactly what you need to explore it.

Collins. Freedom to teach.

Published by Collins
An imprint of HarperCollins*Publishers*
77–85 Fulham Palace Road
Hammersmith
London
W6 8JB

Browse the complete Collins catalogue at
www.collinseducation.com

ISBN 978-0-00-726625-8

Keith Gordon, Kevin Evans, Brian Speed and Trevor Senior assert their moral rights to be identified as the authors of this work.

British Library Cataloguing in Publication Data
A Catalogue record for this publication is available from the British Library.

Extra Functional Maths material written by Greg and Lynn Byrd
Commissioned by Melanie Hoffman and Katie Sergeant
Project managed by Priya Govindan
Edited by Brian Ashbury
Proofread by Amanda Dickson
Design and typesetting by Jordan Publishing Design
Covers by Oculus Design and Communications
Covers managed by Laura Deacon
Illustrations by Nigel Jordan, Tony Wilkins and Barking Dog Art
Printed and bound by Printing Express, Hong Kong
Production by Simon Moore

Acknowledgments
The publishers thank the Qualifications and Curriculum Authority for granting permission to reproduce questions from past National Curriculum Test papers for Key Stage 3 Maths.

The publishers have sought permission from AQA, OCR and EDEXCEL to reproduce past GCSE exam papers.

The map on page 166 is reproduced by permission of Ordnance Survey on behalf of HMSO. © Crown copyright 2008. All rights reserved. Ordnance Survey Licence number 100048274.

The publishers wish to thank the following for permission to reproduce photographs:

p.14-15 (main image) © VisualHongKong / Alamy, p.38-39 (main image) © Gilbert Iundt / TempSport / Corbis and (inset image of flag) © Andrew Paterson / Alamy, p.74-75 (main image) © V. J. Matthew / istockphoto.com, p.94-95 (main image) © Brandon Alms / istockphoto.com, p.108-109 (main image) © Josef Philipp / istockphoto.com, p.124-125 (main image) © Elena Schweitzer / istockphoto.com, p.136-147 (main image) © Comstock / Corbis and (inset image of violin case) © Nancy Louie / istockphoto.com, p.148-149 (main image) © Laurence Gough / istockphoto.com, p.166-167 (main image) © Guy Nicholls / istockphoto.com, p.180-181 (main image) © Cornel Stefan Achirei / istockphoto.com, p.236 (main image) © Brian Kelly / istockphoto.com, p.238 (main image) © Chris Elwell / istockphoto.com, p.240 (main images) © Sharon Day / istockphoto.com, p.242 (main image) © David Lyons / Alamy

Every effort has been made to trace copyright holders and to obtain their permission for the use of copyright material. The authors and publishers will gladly receive any information enabling them to rectify any error or omission at the first opportunity.